Piezoelectric Energy Harvester: Applications and Research Advances

By
ASHUTOSH ANAND

DEPARTMENT OF ELECTRONICS AND COMMUNICATION ENGINEERING
SCHOOL OF ENGINEERING
PRESIDENCY UNIVERSITY
RAJANAKUNTE, BENGALURU, INDIA
2024

Dedicated to my parents Mr Ramnath Singh and Mrs Dharmshila Devi
and my wife Mrs Prity Mandal

Acknowledgement

It gives me immense pleasure to express my heartfelt gratitude and indebtedness to Dr. Sudip Kundu, Assistant Professor, Dept of E.C.E, N.I.T Rourkela and Dr.Neela Chattoraj (Associate Professor) Birla Institute of Technology Mesra Ranchi.

I offer my indebtedness to all faculty members of the Electronics & Communication Engineering Department of Presidency University Bengaluru for their support and encouragement. I wish to express my sincere gratitude to my colleagues Dr Abhishek Pandey (Assistant Professor, Usha Martin University), Dr Manish Kumar (Assistant Professor, G.D Goenka University), Dr Abhishek Kumar, Dr. Geetanjali Singh, Dr Deepak Prasad, Dr Ajit Kumar (Assistant Professor, ECE, Presidency University Bengaluru) and others for their invaluable suggestions during this book.

The present work certainly would not have been possible if I had not been blessed with the environment of love, joy, and understanding created so generously by my parents, brothers, and lovely wife, though I have not been able to harness it in a scientific way!! I am indebted to several individuals who have contributed either directly or indirectly to complete this work successfully. My most sincere appreciation goes to all of them. Last but not least, I would like to thank the ALMIGHTY GOD for his blessings.

Name: ASHUTOSH ANAND
Email ID: ashunitjsr@gmail.com

Preface

Over the past ten years, energy harvesting from ambient waste energy has become a key technique for wireless applications, allowing low-powered electronics to operate. This technique aims to recharge storage devices, such batteries and capacitors, and/or supply distant sources of electricity. Researchers and businesspeople have been enthralled with the field of energy harvesting because of its previously indicated possibilities. The idea offers financial benefits by potentially lowering maintenance costs and has ecological implications by minimising the chemical waste generated when batteries need to be replaced. Increasing public safety is also a benefit of the ability to enable wireless monitoring applications like structural health monitoring. Researchers and businesspeople have been enthralled with the field of energy harvesting because of its previously indicated possibilities. As a result, new goods and scholarly studies have proliferated. The development of low-power-consuming electronics and the requirement to offer wireless solutions for sensing issues have prompted the growth of energy harvesting research. Utilising the piezoelectric effect to transform ambient vibration into useable electrical energy is one of the most researched applications. This application of the piezoelectric effect is the basis of the majority of vibrational energy harvesting equipment on the market today. This book focuses on the comprehensive electromechanical modelling of piezoelectric energy harvesters for a range of uses. As a result, new goods and scholarly studies have proliferated. The development of low-power-consuming electronics and the requirement to offer wireless solutions for sensing issues have prompted the growth of energy harvesting research. This book focuses on the comprehensive electromechanical modelling of piezoelectric energy harvesters for a range of uses.

A perpetual expansion in semiconductor devices has led to technological progress in electronic devices such as portable gadgets, automation systems, transmitters, implanted biomedical devices, and sensors. Conventional batteries generally power these devices. Replacement of batteries from any electronic device becomes very tedious when deployed in remote locations or in-vivo. Therefore harvesting energy from the environment and human body activity makes significant development over decades. The principle of piezoelectricity has been used to design the piezoelectric energy harvester (PZEH) for generating electrical energy from the surrounding vibration. The massive popularity of these energy harvesters is due to the possibility of miniaturization. The main challenge in the design of such energy harvesters is to achieve a low resonant frequency while keeping the harvester small. Another challenge is to overcome the frequency dependency of the piezoelectric based energy harvesters.

Various structural modification methods and bandwidth techniques have been employed in this book to address these issues. Conventional rectangular cantilever structure is modified to tapered cantilever structures. Single and multiple perforations are introduced at suitable positions in the cantilever structure to reduce the design's resonant frequency. The tapering and perforation also increase the stress distribution in the cantilever. It helps in increasing the output voltage and output power of the harvester.

The next part of the book, tries to improve the performance of the PZEH by using non-uniform substrate thickness. Generally, the conventional cantilever structure with a uniform thickness has used to generate electrical energy. The stress and strain distribution in the traditional design of the cantilever is maximum at the fixed end and gradually decreases towards the free end. It results in the under-utilization of the piezoelectric layer at the free end. The tapered substrate thickness helps in reducing the resonant frequency, improves stress distribution, and generates more output voltage and power. Both analytical and finite element method (FEM) analysis using COMOSL Multiphysics have performed to investigate the effect of tapered substrate thickness on the PZ cantilever beam.

To enhance the PZEH's performance, we have suggested an L-shaped cantilever construction in this chapter. The L-shaped contributes to the cantilever structure's homogeneous stress distribution in addition to helping to lower the resonant frequency. Each cantilever beam's output voltage, power, and stress distribution have been measured.

The rectangular spiral cantilever structure has been proposed for powering the battery of the pacemakers. The dimensions of the designed structures are within the permitted size of the modern IMDs while keeping resonant frequencies of the structures suitable for respective applications. The design of a spiral cantilever with proof-mass helps increase the effective length of the cantilever while maintaining the compactness of the cantilever beam.

The piezoelectric cantilever structure is frequency-dependent and generally has a narrow bandwidth. However, the available ambient vibration is distributed over a range of frequencies. The wide bandwidth of the EH is needed to generate high output voltages over a range of frequency. The operating bandwidth of the EH increases as the number of beams are increased, provided the resonant frequencies of the beams differ from each other by a sufficient margin. A parallel multi-beam structure is proposed to increase the bandwidth. In this proposed structure, the top electrodes of the beams are connected by the metal layer (in this case, aluminium), and the bottom electrodes are considered at the ground potential. This book discussed the concept of the coupling effect present in the piezoelectric multiple-plate cantilever structures. The vibrations of one PZ cantilever tend to affect the vibration and output of the neighbouring PZ cantilever structure. A qualitative explanation and finite element method analysis using COMSOL Multiphysics have been presented to explain the coupling effect between cantilever plates.

Another attempt has been made to improve the bandwidth of the PZEH by introducing non-linearity using permanent magnets in the EH. A dual-beam structure with magnetic tip-mass connected to the proof mass is proposed to enhance the bandwidth of the PZEH. The magnets arranged such that there would be a repulsive magnetic force between them. The increase in the permanent magnet's magnetic field intensity helps improve the stress distribution within the cantilever structure and improves the output voltage and power.

Key words: Vibration, Energy Harvester, MEMS, Piezoelectric, Tapered Cantilever, Perforation, Multi-perforation, Spiral, Multi-beam, Bandwidth, Magnetic proof mass.

Contents

List of Figures

List of Tables

List of Abbreviations

$MEMS$	Micro-electro-mechanical system
$CMOS$	Complementary metal oxide semiconductor
EH	Energy harvesting
$PZEH$	Piezoelectric energy harvester
PZ	Piezoelectric
WSN	Wireless sensor node
GPS	Global positioning system
IMD	Implanted medical device
$HAVC$	Heating, ventilation, and air conditioning system
IoT	Internet of things
PZT	Lead zirconate titanate
ZnO	Zinc oxide
Si	Silicon
Al	Aluminium
d_t	Reverse piezoelectric coefficient
D	Electric displacement or electric flux density
ε^s	Dielectric permittivity under constant strain
ε^s	Dielectric permittivity under constant stress
E	Electric field in z direction
L	Length of the cantilever
b	Width of the cantilever
$q_{zx}(t)$	Charge generated in a plate in absence of external field
$q_{zx,total}(t)$	Charge generated in the plate in the presence of external field
S^E	Matrix of compliance coefficient
S	Mechanical strain
T	Mechanical stress
v	Poisson's ratio
S_P	Strain at the middle of the piezoelectric layer
S_S	Strain at the middle of the substrate layer
t_P	Thickness of the piezoelectric layer
t_{PC}	Distance between centre of the piezoelectric layer and neutral axis
t_S	Thickness of the substrate layer
T_P	Mechanical stress on the piezoelectric layer
T_S	Mechanical stress on the substrate layer
w	Transverse deflection of the plate
$V(t)$	External voltage applied across a plate
$V_i(t)$	Voltage generated by PZ Plate
Y_P	Young's modulus of the piezoelectric layer
Y_S	Young's modulus of the substrate layer

Z_N	Z coordinate of the neutral axis
Z_P	Z coordinate of the piezoelectric layer
Z_S	Z coordinate of the substrate layer
T_{pxx}	Applied stress in X plane
T_{pyy}	Applied stress in Y plane
T_{pxy}	Applied stress in XY plane
S_{pxx}	Bending strain in X plane
S_{pyy}	Bending strain in Y plane
S_{pxy}	Bending strain in XY plane
D_r	Flexural rigidity of the plate
SRC	Simple Rectangular cantilever
$RCWM@5mT$	Rectangular cantilever with a magnetic proof mass of 5mT
$DBWOM$	Dualbeam without magnetic proof mass
$DBWM@5mT$	Dualbeam with magnetic proof mass of 5mT
$DBWM@10mT$	Dualbeam with magnetic proof mass of 10mT
$DBWM@20mT$	Dualbeam with magnetic proof mass of 20mT
$DBWM@30mT$	Dualbeam with magnetic proof mass of 30mT

Chapter 1

Introduction to piezoelectric energy harvester

1.1 Background

The tremendous advancement in the field of the semiconductor industry makes it feasible to produce miniaturized electronic devices. These miniaturized devices open a new door in the field of health care, which in recent years make a great jump in the field of bio-implants. The wireless sensors nodes (WSN) that are used in many areas such as collecting data from the deep bottom of the sea [1], in data distribution-based applications [2], [3] controlling the adverse effect due to volcano [4], avalanche rescue [5], and underground monitoring [6]. These devices mostly power by conventional batteries. These applications pose a formidable challenge in replacing battery like in the case of a pacemaker which may cost surgery to the patient. The miniaturization of the battery system is quite difficult due to the limitation in the current technology. Even though the power consumption of these devices is low, the limited life span of the battery and chemical side effects reduces the overall life of the devices, which is another important challenge. Although some bio-compatible batteries [7] have larger life period, but eventually, it also requires recharging or replacement and other replacement related complications.

Therefore there is a need to adopt a necessary and efficient action that can perform or resolve the replacement of a battery-operated device. There are few drawbacks of the conventional/battery-operated method, so an energy harvesting method has been adopted. The conversion of ambient energy from one form to another is known as energy harvesting. The environment provides a limitless amount of renewable energy from wind, water flow, ocean waves, and solar energy. These renewable sources generate power on the macro-scale, which is unsuitable for low-power electronic devices or sensors. The different micro-scale energy sources are vibrations from machines, mechanical stress, strain from high-pressure motors, manufacturing machines, and waste rotations. Chemical, biological sources, and radiation can be considered ambient energy sources. Besides these energy sources, the human body also generates mechanical and thermal energy through walking, running, and many different physical activities. Energy harvesting from these micro-scale energy sources can offer a plausible solution to the shorter battery life and need for frequent replacement. Table 1.1 shows the fundamental difference between conventional methods versus the energy harvesting method. Therefore, there is pressing demand from the health care and disaster management council for devices with longer battery life and without the need for battery replacement. Energy harvesting can resolve this problem without harming or polluting the environment.

Table 1.1: Battery operated versus energy harvesting sensor

Features	Battery Operated Sensor	Energy Harvesting Sensor
Source of Energy	Charged battery	Environment/Human Body
Preservation Cost	High, recharging and replacing the battery	Low, Self-sustaining
Constraint	Energy efficient, long life battery	Energy-neutral
Quality of service	As low as possible	As high as possible
Predictability	High, battery models	Low

Table 1.2: Comparison between the different ambient energy source

Energy Source	Transducer	Output Power	Requirement
Solar (Outdoor)	Photovoltaic Cells	10-15 mW/cm^2* [8]	AM 1.5 (Sunlight)
Solar (Indoor)	Photovoltaic Cells	10-100 $\mu W/cm^2$ [9]	Indoor Light 1-10 W/m^2
Thermal	Thermoelectric generator	20 $\mu W/cm^2$ [10]	Temperature Gradient $>10^o C$
Air Flow	Micro Windmill	20 $\mu W/cm^2$ [11]	5 m/s wind speed
RF Radiation	RF Antenna	10 $\mu W/cm^2$ [12]	MPE limit 1-5 mW/cm^2
Vibrations	Piezoelectric	300 $\mu W/cm^3$ [13]	Frequency matching with ambient vibration
	Electrostatic	100 $\mu W/cm^3$ [13]	External Voltage Source
	Electromagnetic	400 $\mu W/cm^3$ [14]	Magnetic field intensity

*Artificial light o/p 100 W/cm^2

There are different approaches for energy conversion, such as solar, thermal, chemical, RF radiation, mechanical vibration, that have been reported in the last decade. Table 1.2 compiles the different ambient sources of energy and their requirement. Mechanical vibration is the most popular out of all these methods, which can provide sufficient energy to power low-power devices. The vibrations from machines, waste rotations, movement of the human body such as cardiac/ lung motion, blood circulation, muscle relation, and contraction can be converted to electrical energy by the mechanical-based energy harvester. The different techniques that can harvest mechanical vibration energy to useful electrical energy are electromagnetic, [15], [16] electrostatic [16], [17] and piezoelectric mechanism [18], [19], [20]. The piezoelectric energy harvester (PZEH) can convert mechanical vibration into electricity without any external voltage supply. It helps in designing the simple architecture of this mechanism as compared to the electrostatic and electromagnetic mechanisms. The simple architecture of the piezoelectric mechanism leads to the miniaturized size, which is more desirable to the MEMS technology, where micro-machining techniques must create the structures. So piezoelectric energy harvester can be easily compatible with the MEMS technology. It also has a high electromechanical coupling effect than the other two mechanisms. Due to these advantages, PZEH is preferred over others and widely studied in the last decade.

Table 1.3: Different source of vibration energy [21]

Source of Vibration	Frequency (Hz)	Acceleration (m/s^2)
Human Walking	2	0.4
Passenger automobile engine	200	12
Base of 3-axis machine tool	70	10
After closing the door	125	3
Blender machine	121	6.4
Washing and drying machine	121	3.5
HVAC vents in commercial buildings	60	0.2-1.5
Instrumental panel of car	13	3
Microwave oven	121	2.5
Windows beside busy street	100	0.7
Footbridge	0.9-1	-

Since the PZEH works more efficiently in the proximity of an excitation frequency, the designed resonant frequency of the cantilever structure of the PZEH should be close to the ambient vibration frequency. Table 1.3 gives the list of different sources of vibration along with their respective accelerations and frequency. So, there are two main challenges in the design of any PZEH. The first is to achieve the low frequency that should match the vibration frequency of the target ambient vibration, and the second is to achieve the high bandwidth. The broadband energy harvester can harvest electrical energy from finite frequency intervals. So, the EHs must have a low target resonant frequency with a broader bandwidth.

1.2 Techniques of vibration energy harvester

1.2.1 Electrostatic Energy Harvesting

Electrostatic energy harvesting utilizes a variable capacitor to convert mechanical vibrations to electricity. In a simple parallel plate capacitor, the capacitance is given by

$$C = \varepsilon_o \varepsilon_r \frac{A}{d} \tag{1.1}$$

Where ε_o is the permittivity of free space, ε_r is the relative permittivity, A is the area of the plate overlap $(A = lw)$, and d is the plate spacing. The voltage, V is related to the stored charge, Q by,

$$V = \frac{Q}{C} \tag{1.2}$$

The electric energy is given by

$$E = \frac{1}{2} C V^2 \tag{1.3}$$

If an initial constant voltage is provided, an electric field is induced between the plates, and the plates get charged to Q and –Q respectively. Now, generally one plate is kept fixed and the other is movable. Now mechanical vibrations cause the movable plate to be displaced with respect to the fixed plate, and as a result the plate separation changes. The change results in a change in capacitance. As the voltage is kept constant the change in C will result in change in E. Generally, they have structure similar to accelerometers or gyroscopes. A design having an inertial mass with several comb fingers is considered. By configuring the dimensions of inertial mass and the crab leg structures, which support the inertial mass, resonance frequency of the structure can be tuned to desired range. Typical electrostatic energy harvester designs are shown in Fig. 1.1. In-plane overlap and in-plane gap closing type of harvesters [22] are used to convert the vibrations which are in plane with the harvester. The out-of-plane gap closing type [22] of harvester is used to convert vibrations which are perpendicular to the plane of the harvester.

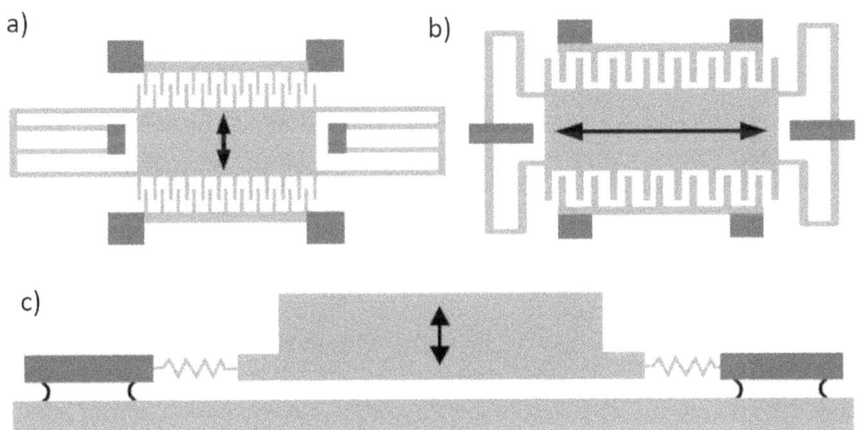

Figure 1.1: Structures of electrostatic energy harvester, (a) in-plane overlap, (b) in-plane gap closing, (c) out-of-plane gap closing converter.[22]

Although for electrostatic energy harvesters are fabrication is favourable, their use in many applications is limited by the polarization requirement of the structures. They need an external voltage source to kick-start their operation. Also, they have high output impedance especially at low frequencies. When compared with piezoelectric harvesters, displacement range of the electrostatic harvesters is limited due to pull-in voltage. The low displacement leads to low power density.

1.2.2 Electromagnetic Energy Harvesting

According to Faraday's Law of Electromagnetic induction, an electric current is induced in a closed circuit when the magnetic flux through any surface bounded by the conductor changes. Using this law, magnetic transducers convert vibration energy into electrical energy through magnetic induction. Input vibration results in relative motion between a magnet and a coil, which leads to a time-varying flux and induced voltage, as shown in Fig. 1.2. The voltage induced by the change in magnetic flux causes current to flow in the coil and delivers electrical energy to an external load.

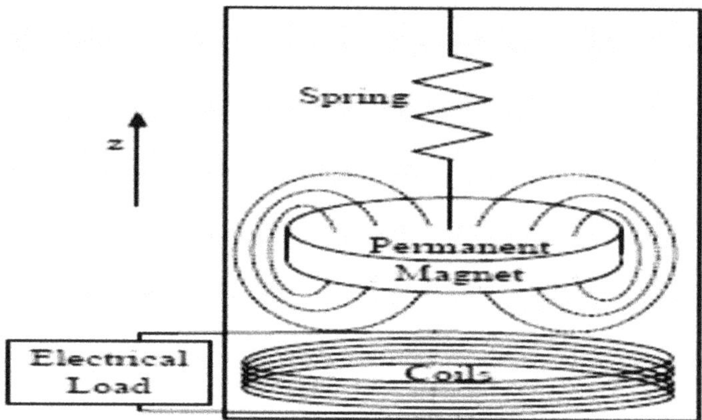

Figure 1.2: Magnetic transducer schematic diagram

For electromagnetic energy harvesters, cantilever beam structures have been widely studied in literature [15] [16] [23] [24]. Other than cantilever structures [25], placed an array of beams in a magnetic field and patterned coils on the surface of beams. The electromagnetic transducers offer the following benefits than the electrostatic transducers:

1. They provide relatively higher power densities than electrostatic transducers.

2. They do not require any external source to provide a kick-start to their operation.

In spite of being advantageous than the electrostatic energy harvesters, the major drawbacks of electromagnetic transducers are as follows:

1. They are not easily compatible and integrable with MEMS fabrication processes like batch processing.

2. Their performance in terms of power output degrades with decrease in dimension.

1.3   Piezoelectric energy harvesting

The piezoelectric materials show the linear relationship between electrical and mechanical parameters. The piezoelectric materials can generate electrical energy when the external stress is applied on the surface, known as the direct piezoelectric effect. There will be mechanical deformation in the piezoelectric plate when an electric field is applied across the piezoelectric plate. This phenomenon is called the reverse piezoelectric effect. Fig. 1.3a, shows the direct piezoelectric effect, in which the applied force generates the electric current, whereas, in Fig. 1.3b, there is a deflection in the PZ plate when the external electric field is applied across the plate. So, the fundamental equations [20], [26], [27] to find the developed mechanical strain (S) and the electric displacement (D) in the piezoelectric materials under given mechanical stress, T and electric field, E is given in Eqs. (1.4a) and (1.4b), respectively.

$$D = d.T + \varepsilon^{T}.E, \tag{1.4a}$$
$$S = s^{E}.T + d_{t}.E, \tag{1.4b}$$

Here, s^{E} is strain under zero or constant electric field and ε^{T} is the dielectric permittivity under zero or constant stress. d and d_{t} are the piezoelectric coefficient and reverse piezoelectric coefficient respectively. Eq. (1.4a) represent direct piezoelectric effect and Eq. (1.4b) represent reverse piezoelectric effect.

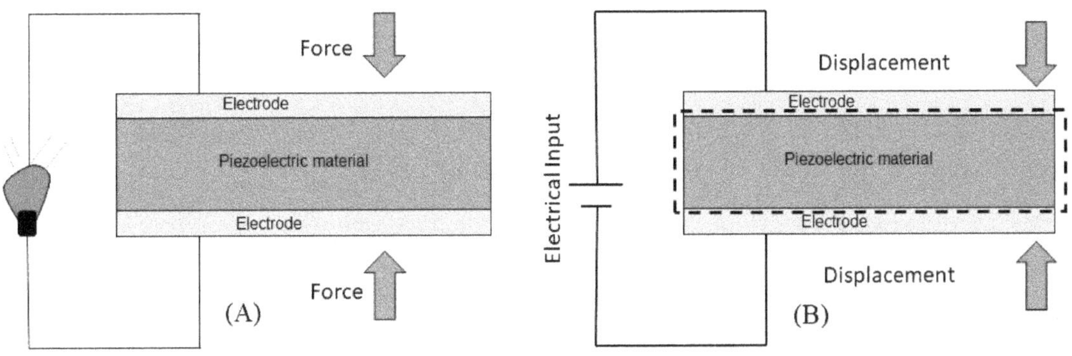

Figure 1.3: (a) Direct piezoelectric effect (b) Reverse piezoelectric effect

The above equations are fundamentally applicable for different directions of acting stress and the corresponding generated electric field. There is two coupling mode for the piezoelectric materials 31 modes and 33 modes. Commonly, stress occurs in the lateral direction (i.e., x-direction, which is denoted by 1) and the electric field is generated perpendicular to it (i.e., z-direction, which is denoted by 3). This mode is called 31 modes. In the 33 modes, electric field and stress occurred in the same direction. The direct piezoelectric effect and reverse piezoelectric effect in 31 modes are given in Eqs. (1.5a) and (1.5b).

$$D_3 = d_{31}.T_1 + \varepsilon_{33}^T.E_3 \tag{1.5a}$$
$$S_1 = s_{11}^E.T_1 + d_{31}.E \tag{1.5b}$$

The piezoelectric coefficient usually quantifies the performance of the piezoelectric materials (d_{3i}). The piezoelectric coefficient is the open circuit charge density ratio, and the applied stress and its unit are C/N. Typically, the d_{33} coefficient is higher than the d_{31} coefficient. However, the 31 modes are most used modes since it has a large strain in the lateral direction.

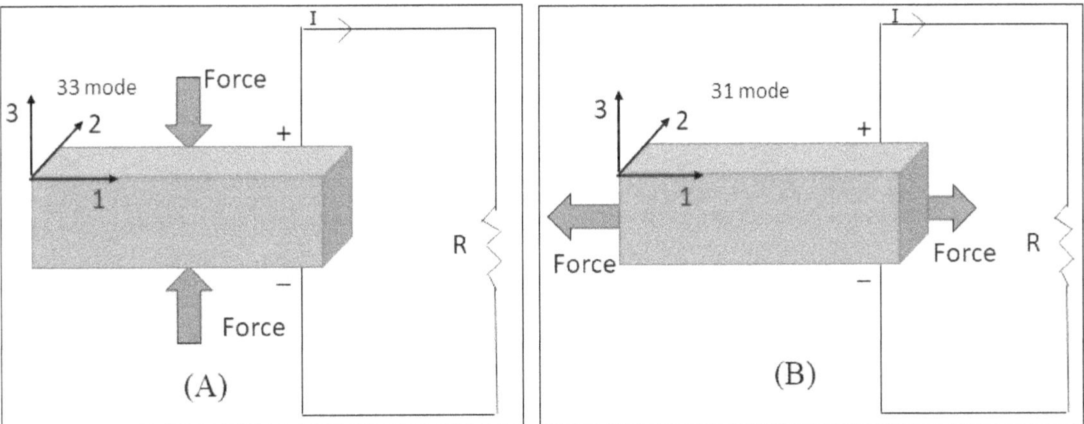

Figure 1.4: Modes of piezoelectric materials (a) 33 mode (b) 31 mode

The piezoelectric energy harvester is the most used cantilever type structure to convert mechanical vibration to electrical energy. The cantilever type structure can produce significant mechanical strain during oscillation. The fundamental frequency is generally much lower than the other mode of vibration in the cantilever structure. The cantilever structures can be bimorph or unimorph cantilevers. Bimorph has two piezoelectric layers, which are bonded together with shim at the centre of the design. When operated in the 31 modes, the top layer of the PZ layer is in elongation mode, and the bottom PZ layer is in compression and harvest electrical energy using the PZ effect. The unimorph configuration PZ layer is a sandwich between two electrode layers on the top of the substrate layer.

The charge generated in the PZ layer can be parallel or perpendicular to the applied mechanical strain depends upon the 31 modes or 33 modes of operation. The open-circuit voltage V_{oc} produced in the PZ layer is given by Eqs. (1.6).

$$V_{oc} = \frac{d_{ij}}{\varepsilon_o \varepsilon_r} \sigma_{ij} t_p \tag{1.6}$$

Here, d_{ij} is the piezoelectric constant, $\varepsilon_o, \varepsilon_r$ is the air permittivity and relative permittivity of the piezoelectric material and σ_{ij} is the stress in the PZ layer and t_p is the thickness of the PZ layer.

1.4 Energy Harvesting Basics

Rigid body vibration is a common occurrence in nearly all dynamical systems and can be attributed to various sources, including uneven mass within the system and material deterioration. Each system exhibits a distinct characteristic behaviour that can be summed up in two terms: natural frequency and damping constant. Usually, the dynamic properties of a vibrating body related to energy harvesting are studied using a lumped spring mass system with one degree of freedom. Linear response of the system can be easily visualised and analysed with the help of single degree of freedom. Fig 1.5 shows the multilayer Cantilever beam with tip mass, and its equivalent lumped spring mass system of a vibrating rigid body with external excitation. In PZEH, cantilever with proofmass is the most common used configuration, in which the stiffness of the structure depends on applied load, material property and area cross-section perpendicular to the vibration.

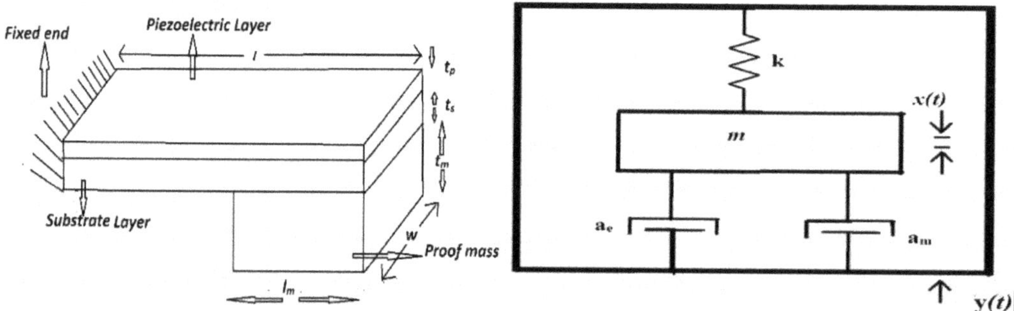

Figure 1.5: (a) Multilayer Cantilever beam with tip mass, (b) equivalent lumped spring mass system of a vibrating rigid body

The general model for the conversion of vibrotational kinetic energy of mass to electrical energy can be analyzed by simple linear system, which can be shown by schematic in figure 1. The system can be explained mathematically by [13]

$$m\frac{\partial^2 z}{\partial t^2} + (a_e + a_m)\frac{\partial z}{\partial t} + Kz = -m\frac{\partial^2 y}{\partial t^2} \tag{1.7}$$

Where x is the deflection of spring, y is the inertial displacement, $z = x - y$ is the total displacement, m is the mass, a_e is the electrically induced damping coefficient a_m is the mechanical induced damping coefficient and k is the spring constant. The energy conversion from vibrating mass to electric energy is alike linear damper with mass spring system, which is the main idea behind this model. Since the conversion of energy is due to loss of mechanical kinetic energy so above model can be used for piezoelectric energy harvester though electrical system effect on mechanical system is not linear. The loss in power of mechanical system by a_m, electrically induced damping is gain in power by electrical system. The electric induced force is a_e x. A damping coefficient ζ, dimensionless quantity is ratio of system damping to the critical damping as,

$$\zeta = \frac{c}{c_c} = \frac{c}{2\sqrt{mK}} \tag{1.8}$$

The natural frequency of the spring mass damper system is given as

$$\omega_n = \sqrt{\frac{K}{m}} \tag{1.9}$$

Here, ω_n is the resonant frequency, $K = \frac{3EI}{L^3}$ is the spring constant, m is the mass of the cantilever, E is the modulus of elasticity and $I = \frac{1}{12}bh^3$ is the moment of inertia and L is the length of the beam. Here b and h are the width and thickness of the beam in transverse vibration.

The ratio of output z(t) and input y(t) can be obtained by applying Laplace transform with zero initial condition on Eq. 1.7 as,

$$\left|\frac{Z(s)}{Y(s)}\right| = \frac{s^2}{s^2 + 2\zeta\omega_n s + \omega_n^2} \tag{1.10}$$

The time domain of the response can be obtained by applying inverse Laplace transform on Eqn. 1.10 and assuming the external excitation as $y = Y sin(\omega t)$.

$$z(t) = \frac{(\frac{\omega}{\omega_n})^2}{\sqrt{(1-(\frac{\omega}{\omega_n})^2)^2 + (2\zeta\frac{\omega}{\omega_n})^2}} Y sin(\omega t - \phi) \tag{1.11}$$

here $\phi = \frac{C\omega}{K-\omega^2 m}$.

The product of force and velocity gives the power generated. The power converted is given by

$$P = 1/2a_e(x^2) \tag{1.12}$$

The following expression for power can be derived from the eq 1.7 and eq 1.12.

$$|P| = \frac{m\zeta_e Y^2 \omega_n \omega^2 (\frac{\omega}{\omega_n})^2}{(1-(\frac{\omega}{\omega_n})^2)^2 + (2\zeta_t\frac{\omega}{\omega_n})^2} \tag{1.13}$$

Where Y is the displacement and P is the output power, ζ_e is an electrical damping ratio ($a_e = 2m\zeta_e\omega_n$), ζ is the combined damping ratio ($\zeta = \zeta_e + \zeta_t$), ω is input frequency and ω_n is the natural resonant frequency of the system.

The maximum power can be obtained by setting the operating frequency as natural frequency and $\zeta_m = \zeta_e$ which is given by,

$$|P| = \frac{mY^2\omega_n^2}{4\zeta} \tag{1.14}$$

From the Eqn 1.14 it may be observed that the maximum power can be obtained from the PZEH when we increase the resonant frequency, mass, and amplitude and lowering damping coefficient.

1.4.1 Modelling of Piezoelectric plate attached to long cantilever beam

There are many cases where the piezoelectric plate is attached to the long cantilever beam, it becomes necessary to determine the stress distribution along the beam's length as a function of stimulation frequency.

Here, we provide a basic, step-by-step process for determining the stress distribution along a continuous beam, which can be utilised to determine the location of piezoelectric plates.

1. In order to determine the relative displacement, which is a function of time and position, using the governing equation of motion. For a given boundary condition, the basic Euler-Bernoulli beam equation can be used to determine the curvature and transverse displacement of a beam. It is represented as follows:

$$EI\frac{\partial^4 w(x,t)}{\partial x^4} = -m_a\frac{\partial^2 w(x,t)}{\partial t^2} \tag{1.15}$$

   here $m_a = \rho A$, is the mass per unit length and A is area of cross-section.

2. Assuming the mass of the cantilever as M and Mass of the proof mass as M_v and solving the differential equation and applying the appropriate boundary condition, which is given as:

$$w(0,t) = \frac{\partial w(0,t)}{\partial x} = 0 \tag{1.16a}$$

$$\frac{\partial^2 w(L,t)}{\partial x^2} = 0; \tag{1.16b}$$

$$EI\frac{\partial^3 w(L,t)}{\partial x^3} = M\frac{\partial^2 w(L,t)}{\partial x^2} \tag{1.16c}$$

3. The general solution of eqn 1.15 can be obtained by using the method of separation as

$$w(x,t) = W(x)Q(t) \tag{1.17a}$$

$$W(x) = C_1 Cos(\lambda\frac{x}{L}) + C_2 sin(\lambda\frac{x}{L}) + C_3 Cos(\lambda\frac{x}{L}) + C_4 Sin(\lambda\frac{x}{L}) \tag{1.17b}$$

4. After applying the boundary condition and solving for the unknown C's. The natural frequency for the transversal motion of the cantilever beam can be obtained analytically is given by the Euler Bernoulli equation as

$$f_i = \frac{1}{2pi}\left(\frac{\lambda}{L}\right)^2\sqrt{\frac{EI}{\rho A}} \tag{1.18}$$

where i is the mode index, ρ is the mass density, A is the cross-sectional area of beam, and L is the length of the beam.

5. The solution of equation 1.15 for the cantilever beam as derived by Erturk and Inman (2007) is given by

$$w(x,t) = W(x)Q(t) = \omega^2 \sum_{r=1}^{\infty} \frac{W(x)(\psi)}{\omega_r^2 - \omega^2 + i2\zeta\omega_r\omega} \tag{1.19}$$

where

$$W(x) = C_r cos(\frac{\lambda x}{L}) - cosh\frac{\lambda x}{L} - \beta[sin\frac{\lambda x}{L} - sinh\frac{\gamma_j x}{L}]$$

$$\beta = \frac{mL(sin\lambda - sinh\lambda) + \lambda M(cos\lambda - cosh\lambda)}{mL(sin\lambda + cosh\lambda) - \lambda M(sin\lambda - sinh\lambda)}$$

$$Q(t) = \frac{\psi\omega^2}{\omega_r^2 - \omega^2 + i2\zeta\omega_r\omega}y_0 e^{j\omega t}$$

$$\psi = -M\int_0^L W(x)dx + M_v W(L)$$

6. The generated strain on the surface of the beam at a distance y from the neural axis can be obtained by taking second degree partial derivative of transverse displacement w(x,t)

$$\varepsilon(x) = -y\frac{\partial^2 w}{\partial x^2} \tag{1.20}$$

The stress generated in the beam is given by the Hooke's law as $\sigma(x) = E\varepsilon(x)$.

Now suppose the PZ plate is bounded by the beam, then the voltage generated by the PZ materials like PZT, ZNO or AlN can be estimated by taking the product of the stress generated and PZ voltage coefficient assuming the 31 mode of vibration as:

$$V(x/L) = g_{31}E\varepsilon(x/L)L_b \tag{1.21}$$

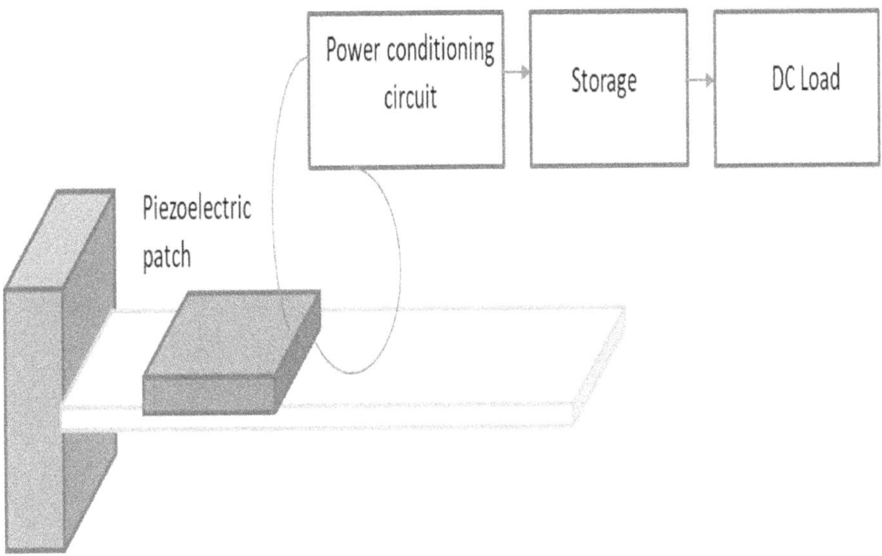

Figure 1.6: Typical model of piezoelectric energy harvesting mechanism

The output power generated by the PZ cantilever connected with the resistive load of value R is given by

$$P = \frac{V^2}{R} = \frac{1}{R}g_{31}E\varepsilon(x/L)L_b^{\ 2} \tag{1.22}$$

where L_b is the length of piezoelectric crystal bonded to substrate beam

1.5 Literature survey

1.5.1 Performance enhancement techniques in piezoelectric energy harvester

The typical and the complete model of piezoelectric-based energy harvester can be represented as in Fig. 1.6 and Fig. 1.7. The performance of the PZEH depends on its shape, structure, and the selection of the piezoelectric material. Eq. (1.9) gives the equation of the resonant frequency of a piezoelectric cantilever structure.

The Piezoelectric energy harvester is generally used in low-frequency application, so researchers over the year tried to improve the output performance of the piezoelectric energy harvester. They tried to reduce the resonant frequency, improve the bandwidth of PZEH, and tried to improve the compatibility with MEMS and CMOS technology.

A. Techniques to reduce resonant frequency of PZEH

Low-level vibrations occur on many household appliances, everyday objects and around buildings. The fundamental frequency is generally below 100 Hz. Some of the portable system can use the miniaturized EH which can be functional at the low frequency ambient vibration. Mostly the implanted medical devices operated at such low frequency such as pacemaker, cardiac defibrillator. These devices requires the energy harvester with the miniaturized size which can work at such low frequency and able to generate enough electric power. So if the resonant frequency of the designed device is higher than target frequency range, then they will not be able to generate enough power. So, the main aim of the researchers over a period of time was to reduce the resonant frequency of the PZEH.

The resonant frequency of the EH can be reduced by increasing the length, or by using proof mass at the free end or by modifying the shape and size of the cantilever structure. So this subsection review the literatures in the above mentioned points.

Use of proof mass to reduce resonant frequency   Roundy et al. [22] in 2003 designed the rectangular bimorph cantilever with proof mass using PZT to reduce the resonant frequency of 120 Hz. Roundy et al. [28] again in 2004 showed that the use of the proof mass was able to reduce the resonant frequency without increasing the size of the cantilever. Shen et al. [29] in 2008

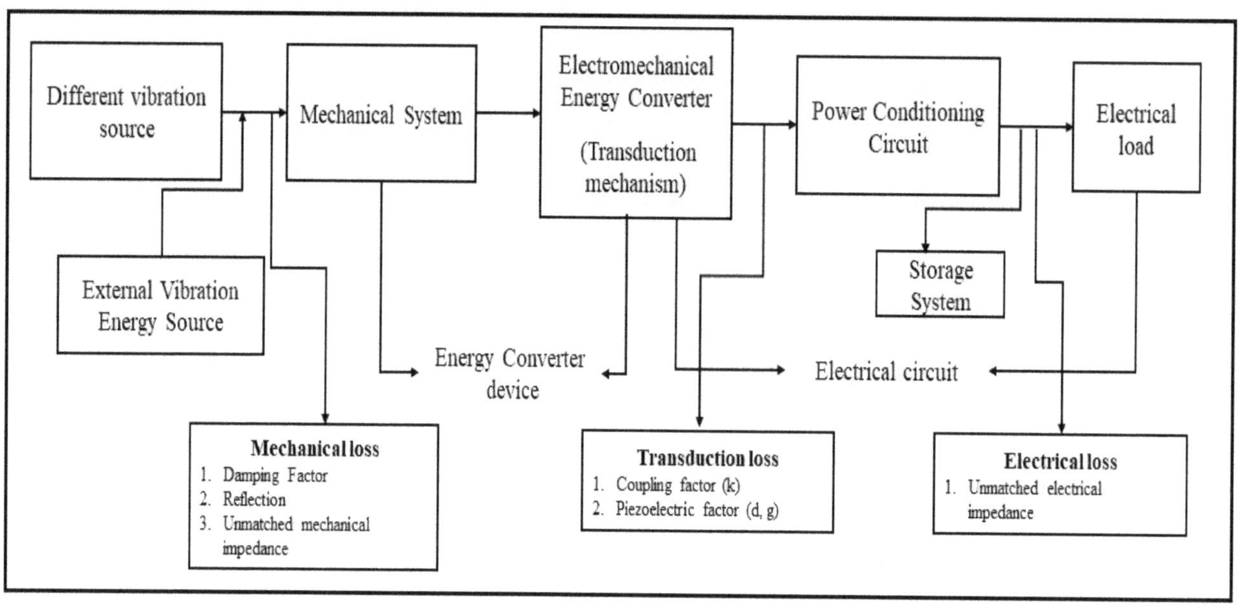

Figure 1.7: Complete model of PZEH

designed the unimorph PZT cantilever with the integrated Si proof mass to achieve low resonant frequency and high cantilever deflection. The dimension of the fabricated device was 4.800 mm × 0.400 mm × 0.036 mm, and the size of the proof mass was 1.36 mm x 0.940 mm x 0.456 mm.

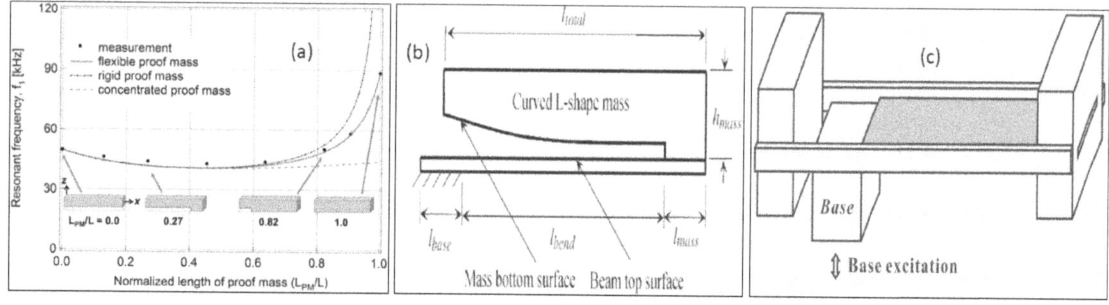

Figure 1.8: (a) Effect of size of proof mass on resonant frequency [30] (b) Piezoelectric harvester with curved L-shaped mass [31] (c) H-shaped cantilever structure [32]

Kim et al. [30] in 2011 investigated the effect of proof mass size on micro-cantilever with the flexible proof mass on the performance of the EH in terms of the resonance frequency and strain distribution. Li et al. [31] in 2010 used an L-shaped proof mass to reduce resonant frequency and achieved a low resonant frequency and higher output power. A power density of 1.45 mW/cm^2 was generated at excitation of 0.75g at the resonant frequency of 65.1 Hz. Gaun et al. [32] in 2013 used the H-shaped proof mass to improve the strain distribution of the PZEH device. Miller et al. [33] in 2013 used the sliding proof mass to tune the resonant frequency of the fixed-fixed beam. Lumentut et al. [34] in 2016 designed the arbitrarily shaped proof mass and developed the parametric design based model for the damped vibration PZEH. Jia et al. [35] in 2016 presented the mass tuning of the proof mass to optimize the generated output power of the energy harvester. They found that the proof mass occupying about 60-70% of the length of the cantilever was the optimum length to maximize the generated output power.

A summary of all the EHs with proof mass is tabulated in Table 1.4.

Structural modification to reduce resonant frequency   The geometrical structure of the cantilever plays a vital role in enhancing the efficiency of PZEH. Many researchers tried different structural modifications to reduce the resonant frequency and improved the performance of PZEH. Some researchers tried to increase the effective length of the cantilever structure to reduce the resonant frequency. Karami et al. in 2012 [38] designed a zigzag energy harvester for low frequency. They showed

Table 1.4: Summary for energy harvester with proof mass

Reference and Year	Material and Dimension	Resonant Frequency	Output Parameter
[22][28] 2004, 2003	PZT, 1 cm^3	120 Hz	Power- 250 μW
[29] 2008	PZT, 4.8× 0.4 × 0.036 mm^3	461.15 Hz	output voltage -160 mVpk; power-2.15 μW at 2g
[30] 2011	Si , 220.7 μm × 20.7 μm × 3.07 μm		The longer and distributed proof mass induces more strain, implying increased power generation of piezoelectric energy harvesters.
[31] 2010	PZT, 32 × 3.2 × 0.241 mm^3	65.1 Hz	A power density of 1.45 mW/cm^3 was achieved at 0.75g sinusoidal acceleration. The harvester generates 49 μW at walking speed of 3 mi/h.
[32] 2013	PZT , 81× 20 × 1.3 mm3	35.7 Hz	Open circuit voltage - 77.6 V, Load Voltage - 32 V
[36] 2012	AlN , 8.375 mm ×7.8mm×10.8μm	(58 $\pm$ 2) Hz, (75 $\pm$ 2) Hz and (105 $\pm$ 2) Hz	Vp/Pp = 1.7/32, 2.3/63 and 3.2/128 $V/\mu W$
[35] 2016	AlN , 3.5 mm × 3.5 mm	210 Hz	1.78 μW at 0.6 m/s^2 and up to 20.5 μW at 2.7 m/s^2
[37] 2019	PZT , 20×4×3 mm^3	232 Hz	Output Voltage- 9.1 mVpp and Output Power- 0.13 nW.

resonant frequency and output power variation with different dimensionless parameters such as damping, tip mass, number of members, stiffness of beam, etc. Abdeljaber et.al [39] designed a linear zigzag meta-structure cantilever for low frequency vibration. They used genetic algorithm to optimize the dimension of the zigzag.

Liu et al. [40] in 2006 designed an S-shaped cantilever beam for harvesting energy at a low frequency below 30 Hz and acceleration below 0.4g. Shindo and Narita [41] in 2014 also designed the S-shaped cantilever. They showed that the resonant frequency and output voltage depends on the waviness ratio and proof mass. The designed S-shaped cantilever structure generated an output voltage of 34 V at 40 Hz. Kim et al. [42] developed a circular-shaped cymbal transducer to investigate the energy harvesting capabilities, and produced a power of 39 mW across 400 Kohm resistor at 100 Hz resonant frequency.

Some researchers tried to modify the shape of the cantilever to reduce frequency and improves the stress distribution. White et al. [43] in 2001 also uses PZT to develop the triangular shaped EH that produces the output power of 2 μW under 9 mm of vibration amplitude at 80 Hz. Glynne-jonnes et al. [23] in 2001 developed a thick film PZT based tapered cantilever to generate the output power of 3 μW under 0.8 mm vibrational amplitude at the frequency of 80.1 Hz. Roundy et al. [22], [28] in 2003 and 2004 uses PZT in PZEH to investigate the performance of rectangular bimorph cantilever. It generated the output power of 250 μW at the resonant frequency of 120 Hz and excitation acceleration of 2.5 m/s^2. Mateu and Moll [44] in 2005 proposed that a triangular-shaped cantilever with a larger fixed end could endure the higher strain and had more significant deflection, which resulted in a higher power than a rectangular cantilever beam of the same size. In 2005, Roundy et al. [16] found that strain distributed were more evenly in the trapezoidal structure than in rectangular cantilever. The trapezoidal design can generate twice the energy as a rectangular structure. Baker et al. [45] in 2005 showed that the tapering of the rectangular cantilever at the free end increased the strain distribution along the length of the cantilever and improved the power density of the PZEH. It increased the output power by 30 % at resonant frequency 125 Hz by evenly distributing strain. Muthalif and Nordin [46] show that under the same applied load the truncation of a cantilever beam improves the strain distribution. They also show that triangular cantilever structure has a double average strain along the length than the normal rectangular cantilever structure of the same fabrication area and generate a higher output voltage. Hosseini and Nouri et al. [47] in 2016 reported that the strain distribution in the triangular cantilever is more than the rectangular and trapezoidal cantilever. Ayed et al. [48] show that the quadratic shaped cantilever beam generates twice the electrical energy than the rectangular shaped rectangular cantilever beam.

Dipta et al. [49] in 2018 designed the perforated tapered cantilever within 5 mm length to power the machine health monitoring system. They found that tapering towards the free end and perforation reduces the resonant frequency and improved the stress and strain distribution along the length of the cantilever. The designed structure generated an output voltage of 8.5 V and the peak output power of 3.61 μW at a resonant frequency of 101 Hz.

Sriramadas et al. [50] improve the performance of the bimorph piezoelectric harvester by the use of multistep thickness profile of the piezoelectric layer. The introduction of the multistep thickness profile helps in reducing the resonant frequency and increase the generated output power by 90 %. Paquin et al. [51] studies the effect of a variable thickness beam harvester on its electro-mechanical performance. They found that tapered beams have more uniform strain distribution across the PZ materials and improves the EH performance by 3.6 times. Ibrahim et al. [52] presented a comparison between the thickness tapered beam and width tapered beam. They show that beam truncated in thickness has 18% lower resonant frequency and 6.4% higher output power than beam truncated in width. Zhang et al. [53] presented a variable cross-section PZEH to obtain the electrical energy from the longitudinal motion of near shore sea wave. They found that variable cross-section PZEH has larger efficiency in terms of more uniform and bigger surface strain than conventional EH. Kundu et al. [54] show that a variable thickness profile in PZEH can achieve uniform stress along the length. They found that proposed PZEH generates 20% higher output power than the traditional cantilever beam with uniform thickness.

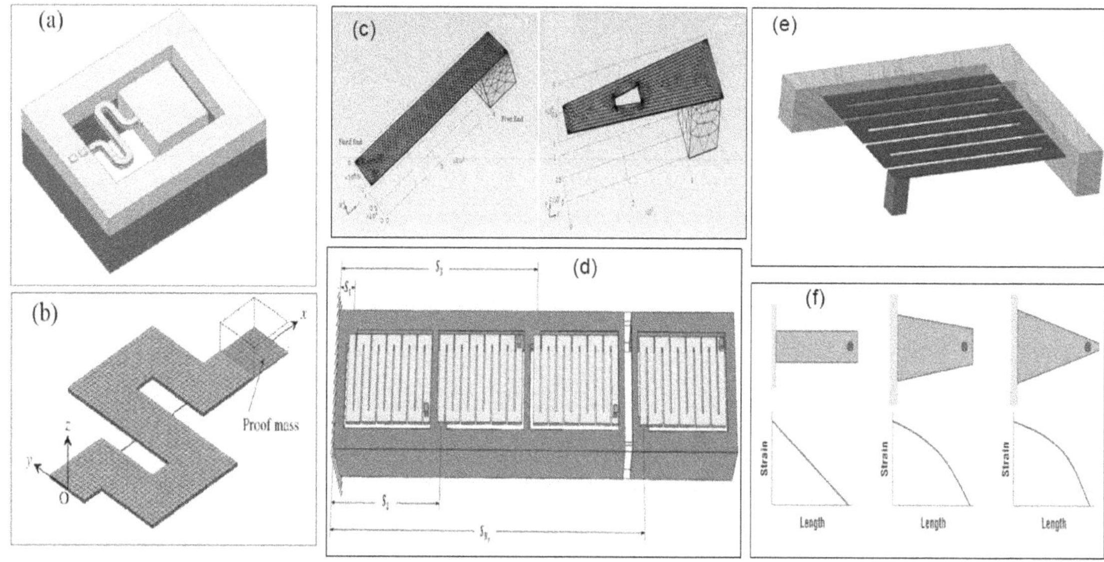

Figure 1.9: (a) S-shaped cantilever [40] (b) S-shaped piezoelectric cantilever [41] (c) Rectangular cantilever and perforated tapered cantilever [49] (d) A meta-structure consisting of the cantilever channel coupled with zigzag inserts [39] (e) Zigzag structure [38] (f) Relative strain profiles for alternative beam geometries [16]

After discussing the major structural modification techniques to reduce the natural frequency, we are tabulating the brief summary of all these techniques in table 1.5.

B. Different techniques to improve the bandwidth of PZEH

The ambient vibration is random, periodic, and mainly varies in the low-frequency region (e.g., a vibration of machines, concrete structure and motion of the human body). The ambient vibration has a wide bandwidth rather than a sharp peak. Most of the piezoelectric EH work efficiently around the resonant frequency and has a narrow bandwidth. The slight variation in the environmental frequency results in a sharp decrease in the output efficiency of EHs. Hence increase in bandwidth is needed to maximize the output power of EHs. Many researchers have used different techniques to increase the bandwidth. Several models have been proposed for the wideband energy harvesters [55], [56], [57] such as the use of a fluid or movable mass [58], use of several unconnected cantilever beams [59], an array of piezoelectric beams connected through springs [60], the use of

Table 1.5: Summary of different structural modification techniques to reduce natural frequency of energy harvester

Reference, Year	Material and Shape	Resonant Frequency	Output Parameter
[43] 2001	PZT, Triangular	80 Hz	Voltage-1.2 V, Power -2 μW
[23] 2001	PZT, Triangular	80.1 Hz	$3 \mu W$
[28][22] 2003, 2004	PZT, Rectangular	120 Hz	power-250 μW
[21] 2005	PZT, Trapezoidal	120 Hz	$375 \mu W / cm^3$.
[45] 2005	PZT, Trapezoidal	125 Hz	300 μW per cubic centimeter
[40] 2012	PZT, S-shaped	30 Hz	Voltage- 42 mV, Power- 0.3 μW
[41] 2014	PZT, S-Shaped	40 Hz	Voltage-40V
[49] 2018	ZnO, Perforated tapered	101 Hz	Voltage-8.5 V, Power-3.61 μW

parallel connection of single beam structures [61], use of stoppers, use of magnetic proof mass, etc. Some of the main methods have been described here.

Multiple-beam method to increase bandwidth of PZEH   Different researchers over the period used the multiple cantilever beam to increase the bandwidth by increasing the degree of freedom. Liu et al. [55] developed a MEMS-based power generator array for vibrational energy harvesting to increase the bandwidth. An array structure of three cantilevers of length 2-3.5 mm and width 0.75-1 mm were operated with 226-234 Hz bandwidth. The prototype generated the output power of 3.98 μW and output voltage of 3.93 V at the load resistance. Xue et al. [62] integrated the multiple bimorphs of different aspect ratios to increase the operating frequency of the EH. The series and parallel connection of bimorph was investigated on frequency bandwidth and found that connecting multiple bimorphs can increase frequency bandwidth. They found that bandwidth could moved to dominant frequency domain by increasing or decreasing the number of parallel bimorphs. The combination of the mixed pattern increased the output power as well as moved the frequency domain. Shahruz et al. [63] had designed a mechanical bandpass filter using an ensemble of beam mass systems for energy scavenging. They showed that the maximal frequency band of a bandpass filter was independent of the dimension of the beam and masses of the proof mass.

Bandwidth improvement of PZEH with stopper   Many researchers had showed that the use of stopper in a cantilever system could increase the bandwidth. The mechanical stoppers in the cantilever could induced the piecewise-linear hardening restoring effect. There would be sudden jumps in spring stiffness when the cantilever and stopper would touch each other. Huicong Liu et al. [64] used the stoppers on one side and both sides of the cantilever for the wide-band frequency response. The operating bandwidth ranged from 30-48 Hz corresponds to 34 to 100 nW at an acceleration of 0.6g in configuration 2. In contrast, in configuration 1, output power was slightly higher from 72 to 114 nW in the operating bandwidth range of 32 to 42 Hz. They showed that the output voltage and operating frequency range could be adjusted by changing the distance of the stopper. Dhakar et al. [65] proposed a PZEH consist of a composite cantilever beam with proof mass at the free end to overcome low output power at low frequency and limitation of harvesting mechanisms at narrow frequency range. They also used the mechanical stopper to improve the bandwidth and successfully increased the bandwidth from 5 Hz to 16 .4 Hz. Zhou et al. [66] investigated the different configurations of the stopper to enhance the harvesting performance of PZEH. They observed that there was a increase in bandwidth by increasing the stopper's stiffness, decreasing the space between stopper and cantilever and moving the stopper towards the free end. Still, it also resulted in the reduction of the harvested peak average power.

    The operation bandwidth of these EH that used a piece-wise linear model depends on the cantilever's spring constant, level of excitation, and the presence of non-linear restoring force. A stopper in the PZEH system may help to achieve the resonance effect if the overlapping distance is finely adjusted. The aforesaid mechanical impact may increase the mechanical instability, increase the risk of breakage, and reduces the long-term durability of a piezoelectric cantilever.

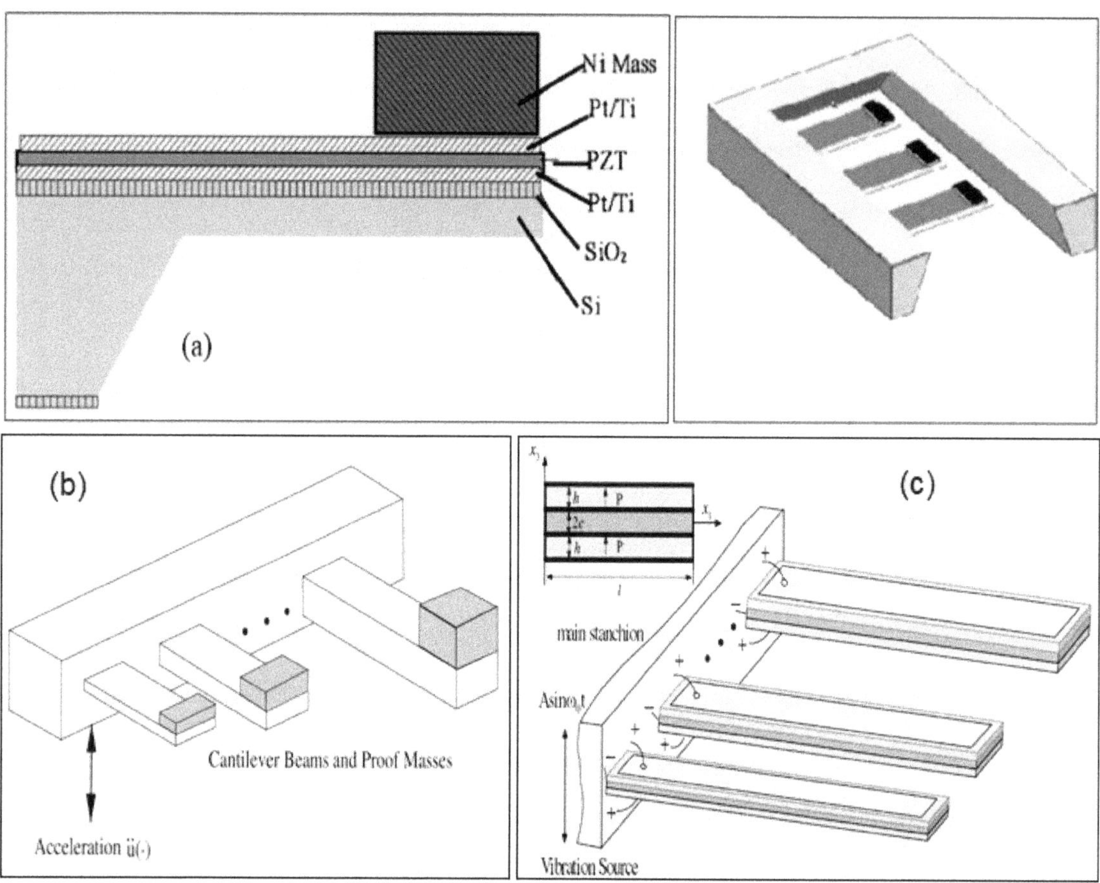

Figure 1.10: (a) Schematic configuration of single cantilever beam and micro power generator array [55] (b) A band pass filter using ensemble of beam mass system. [63] (c) A schematic illustration of a piezoelectric bimorph harvesting system [62]

Bandwidth improvement of PZEH using magnetic proof mass   Non-linearity in the PZEH can improve the output voltage and bandwidth. One of the methods to introduce non-linearity is the use of magnetic proof mass in the magnetic environment. The relative alignment, position, and arrangement of the magnet can introduce non-linearity in the system. Many researchers tried different configurations to improve the efficiency and operating bandwidth of PZEH. They tried to introduce magnet in the system to achieve monostable, [67], [68] bi-stable [69], [70], [71] or tri-stable state [72], [73], [74], [75] to increase the bandwidth.

Challa et al. [67] designed an EH of length 34 mm and tuned the resonant frequency with the magnetic force by changing the relative position of the magnets. This method helped to adjust $\pm$ 20% of the resonant frequency of the PZ cantilever beam. The cantilever successfully tuned in the frequency range of 22-32 Hz and generated the output power of (240-280) μW. Stanton et al. [69] showed that the non-linear EH was capable of increasing the bandwidth of the device and experimentally verified that the non-linear response could outperformed the linear response. Zhou et al. [71] tried to broadband enhancement by altering the angular orientation of the external magnets. They also showed that magnetic inclination plays a vital role in improving the bandwidth. They have achieved the bandwidth of (4-22) Hz by changing the angular orientation of the magnet. Zhou et al. [72] designed a tri-stable PZEH using the doubly magnet-coupled EH. The different magnetic coupling and non-linear characteristic responses had been obtained by adjusting the horizontal distance between the EHs. It helps in achieving the bandwidth of (5-14) Hz and generated the maximum output voltage of 20 V and output power of 0.16 mW. Zhou et al. [73] numerically and experimentally investigated a tri-stable harvester with a triple-well potential induced by a magnetic field at different harmonics in the frequency range of (1-20) Hz. They show that the tri-stable configuration is better than the bi-stable configuration and helps to achieve higher output energy on the broader frequency range. Zhou et al. [76] tries to achieve a penta-stable state by adjusting the position and orientation of permanent magnet and hence improve the efficiency. Tan et al. [77] tries to device a method to calculate magnetic force in the vibration and energy harvesting efficiency of the piezoelectric energy harvester. Zhu et al. [78] designed (13 x 5) mm^2 cantilever beam for the electromagnetic micro-generator. The resonant frequency of the

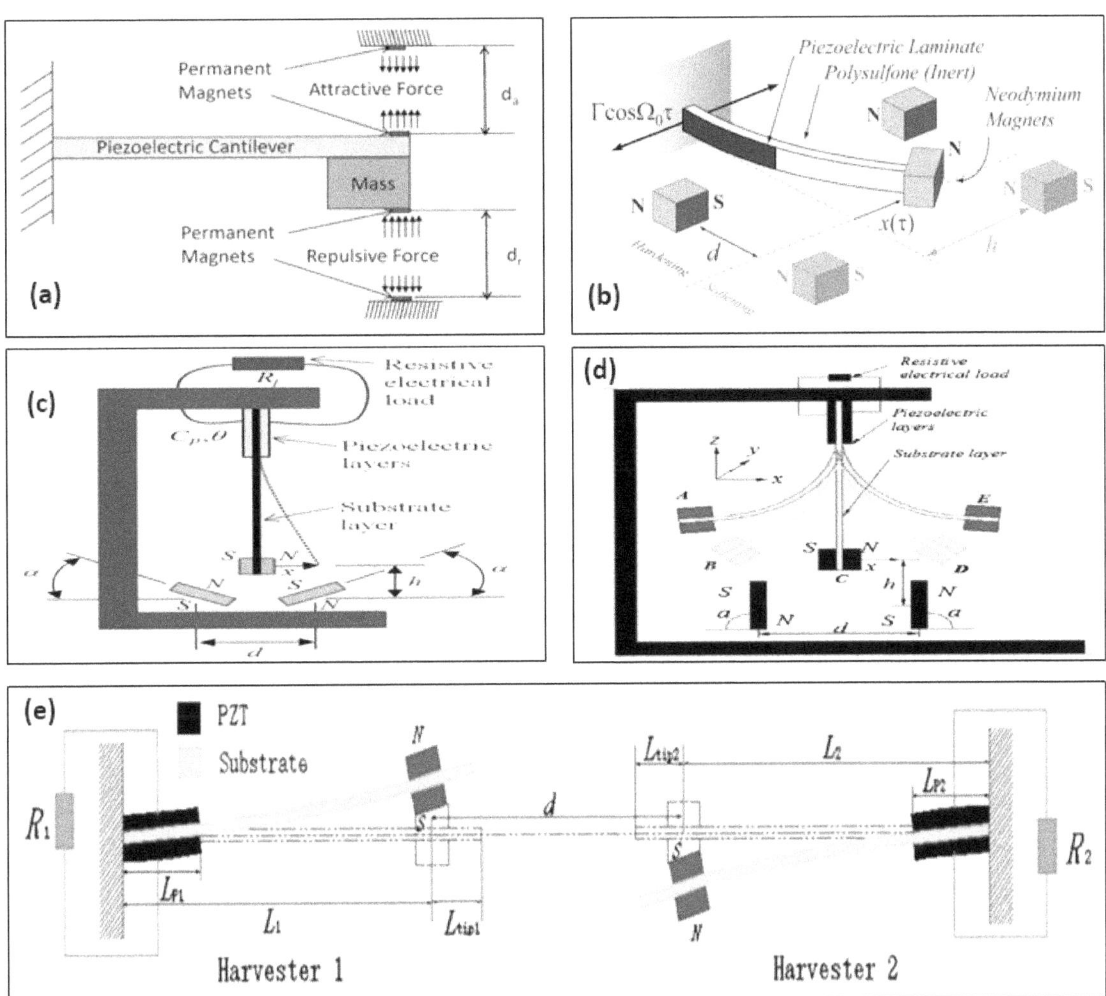

Figure 1.11: Schematic of (a) the resonance frequency tunable energy harvesting device [67] (b) the nonlinear piezoelectric cantilever with a permanent magnet end mass interacts with the field of oppositely poled stationary magnets [69] (c) the bi-stable PZEH with rotatable external magnets [71] (d) the tri-stable PZEH [73] (e) a doubly magnet-coupled energy harvesting system (DMEHS) [72]

cantilever has been tuned with the help of attractive force of axially aligned permanent magnet. Wei-jiun et al. [79] designed a 98 mm dual cantilever to enhance the bandwidth of the EH with permanent magnet on a dual cantilever. D. Guo et al. [80] also designed 12 cm long array of cantilevers to enhance the frequency bandwidth with the magnetic tip mass and increase the performance of EH.

The summary of the bandwidth enhancement techniques for PZEH is given in table 1.6.

1.5.2 Wearable and implantable PZEH

The advancement in EH has increased the need for a portable or wireless electronics system with an enhanced life span for a wide variety of applications. This section tries to demonstrate the different applications of the PZEH, which mainly includes implantable medical or wearable devices, harvesting the vibration energy for self-powered wireless sensors, and health monitoring devices. A wearable EH system uses the mechanical energy of the human motion to harvest electrical energy, which is properly rectified and regulated by the power conditioning circuits and stored the electrical energy in the storage device like rechargeable battery or capacitor. This harvested energy helps in achieving sustainable wearable products, wireless sensors nodes and system.

The different mechanical energy source available due the various human activity had been complied by the González et al. [83]. All human activities had been divided into two category, first one was continuous activity like blood flow and breathing etc. and second category was discontinuous activity such as movement of hand, walking etc. Niu et al. [84] also studied about the

Table 1.6: Summary of bandwidth enhancement techniques for piezoelectric energy harvester

Reference and Year	Material and Shape	Operating Frequency	Output Parameter
[55] 2008	PZT, Arrayed device	226-234 Hz	Voltage - 3.93 V, Power - 3.98 μW
[62] 2008	PZT-5H, Multiple piezoelectric bimorphs in series and parallel connection	82-133 Hz in mix pattern	Max. Power - 141 μW in mix pattern
[63] 2006	Ensemble of beam mass system	-	-
[81] 2015	PVDF, Pillar structure	62 Hz	Voltage - 4.5 V, Power - 58.4 μW
[20] 2020	ZnO, Coupled four beam structure	(135-150)Hz	Voltage - 8.25 V, Power - 22.7 μW
[64] 2012	PZT, PZT elements parallel arrayed on the supporting beam	18 Hz (30–48 Hz)	optimal power ranges from 34 to 100 nW
[65] 2013	5A Navy Type II piezoceramic, piezoelectric rectangular bimorph with stopper at free end	16.4 Hz	Voltage - 8 V
[82] 2016	Macro fiber composite (MFC) sheet,	7.4 Hz	Output Power - 429 μW and 411 μW for first and second resonances respectively.
[66] 2020	PZT, Rectangular cantilever beam with stopper	26.4 - 43.7 Hz	Output Power - 4.4 mW and 3.4 mW .
[67] 2008	Rectangular cantilever	22-32 Hz	output Power- (240-280)μW
[69] 2019	PZT-5H, Rectangular cantilever	10 Hz	Power - 5.2 mW
[71] 2013	PZT-5A, Rectangular cantilever	4-22 Hz	
[73] 2014	PZT-5A	3.5–11.8 Hz	
[72] 2015	PZT, A doubly magnet-coupled rectangular cantilever	5-14 Hz	Voltage- 20 V, Power - 0.16 mW

different energy source associated with different human body movement. They found that the motion of hip, ankle, knee, elbow and shoulder could produce the power upto 39.2, 69.8, 49.5, 2.1, and 2.2 W respectively. The discontinuous human motions or activities had attracted attention of many scientist and researchers to conduct the research in the field of bio-mechanical EH system. One of the most early attempt to harness the power of human activities had been done using shoe-inserted EH system because of its simple and easy implementation. Kymissis et.al [85] in 1998 and Shenck and Paradiso [86] in 2001 presented the piezoelectric shoe which used the parasitic power generated from walking. The PVDF bimorph hexagonal stave was mounted under the insole to extract energy from the walking as shown in Fig. 1.12. Shoe insole pedometer was developed by Ishida et al. in 2012 [87] to harvest the flexible large area electrical energy. It consists of 2 V organic pedometer circuit, PVDF roll based pulse-generator and other PVDF for harvesting energy. Renaud et al. showed that the motion of wrist and arm during walking could be a used to harvest energy or power. They had proposed the non-resonant system to describe the motion of arm and wrist. They had developed an analytical model and showed that the maximum power of 40 μW could be generated while walking.

The low power requirement of portable electronic and biomedical devices makes it feasible to power these devices by energy harvesting techniques. The different human activities such as walking, running, breathing, movement of the arm, or tiny bio-mechanical movements of muscles and organs inside the body (e.g., heartbeat, blood flow, eye blinking or muscle stretching, contraction/relaxation of the diaphragm and lungs, etc.), can be used to harness electrical energy.

The early implantable medical devices was dated back to 1958 with the implantable pacemaker [93]. Since then, implanted medical devices have been continuously used for tackling different health problems. In 1996, Staner [94] investigated the possibility of harnessing energy from a human source like chest motion during breathing and footstep during walking. Goto et al. [95] investigated the feasibility of using the automatic power-generating system of a quartz watch to power a pacemaker. A system attached to a dog's heart successfully generated 13 mJ of energy per heartbeat, showing that the automatic power-generation system could power a pacemaker. Clark et al. [96] analysed powering of in-vivo MEMS with piezoelectric transducer

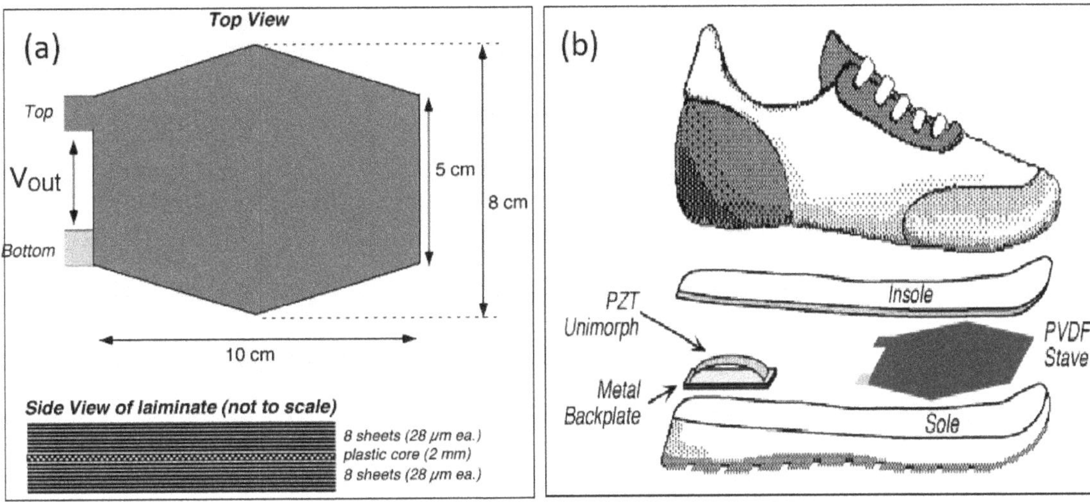

Figure 1.12: (a) Layout of the PVDF power insole [85], [86] (b) piezoelectric energy scavenging in shoes [85], [86]

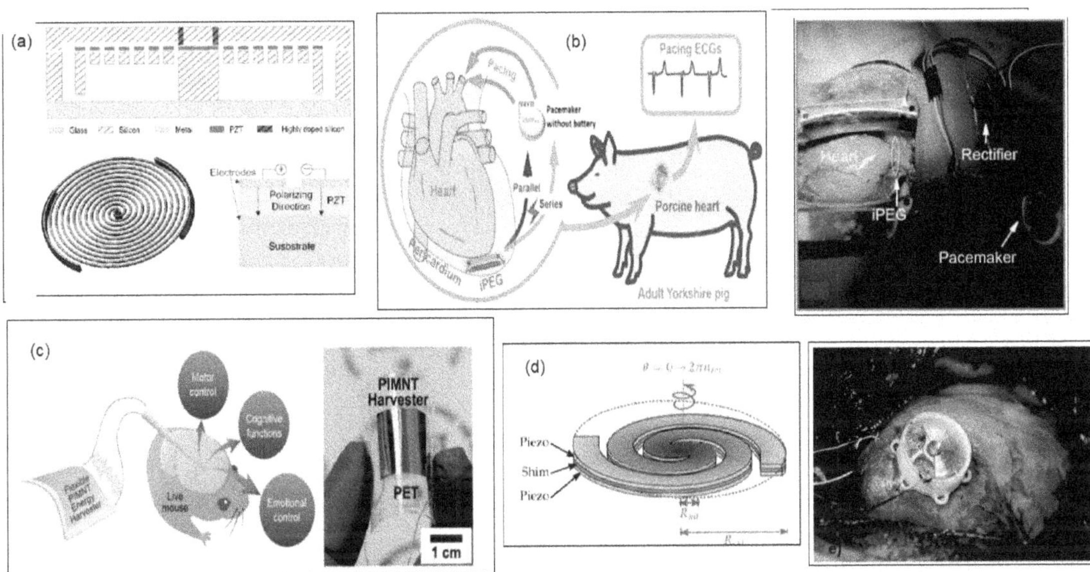

Figure 1.13: (a) Schematic structure of the SPEH [88] (b) mechanism of energy harvesting using pig's heart [89] (c) deep brain stimulation (DBS) applications using the flexible PIMNT energy harvester [90](d) multi-arm bimorph piezoelectric spiral cantilever [91] (e) in-vivo pacing:pacemaker sutured on the heart and inhibited by the magnet [92]

by actuating square thin plate from blood pressure. Q. Niu et al. [88] in 2009 proposed a MEMS-based spiral piezoelectric energy harvester (SPEH) for artificial heart wireless energy transmission. This SPEH energy harvester decreases the frequency and the size of a harvester. The SPEH uses PZT-4D PZ material with thickness 2 μm at 5g acceleration along the X-axis. They were able to generate peak to peak putput voltage of 40 V, current of 340 mA and an output power of 25.12 μWm. Martin Deterre et al. [91], [97] in 2011 developed an energy harvesting system for cardiac implant application. They achieve a power of 100 µW for the 0.5 cm^3 at 3.5g. The dimension of the system is $15 \times 7 \times 5 \ mm^3$, and the volume of the proof mass is 200 mm^3. They achieved a resonant frequency of 25 Hz. Zurbuchen et al. [92] designed an energy-harvesting mechanism derived from the working of a Swiss wristwatch and, combining this with a pacemaker, performed an $in-vivo$ study on a pig's heart for 30min. The outer diameter and the thickness of the prototype device were 27 mm and 8·3 mm, respectively, which makes its use impractical for the modern pacemaker. Ansari and Karami [98], [99] proposed a fan-folded structure to achieve low frequency. They show that the proposed structure could produce sufficient energy to power a pacemaker. However, the use of lead zirconate titanate (PZT) as piezoelectric material makes it harmful for human use, and an 18·4g (1g = 9·8 m/s^2) tip mass is too heavy for the pacemaker. Hwang et al. [100] reported a self-powered pacemaker that generated an output voltage of 8·2

V and an output current of 145 mA. Rufer et al. [101] proposed a rectangular cantilever of length 40 mm to achieve a resonant frequency of 15 Hz. The structure generated an output voltage between 1·5 and 4V and an output power between 6 and 18 mW. Jay et al. [102] proposed a rectangle-shaped EH of length 32 mm with a resonant frequency of 47 Hz to power a pacemaker. Jackson et al. [103] presented an aluminium nitride (AlN)-based EH to power a leadless pacemaker. The dimensions of the proposed structure were 8mm × 4mm × 4·6 mm, and it generated 2·92 mW of output power at a resonant frequency of 28·5 Hz at 0·15g acceleration. Anuruddh et al. [104] designed a spiral-shaped PZEH with the natural frequency in the range of 1.1 to 1.3 Hz. The maximum output voltage obtained from the 6 mm harvester is 0.9 V which is insufficient to power the pacemaker. The boosted output voltage with 80 % and 90 % duty cycle is 6 V and 7 V, respectively. Ning Li et al. [89] designed a generator with an elastic skeleton and piezoelectric composite. It can pace the porcine heart with the electrical energy generated from the heartbeat without any external energy storage device. The harvester can generate high output current of 15 µA in vivo over state of the art.

Many different researchers had tried to increase the lifespan of cochlear implant (CI) using the techniques of EH. Beker et al. [105] developed a micro-scale energy harvester to convert vibrations of an eardrum into electricity. They proposed two applications of the method, first is using this electricity to power the CI's battery, second is using this electricity for stimulating the auditory nerve. The size of the harvester footprint was 6×6 mm^3, and the resonant frequency was 474 Hz. Yip et al. [106] developed a fully implantable cochlear implant SoC with piezoelectric sensors, which had been integrated with implantable acoustic sensing system, sound processing system, and proof in concept.

Hwang et al. [90] reported a high performance flexible $(Pb(In_{1/2}Nb_{1/2})O_3 - Pb(Mg_{1/3}Nb_{2/3})O_3 - PbTiO_3)$ PIMNT thin-film based PZEH to power the deep-brain stimulation in mice. They reported that slight bending of the device generates a very high current of 0·57 mA.

The summary of different application related to the piezoelectric energy harvester is given in table 1.7.

Table 1.7: Summary of different application related to the piezoelectric energy harvester

Reference and Year	Material and Shape	Operating Frequency	Output Parameter
[105] 2013	Array of rectangular cantilever, PZT	474 Hz	Voltage- 588 mV, Power- 1.33 μW
[107] 2015	Fan folded structure $1 \times 1 \times 1cm^3$, PSI-5A 4E piezo sheets	170 Hz	Power 2.12 μW
[99] 2017	Fan folded geometry, $2 \times 0.5 \times 1cm^3$, PZT	15.79 Hz	Power 16.25 μW
[101] 2013	Rectangular, $40 \times 5 \times 0.38mm^3$, PZT	15 Hz	Voltage 1.5-4 V, Power 6 -18 µW
[102] 2016	Rectangular, $32 \times 12.19 \times 0.194mm^3$, PVDF	47 Hz	Voltage 25 V
[103] 2018	Rectangular, length 8 mm, width 4 mm, thickness 4.6 µW, AlN	28.5 Hz	Power 2.92 μW
[108][18] 2019	Rectangular shaped Spiral cantilever, 6mm×6 mm, ZnO	30.6 Hz	Voltage - 4 V, Power - 5.3 μW
[90] 2015	Rectangular, PIMNT	-	Open-circuit voltage- 11 V, Maximum current -0.57 mA

1.6   Motivation

One of the most critical trends in electronic equipment technology from its origin has been reducing the size and increasing its functionality. Small-scale PZEH is compact, light-weighted, and currently capable of harvesting electrical energy from the ambient source. However, harvesting sufficient energy from the ambient source still be a challenge due to the random nature of the ambient source.

All the literatures discussed above have tried to achieve the lowest possible resonant frequency. For example, in the case of a pacemaker, the target resonant frequency of the designed EHs should be below 50 Hz [98], [99], [107], [109]. Many researchers [92], [98], [99], [100], [107] tried to design the PZEH for pacemakers. They tried to achieve the target resonant frequency, but the size of the harvesters was big. Since the PZEH is a mechanical structure that would have a definite resonant frequency, thereby at that frequency, output voltage and power will be maximum. However, ambient vibration is random, making it challenging to capture all available energy by cantilever design. It has been observed that these cantilever based structures are incapable of operating over a wide range of frequencies [55], [75], [61], [58], [59]. So, there is a need for the design of wideband energy harvesters for deployment in diverse scenarios and applications. Hence, there is a need to increase the bandwidth of EH.

This research gap of reduction in resonant frequency while miniaturizing the size of EH and increasing the bandwidth of the harvester is the primary motivation behind this book.

1.7 Objectives of the book

The objective of this book is to design a MEMS based piezoelectric energy harvester. Briefly, the main objectives of this research work are:

1. Design of the piezoelectric energy harvester with low resonant frequency.

2. Miniaturized the size of the cantilever structure.

3. Design of PZ transducer focussing on the higher output voltage and power.

4. Design of wide bandwidth PZ transducer which can efficiently convert the vibrations exist in the ambient environment to electrical energy.

1.8 Contribution of the book

In this book, the piezoelectric energy harvester is designed using COMSOL MULTIPHYSICS software. The different contributions of the book is given below.

1. The structural modifications in the form of tapering, perforation and multi-perforation have been introduced in the cantilever structure to reduce the resonant frequency and improves output voltage and power. The perforation and multi-perforation not only reduces the resonant frequency but also improved the stress distribution within the cantilever structures. It also helped in increasing the output voltage and power of EH.

2. The book also designed the cantilever structure with tapered substrate thickness. It helped in reducing the underutilization of the piezoelectric layer towards the free end. The tapered substrate thickness reduced the resonant frequency. It improved the stress distribution within the cantilever structure, which resulted in improved the output performance of the piezoelectric cantilever structure

3. The L-shaped PZEH shows the low frequency range can be achieved without increasing the dimension of the cantilever.

4. The spiral-shaped piezoelectric cantilever structure has been designed that can be able to power the modern pacemaker. The spiral shape allowed to increase the length of the cantilever structures without compromising on compactness. The size of the designed spiral cantilever is within the permissible limit of the pacemaker.

5. The multi-beam cantilever structure has been designed to enhance the frequency bandwidth of the energy harvester (EH).

6. The permanent magnet has been introduced in the energy harvesting system to introduced non-linearity in the system. The use of magnetic proof-mass helps in improving the performance and frequency bandwidth of the harvester.

1.9　Organization of the book

The outline of the research work is as follows:

* **Chapter 1:** This chapter contains the introduction to the book, basic piezoelectric principle, literature survey, motivation, objectives, and contribution of the book. The organization of remaining chapters are as follows.

* **Chapter 2:** provides the structural modification of the piezoelectric cantilever structure to enhance the performance. In the first part of this chapter, tapering, perforation and multi-perforation have been introduced in the cantilever structure.

* **Chapter 3:** This chapter shows the design of non-uniform substrate thickness have been discussed. It shows the effect of tapered substrate thickness on resonant frequency, stress distribution, and performance of the cantilever structure.

* **Chapter 4:** Presented the L shaped piezoelectric energy harvester for low frequency range applications.

* **Chapter 5:** present the spiral shaped piezoelectric cantilever structure that can be able to power the pacemaker. In this chapter the effect of design of spiral cantilever on resonant frequency, stress, output voltages and power has been discussed.

* **Chapter6:** develops the multi-beam cantilever structure to enhance the frequency bandwidth. The chapter also develops the mathematical model to show the coupling effect between the multi-beam cantilever structure, which is later verified using the Finite Element Method (FEM) through COMSOL Multiphysics.

* **Chapter 7:** introduces the permanent magnet in the energy harvesting system to introduced non-linearity. The magnetic proof mass has been placed in the vicinity of another permanent magnet to create the magnetic field. This chapter shows that the magnetic proof mass helps improve the performance and bandwidth.

* **Chapter 8:** gives the summary/conclusion of this work. This chapter also includes a list of possible future work.

Chapter 2

Structural modification in the uniform piezoelectric cantilever

2.1 Introduction

Small-sized low-power electronic devices for implanted medical devices (IMDs) [18], [49], [108] wireless communication, [22], [28] military equipment, etc., are being developed as a result of a recent advancement in the field of semiconductor devices. Most of these gadgets run on standard batteries, which have a finite lifespan and require periodic recharging or replacement. Certain gadgets, like pacemakers, are utilised in inaccessible areas such inside machines, far-off regions, or inside the human body. It becomes challenging to replace the batteries in these devices. A machine status monitoring system is one example of this type of application, in which the sensor nodes are positioned inside turbines or induction motors and are difficult to reach. Therefore, there is a high demand for gadgets that have an integrated energy harvesting mechanism for battery recharging. The best energy harvester for vibration-based systems is the one that powers these tiny gadgets.

The multi-perforation in the cantilever construction was suggested in this chapter to enhance PZEH performance. The dynamic machine monitoring system's wireless sensor network, which tracks the condition of the HAVC system (heating, ventilation, and air conditioning system), is powered by the PZ cantilever structure. The HAVC system vibrates at double the line frequency, or roughly 100 Hz (the line frequency in India is 50 Hz). The constant power supply is necessary for this battery-powered device to keep track of the HAVC system's condition. The lifespan of these gadgets can be extended by including an energy harvesting. The difficult part of designing an energy harvester is getting enough output voltage and power while maintaining a resonance frequency range of about 100 Hz without enlarging the cantilever structure's construction area. The cantilever structure's stress distribution is improved and the resonance frequency is decreased by the use of many perforations. The performance of the suggested design is contrasted with that of a cantilever structure of the same dimensions that is rectangular and tapered in shape. For every cantilever beam, the output voltage, power, and stress distribution have been measured. At a resonance frequency of 98.59 Hz, the multiperforated tapered cantilever beam produces the highest output voltage.

2.2 Materials

One important parameter of piezoelectric materials is the charge coefficient d_{ij} (C/N), which connects the charge created in the material on the i-axis with the force applied on the j-axis. Equation (2.1) gives the charge created if force F is applied.

$$q = d_{31}F \tag{2.1}$$

The voltage coefficient, or $g_{ij}(Vm/N)$, is another crucial piezoelectric parameter. It may be found by dividing the generated piezoelectric coefficient by the absolute permittivity, or $g_{31} = \frac{d_{31}}{\varepsilon_o \varepsilon_r}$. Therefore, a material with a higher voltage coefficient value will produce a higher voltage output. The relative permittivity ε_r and value of d_{31} for several PZ materials must be determined in order to determine which piezoelectric material has the highest value of g_{31}. Eq. (1.6) yields the voltage produced by a rectangular piezoelectric block with thickness t_p, area A, and permittivity $\varepsilon_o \varepsilon_r$.

This book compares lead zirconate titanate (PZT) with the piezoelectric voltage coefficient of well-known biocompatible PZ materials. The PZT is not taken into account in this study since it contains lead, which is hazardous to the environment. A variety of PZ materials' PZ properties are displayed in Table 2.1.

Table 2.1: Properties of the piezoelectric materials [18]

Materials	Charge coefficient, d_{31}, (pC/N)	Dielectric constant, ε_r	Voltage coefficient, g_{31}, (Vm/N)
PZT	741	3400	0.217
ZnO	11.34	12.64	0.897
AlN	3.84	10.256	0.374
BaTiO3	149	1200	0.124

The value of g_{31} is highest in the case of ZnO. Hence it will give the best voltage output if the dimensions are the same. So, in this research work, ZnO is used.

2.3   Design and analysis

Here, a cantilever beam is created for the PZEH, maintaining a manufactured length of no more than 5 mm, and a resonance frequency of about 100 Hz. As little as 0.5 μm of thin film deposition can be applied to the substrate using the current thin film deposition technology. The PZ layer has a thickness of 2 μm, while the silicon substrate has a thickness of 13 μm. These differences could offer enough mechanical strength to support the cantilever construction. Sandwiched between the aluminium (Al) electrodes is the ZnO layer. The Al electrode has a thickness of 0.5 μm.

2.3.1   Mathematical modelling

This part is devoted to the development of the piezoelectric plate cantilever structure's analytical model. As seen in Fig. 2.1, an analytical model was built by taking into consideration a simplified cantilever plate consisting of a piezoelectric layer on top of a substrate layer. The substrate layer is t_s thick and the piezoelectric layer is t_p thick. Because of its modest thickness and negligible impact on the cantilever plate's vibration, the electrode affixed to the piezoelectric layer in this simplified cantilever structure is disregarded.

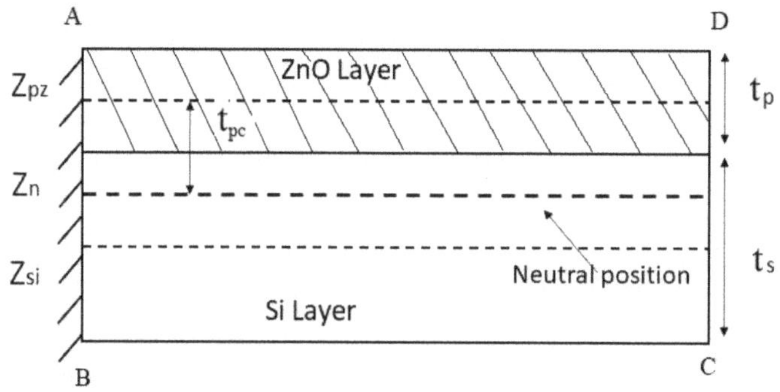

Figure 2.1: Cross-sectional view of simple PZ cantilever structure

The application of external stress on the PZ layer surface in the piezoelectric layer generates an electric field, and vice versa; these phenomena can be explained by applying Eqs. (1.4a) and (1.4b), respectively.

The substrate layer is the normal linear elastic material, so the stress applied (Ts) in the substrate layer is directly proportional to the resultant strain (Ss) as

$$T_s = Y_s \times S_s \tag{2.2}$$

However, applied stress (Tp) in the case of the piezoelectric material produces an electric field (E) in addition to strain (Sp). The x, y, and xy planes are under stress as the rectangular cantilever vibrates vertically. As a result, the piezoelectric layer's applied stress, strain, and electric field are connected as shown in Equations [20] (2.3a, 2.3b, 2.3c).

$$T_{pxx} = \frac{Y_p}{1-v^2} S_{pxx} + \frac{vY_p}{1-v^2} S_{pyy} - d_{31} Y_p E, \tag{2.3a}$$

$$T_{pyy} = \frac{Y_p}{1-v^2} S_{pyy} + \frac{vY_p}{1-v^2} S_{pxxx} - d_{32} Y_p E, \tag{2.3b}$$

$$T_{pxy} = G S_{pxx} - (d_{31} + d_{32}) Y_p E, \tag{2.3c}$$

Where v is the poison ratio, G is the shear modulus and Yp is the young's modulus of the piezoelectric layer.

The cantilever plate deflects away from the neutral axis or mean position when it experiences external stress. The neutral axis's position from the cantilever plate's base can be ascertained using the stress equilibrium, which is provided by Eq. (2.4).

$$\int_{-t_s/2}^{t_s/2} \frac{Y_s}{1-v^2} (Z - Z_n) dz + \int_{t_s/2}^{t_s/2+t_p} \frac{Y_p}{1-v^2} (Z - Z_n) dz = 0 \tag{2.4}$$

The position of the neutral axis can be determined on solving Eq. (2.4), which is given as Eq. (2.5).

$$Z_n = \frac{\frac{Y_p}{1-v^2} t_p (t_s + t_p)}{2 \left(\frac{Y_s t_s}{1-v^2} + \frac{Y_p t_p}{1-v^2} \right)} \tag{2.5}$$

where v_s is the substrate's Poisson's ratio and Z_S and Z_P are the substrate and PZ layer, respectively, centre positions with respect to the plate's base BC.

The cantilever plate's transverse vibration causes the bending strain. The bending strain in the cantilever plates is displayed by the equations (2.6a, 2.6b, 2.6c).

$$S_{pxx} = -(Z_n - Z) \frac{\partial^2 w(x,y,t)}{\partial x^2}, \tag{2.6a}$$

$$S_{pyy} = -(Z_n - Z) \frac{\partial^2 w(x,y,t)}{\partial y^2}, \tag{2.6b}$$

$$S_{pxy} = -(Z_n - Z) \frac{\partial^2 w(x,y,t)}{\partial x \partial y}, \tag{2.6c}$$

The vertical displacement of the plate with respect to the plate base is denoted by $w(x,y,t)$, while the strain in the x, y, and xy planes are indicated by $S_{pxx}, S_{pyy},$ and S_{pxy}, respectively.

Electrical analysis

The piezoelectric plate cantilever structure, which has the piezoelectric plate on the substrate layer, has been taken into consideration for the electrical analysis of the PZEH. This analysis focuses on the electrical effect caused by the ambient vibration vibrating the piezoelectric cantilever structure.

Equations (2.7a, 2.7b, 2.7c) provide the total strain S_P along the three planes in the middle of the PZ layer.

$$S_{pxx} = -t_{pc} \frac{\partial^2 w(x,y,t)}{\partial x^2}, \tag{2.7a}$$

$$S_{pyy} = -t_{pc} \frac{\partial^2 w(x,y,t)}{\partial y^2}, \tag{2.7b}$$

$$S_{pxy} = -t_{pc} \frac{\partial^2 w(x,y,t)}{\partial x \partial y}, \tag{2.7c}$$

where $Z_n - Z = t_{pc}$. The total stress in the middle of the PZ layer, which is given in Eqs. (2.8a, 2.8b, and 2.8c), is obtained by substituting the value of total strain (Sp) in Eqs. (2.3a, 2.3b, 2.3c) from Eqs. (2.7a, 2.7b, 2.7c).

$$T_{pxx} = \frac{Y_p}{1-v^2}\left(-t_{pc}\frac{\partial^2 w(x,y,t)}{\partial x^2}\right) + \frac{vY_p}{1-v^2}\left(-t_{pc}\frac{\partial^2 w(x,y,t)}{\partial y^2}\right) - d_{31}Y_pE, \tag{2.8a}$$

$$T_{pyy} = \frac{Y_p}{1-v^2}\left(-t_{pc}\frac{\partial^2 w(x,y,t)}{\partial y^2}\right) + \frac{vY_p}{1-v^2}\left(-t_{pc}\frac{\partial^2 w(x,y,t)}{\partial x^2}\right) - d_{32}Y_pE, \tag{2.8b}$$

$$T_{pxy} = G\left(-t_{pc}\frac{\partial^2 w(x,y,t)}{\partial x \partial y}\right) - (d_{31}+d_{32})Y_pE, \tag{2.8c}$$

The tension applied in the x, y, and xy planes produces the electrical displacement along the z direction, which is measured separately. An analogous computation is performed for the charge induced in the PZ plate. Initially, the charge that the x-plane stress has generated in the piezoelectric layer is estimated.

To obtain the electric flux density in the PZ layer, which is represented by Eq. (2.9), substitute the value of T_P in the x plane (T_{pxx}) in Eq. (1.5a) from Eq. (2.8a).

$$D_{zx} = d_{31}\left[\frac{Y_p}{1-v^2}(-t_{pc}\frac{\partial^2 w(x,y,t)}{\partial x^2}) + \frac{vY_p}{1-v^2}(-t_{pc}\frac{\partial^2 w(x,y,t)}{\partial y^2}) - d_{31}Y_pE\right] + \varepsilon_{33}^T E \tag{2.9}$$

The external electric field E is 0 since the cantilever plates are oscillating freely. Eq. (2.9) will thus be modified to Eq. (2.10).

$$D_{zx} = -d_{31}\frac{Y_p}{1-v^2}t_{pc}\left[\frac{\partial^2 w(x,y,t)}{\partial x^2}) + v\frac{\partial^2 w(x,y,t)}{\partial y^2}\right] \tag{2.10}$$

The charge created in the PZ plate can be obtained by integrating the electric flux density over the plate area, as shown in Eq. (2.11).

$$\begin{aligned}
q(t) &= d_{31}\int_0^L\int_0^b\left[\frac{Y_p}{1-v^2}(-t_{pc}\frac{\partial^2 w(x,y,t)}{\partial x^2}) + \frac{vY_p}{1-v^2}(-t_{pc}\frac{\partial^2 w(x,y,t)}{\partial y^2})\right] \\
&= d_{31}\int_0^L\int_0^b\left[\frac{Y_pt_{pc}}{1-v^2}\left[(-\frac{\partial^2 w(x,y,t)}{\partial x^2}) + v(-\frac{\partial^2 w(x,y,t)}{\partial y^2})\right]\right]dxdy
\end{aligned} \tag{2.11}$$

where the breadth (b) and length (L) of the plate are specified. Equation (2.11) provides the amount of charge generated by a single vibrating plate in the absence of an external electric field applied across it.

The total electric current created in this plate in the absence of an external electric field is represented by Equation (2.12).

$$I(t) = \frac{q(t)}{dt} = -d_{31}\int_0^L\int_0^b\left[\frac{Y_pt_{pc}}{1-v^2}\left[(\frac{\partial^2 w(x,y,t)}{\partial x^2\partial t}) + v(\frac{\partial^2 w(x,y,t)}{\partial y^2\partial t})\right]\right]dxdy \tag{2.12}$$

If the internal resistance of the PZ plate is assumed to be R, then according to the ohm's law, the voltage obtained across the plate is given by $V_1(t) = I_{zx}(t).R$. The Eq. (2.13) shows the expression of $V_1(t)$.

$$V_1(t) = -R.d_{31}\int_0^L\int_0^b\left[\frac{Y_pt_{pc}}{1-v^2}\left[(\frac{\partial^2 w(x,y,t)}{\partial x^2\partial t}) + v(\frac{\partial^2 w(x,y,t)}{\partial y^2\partial t})\right]\right]dxdy \tag{2.13}$$

Similarly using Eqs. (2.8b), and (2.8c), the voltage generated due to the stress T_{pyy} and T_{pxy} can be calculated which is represented as in Eqs. (2.14) and (2.15) respectively.

$$V_2(t) = -R.d_{32}\int_0^L\int_0^b\left[\frac{Y_pt_{pc}}{1-v^2}\left[(\frac{\partial^2 w(x,y,t)}{\partial y^2\partial t}) + v(\frac{\partial^2 w(x,y,t)}{\partial x^2\partial t})\right]\right]dxdy \tag{2.14}$$

$$V_3(t) = -2Rd_{33}Gt_{pc}\int_0^L\int_0^b\left[\frac{\partial^2 w(x,y,t)}{\partial x\partial y\partial t}\right]dxdy \tag{2.15}$$

Combining Eqs. (2.13), (2.14), and (2.15) yields the total voltage across the PZ plate, which is expressed as $V_4(t) =$

$V_1(t) + V_2(t) + V_3(t)$. The PZ system's electrical component will be regulated by Equation (2.16), which states,

$$V(t) - \frac{1}{C_i} \int I(t)dt - V_4(t) - I(t)R_L = 0, \tag{2.16}$$

In this PZEH system, R_L represents the load resistance, $i(t)$ is the current, and C_i is the PZ layer's internal capacitance, defined as $C_i = (\frac{\varepsilon_o \varepsilon_p A}{t_p})$. where the relative permittivity of the PZ plate and the air permittivity are denoted by ε_p and ε_o, respectively. The voltage produced by ambient excitation in the piezoelectric cantilever structure is denoted by $V_4(t)$.

Mechanical analysis

The mechanical vibration of PZ cantilever structures may be studied using a variety of techniques [20], [22], [28], [110]. The thin plate type cantilever construction described in this book has comparable length and width and low thickness; hence, either of the two dimensions is taken into consideration. The mechanical analysis of the PZ cantilever structure has been explained by the Kirchhoff plate theory [20], [110]. The cross-section in this hypothesis is perpendicular to the plate's axis. The transverse displacement of the cantilever plate is represented by Eq. (2.17) or Eq. (2.18) in accordance with the Kirchhoff plate theory [20], [110].

$$D_r \left(\frac{\partial^4 w(x,y,t)}{\partial x^4} + 2\frac{\partial^4 w(x,y,t)}{\partial x^2 \partial y^2} + \frac{\partial^4 w(x,y,t)}{\partial y^4} \right) + \rho t_p \frac{\partial^4 w(x,y,t)}{\partial t^2} = f(x,y,t), \tag{2.17}$$

$$D_r \nabla^4 w(x,y,t) + \rho t_p \frac{\partial^4 w(x,y,t)}{\partial t^2} = f(x,y,t), \tag{2.18}$$

In this case, the biharmonic operator Δ^4 is provided by Eq. (2.19). The vertical displacement of the plate is denoted by $w(x,y,t)$, the density is ρ, and the flexural rigidity is D_r, as found in Eq. (2.20). The external force acting on the rectangular plate is denoted by $f(x,y,t)$.

$$\nabla^4 = \nabla^2 \times \nabla^2 = \frac{\partial^4}{\partial x^4} + 2\frac{\partial^4}{\partial x^2 + \partial y^2} + \frac{\partial^4}{\partial y^4}, \tag{2.19}$$

$$D_r = \frac{Yt^3}{12(1-v^2)}, \tag{2.20}$$

where v is the Poisson ratio, t_p is the plate's thickness, and Y is the plate's young's modulus. For the cantilever structure to experience free vibration, the external loading is assumed to be zero, or $f(x,y,t)$. A modified version of Eq. (2.18) is Eq. (2.21).

$$D_r \nabla^4 w(x,y,t) + \rho t_p \frac{\partial^4 w(x,y,t)}{\partial t^2} = 0, \tag{2.21}$$

The boundary limit changes from x = 0 to L along the length and from y = 0 to b along the breadth of the rectangular plate, which has length and width of L and b, respectively. Equation (2.21) can be solved using the method of separation of variables, yielding Equation (2.22).

$$w(x,y,t) = W(x,y)T(t), \tag{2.22}$$

Substituting the Eq. (2.22) in Eq. (2.21) [20], [110] will give,

$$\frac{d^2 T(t)}{dt} + \omega^2 T(t) = 0, \tag{2.23}$$

$$\nabla^4 W(x,y) - \lambda^4 W(x,y) = 0, \tag{2.24}$$

where,

$$\lambda^4 = \frac{\omega^2}{\beta^2} = \frac{\rho t_p \omega^2}{D_r}, \tag{2.25}$$

The plate is in sinusoidal oscillation. So, general solution of Eq. (2.23) is to be time dependent Eq. (2.26) [110].

$$T(t) = A.cos\omega t + B.sin\omega t, \tag{2.26}$$

where A and B are arbitrary constant. The solution of displacement dependent equation i.e., Eq. (2.24) can be expressed as Eq. (2.27).

$$(\nabla^4 - \lambda^4)W(x,y) = (\nabla^2 - \lambda^2)(\nabla^2 + \lambda^2)\dot{W}(x,y), \tag{2.27}$$

According to the linear differential equation theory, the superimposition of Eqs. (2.28) and (2.29) will provide the complete solution of Eq. (2.27) [20], [110].

$$(\nabla^2 + \lambda^2)W(x,y) = \frac{\partial^2 W_1(x,y)}{\partial x^2} + \frac{\partial^2 W_1(x,y)}{\partial y^2} + \lambda^2 W_1(x,y), \tag{2.28}$$

$$(\nabla^2 - \lambda^2)W(x,y) = \frac{\partial^2 W_2(x,y)}{\partial x^2} + \frac{\partial^2 W_2(x,y)}{\partial y^2} - \lambda^2 W_2(x,y), \tag{2.29}$$

Considering that the solution $W_1(x,y)$ [20] resembles the harmonic motion, $W_1(x,y)$ may be expressed in the form of for the Eq. 2.28

$$W_1(x,y) = X(x)Y(y), \tag{2.30}$$

where,

$$X(x) = c1.cos\alpha x + c2.sin\alpha x, \tag{2.31}$$

$$Y(y) = c3.cos\beta y + c4.sin\beta y, \tag{2.32}$$

Where, $c1$, $c2$, $c3$, and $c4$ are the arbitrary constant.
The solution of equation (2.28) can be obtained using the product of Eqs. (2.31) and (2.32) as

$$\begin{aligned} W_1(x,y) = &A1 sin\alpha x.sin\beta y + A2 sin\alpha x.cos\beta y \\ &+ A3 cos\alpha x.sin\beta y + A4 cos\alpha x.sin\beta y, \end{aligned} \tag{2.33}$$

In a similar vein, Eq. (2.29) can be solved, with the exception that $\iota\lambda$ is used in lieu of λ. Thus, the solution to Eq. (2.29) contains the components of the product of the sinh and cosh terms. Consequently, it is possible to solve and represent Eq. (2.27) as Eq. (2.34).

$$\begin{aligned} W(x,y) = &C1 sin\alpha x.sin\beta y + C2 sin\alpha x.cos\beta y \\ &+ C3 cos\alpha x.sin\beta y + C4 cos\alpha x.sin\beta y \\ &+ C5 sinh\alpha x.sinh\beta y + C6 sinh\alpha x.cosh\beta y \\ &+ C7 cosh\alpha x.sinh\beta y + C8 cosh\alpha x.sinh\beta y, \end{aligned} \tag{2.34}$$

where $C1, C2, C3, C4, C5, C6, C7, C8$ are the arbitrary constants whose values depend on the initial conditions and $\lambda = \alpha^2 + \beta^2 = \theta^2 + \phi^2$. From Eq. 2.25 as Eq. (2.35), ω may be found.

$$\omega = \lambda^2 \sqrt{\frac{D_r}{\rho t_p}} = \lambda^2 \sqrt{\frac{\frac{Yt_p^3}{12(1-v^2)}}{\rho t_p}} = \lambda^2 \sqrt{\frac{Yt_p^2}{12(1-v^2)\rho}}, \tag{2.35}$$

Since $I = \frac{wt_p^3}{12}$ gives the moment of inertia of the rectangular structure, Eq. (2.35) may be recast as Eq. (2.36). where λ is given by the boundary condition of the plate.

$$\omega = \lambda^2 \sqrt{\frac{YI}{m(1-v^2)}}, \tag{2.36}$$

Here $m = \rho wt_p$ is the unit length mass.

The following lists the two crucial conclusions that may be drawn from the mathematical study mentioned above.

1. According to Eq. (2.11), the voltage produced by the piezoelectric plate is dependent on the applied stress, the thickness of the piezoelectric layer, the piezoelectric coefficient, and the transverse vibration of the cantilever structure..

2. As demonstrated by Eq. (2.36), the resonant frequency of the cantilever structures is dependent upon their moment of inertia and may change depending on their size and shape.

After the mathematical analysis, next section will discuss the simulations and observed results of various cantilever structures.

2.4   Simulations and results

This section uses COMSOL Multiphysics' finite element method (FEM) analysis to verify the theory that was created in the sections that came before it. Cantilever constructions of many kinds have been created and examined. These cantilever structures have undergone a FEM analysis using the COMSOL Multiphysics simulation tool. In COMSOL Multiphysics, solid mechanics and electrostatics physics are used to construct and simulate the plates. All of the structures that were designed have been meshing using standard meshing procedures. The mechanical characterisation of the PZ material is done using solid mechanics physics, whereas the electrical characterization is done using electrostatics physics. By using the reciprocal of the step size, one can obtain the convergence plot of the time-dependent model. At an excitation acceleration of $1g(= 9.8m/s^2)$, all of the planned cantilever structures have been simulated using a damping coefficient of 0.006 Ns/m (or kg/s).

Initially, the cantilever constructions made of rectangular plates were designed and examined. After designing a tapered cantilever structure, a rectangular cantilever structure with a perforation will be constructed. The impact of structural change on cantilever structures is covered in this section.

2.4.1   Rectangular plate structures

With a resonance frequency of 143.16 Hz, the rectangular cantilever structure is constructed using the Kirchhoff plate theory, as covered in Subsection 2.3.1b. Table 2.2 lists the various materials that were employed in the cantilever structure's design along with their corresponding mechanical properties. To determine the rectangular structure's resonant frequency, COMSOL Multiphysics is used for the eigenfrequency analysis. As seen in Fig. 2.2, the variation in the cantilever structure's length, width, and thickness is studied in relation to the variation in the resonance frequency of the rectangular construction with proof mass, while maintaining the other dimensions constant throughout the investigation. As the cantilever structure's length increases, the resonance frequency falls. On the other hand, as Fig. 2.2 illustrates, it progressively rises as the cantilever beam's width and thickness grow.

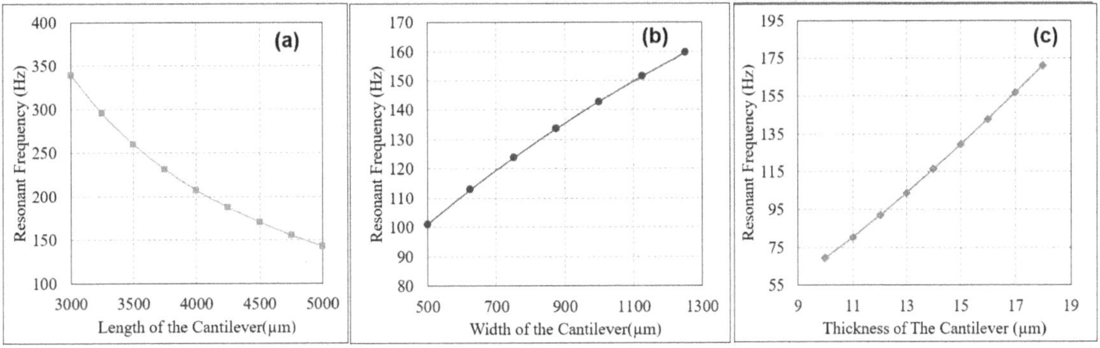

Figure 2.2: Variation in resonant frequency with (a) length (b) width (c) thickness of the cantilever structure

As designing the energy harvester for the HAVC system with a target resonance frequency of approximately 100 Hz is the goal. Thus, as illustrated in Fig. 2.3, a silicon (Si) based rectangular cantilever structure with dimensions of 5000 μm for length, 1000 μm for breadth, and 16 μm for net thickness is designed. Silicon is the lowest layer, with a thickness of 13 μm. Zinc oxide (ZnO) is the piezoelectric layer that sits on top of the Si layer between two Al electrode layers. ZnO has a thickness of 2 μm, while Al layers have a thickness of 0.5 μm. In order to lower the resonance frequency, the Si-based proof mass is fixed to

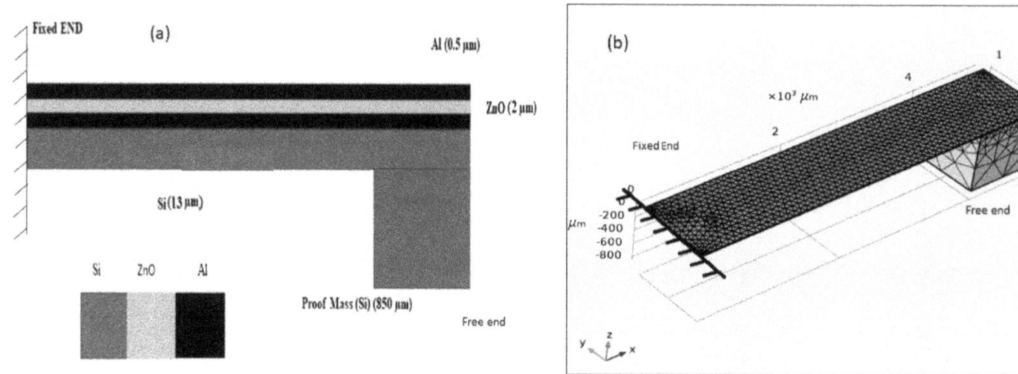

Figure 2.3: Rectangular cantilever structure (a) Side view (b) 3D-meshed view

Table 2.2: Property of the materials used in the cantilever beam [18], [111]

		Materials	
Property	Si	ZnO	Al
Young's modulus (GPa)	170	210	70
Poisson ratio	0.29	0.33	0.35
Density (kgm^{-3})	2329	5680	2700

the free end of the cantilever construction. The proof mass has dimensions of 1000 μm in length, 1000 μm in width, and 850 μm in thickness. The intended rectangular cantilever construction has a resonance frequency of 143.16 Hz.

2.4.2   Structural modification to decrease resonant frequency

Many researchers typically introduce structural modifications to the cantilever beam in order to lower the resonance frequency. [31], [40], [45], [108], [18]. An S-shaped cantilever beam was created by H. Liu et al. [40] in order to reach the low resonance frequency less than 30 Hz. In order to attain a low resonant frequency, Liu et al. [64] constructed a Si cantilever beam with parallel thin PZT film elements and Si proof mass. By introducing structural alteration and perforation in the cantilever beam, the low resonant frequency is obtained by reducing the stiffness of the cantilever structure.

A. Design of tapered cantilever structure

The aforementioned mathematical study demonstrates (as in Eq. (2.36)) that altering the cantilever's shape alters its resonant frequency. As a result, the tapered cantilever structure replaces the rectangular cantilever structure. With Si as the lowest layer, the tapered cantilever structure is constructed in a similar way as the rectangular cantilever structure. On top of the silicon layer, the ZnO layer is positioned between the two aluminium electrodes. The tapered cantilever construction has three widths: 600 μm for the smaller width, 1000 μm for the broader width, and 5000 μm for the length. The Si layer is 13 μm thick, the Al electrode is 0.5 μm thick, and the ZnO layer is 2 μm thick, in that order. The tapering cantilever structure's proof mass, which is affixed at its free end, has dimensions of 1000 μm x 1000 μm x 850 μm. It is possible to fix the tapered cantilever construction at a broader or smaller width. Figures (2.4 (a) and (b)) display the three-dimensional views of the two types of tapered cantilever structures. The tapered cantilever structure positioned at the smaller end has a resonant frequency of 117.17 Hz, whereas the tapered cantilever structure fixed at the broader width has a resonant frequency of 179.23 Hz. As the goal is to lower the cantilever structure's resonant frequency, it rises in the case of a tapering cantilever with a wider end fixed. We won't be discussing the tapered with wider end fixed any further. Thus, a tapered cantilever structure will be defined as one that is fixed with a decreased width.

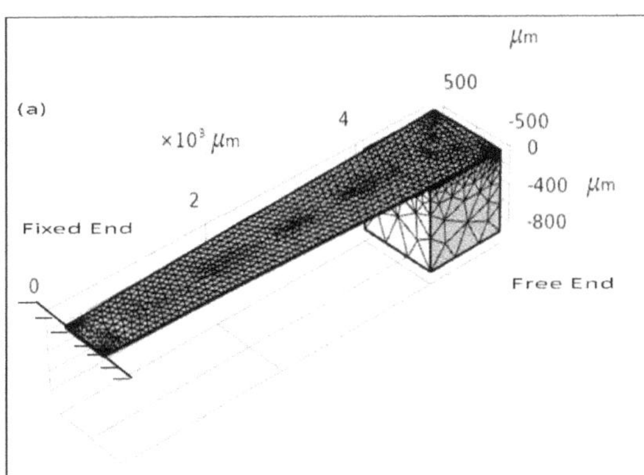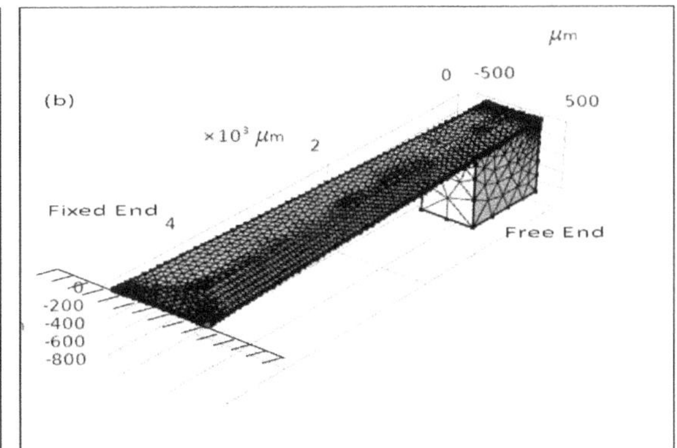

Figure 2.4: 3D-meshed tapered cantilever (a) smaller width fixed (b) wider width fixed

B. Perforation in the cantilever structure

Reducing the cantilever structure's spring constant—which can be done by using the proof mass or by changing the cantilever structure's shape—will change the resonance frequency of the structure. As was covered in the section above, the cantilever structure already incorporates the proof mass and a change in shape. Although it will result in an increase in the cantilever structure's size, lengthening the structure can also lower the resonance frequency. The mechanical stability will be jeopardised by the thickness decrease. For this reason, a perforation is added to the cantilever construction in order to lower the resonance frequency without growing it. The perforation in the cantilever constructions was introduced using two distinct ways. The impact of a single large perforation and multiple perforations on the resonant frequency, stress distribution, and electrical output of the cantilever structure have been investigated. Initially, the cantilever structure's single perforation is examined, and then its multi-perforation.

Single perforation in the cantilever structure

Originally, the rectangular cantilever structure was designed with a single perforation to lower the spring constant of the cantilever structure. The rectangular cantilever structure's perforation measures 1200 μm in length. The perforation's diameter and thickness are 500 μm and 16 μm, respectively. The hole is equally spaced from the lateral dimension and begins at 1300 μm from the fixed end. The cantilever structure's proof mass, which is affixed at its free end, has dimensions of 1000 μm x 1000 μm x 850 μm. Fig. 2.5 (a) illustrates the rectangular perforated cantilever structure, which is the cantilever structure that results from the introduction of perforation. The rectangular perforated cantilever structure shares the same dimensions and layer distribution as the rectangular cantilever structure. Rectangular perforated cantilever structures have a resonance frequency of 125.25 Hz, as opposed to rectangular cantilever structures' 143.16 Hz. After examining how the perforation affects the resonance frequency, the dimension mentioned above was chosen. By adjusting one parameter at a time and holding the other parameters constant, the variation of the resonant frequency is investigated in relation to the variation of the length, width, and position of the perforation from the fixed end. The fluctuation of the resonant frequency with the perforation settings is depicted in Fig. 2.6.

As the length and width of the hole expand, the resonant frequency falls, as seen in Fig.2.6. On the other hand, when the perforation moves further from the fixed end, its value grows. In order to further lower the resonance frequency, perforation is added to the tapered cantilever structure after the benefits of perforation in the rectangular cantilever structure have been discussed. The tapered cantilever structure displays the tapered-shaped hole. It improves the tapered perforated cantilever structure's mechanical stability.

The tapered perforated structure is set at a narrower width and has the same dimensions as the tapered cantilever structure. The tapered cantilever structure's distinct layer is the same as itss. The tapered shaped perforation has a length of 1200 μm and a width of 400 μm and 500 μm, which are its smaller and larger widths, respectively. Similar to the rectangular perforated cantilever structure, the perforation begins at 1300 μm from the fixed end. The proof mass is 1000 μm x 1000 μm x 850 μm in dimension.

The dimension of the tapered perforated structure is the same as that of the tapered cantilever structure, and it is fixed at a

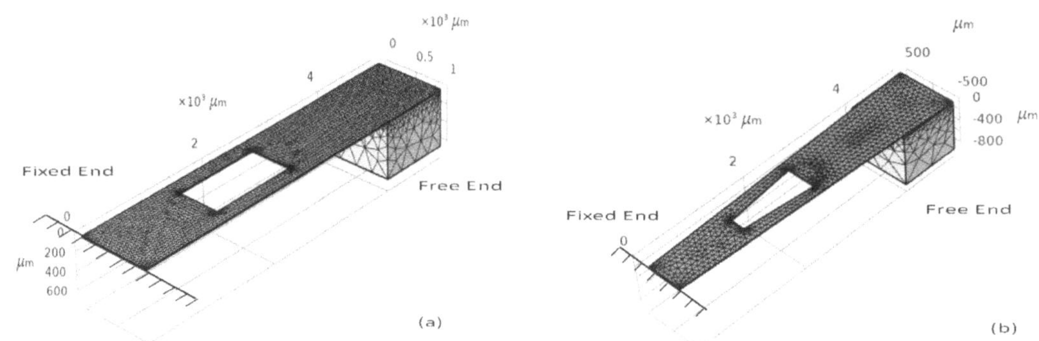

Figure 2.5: 3D-meshed (a) rectangular perforated cantilever (b) tapered perforated cantilever

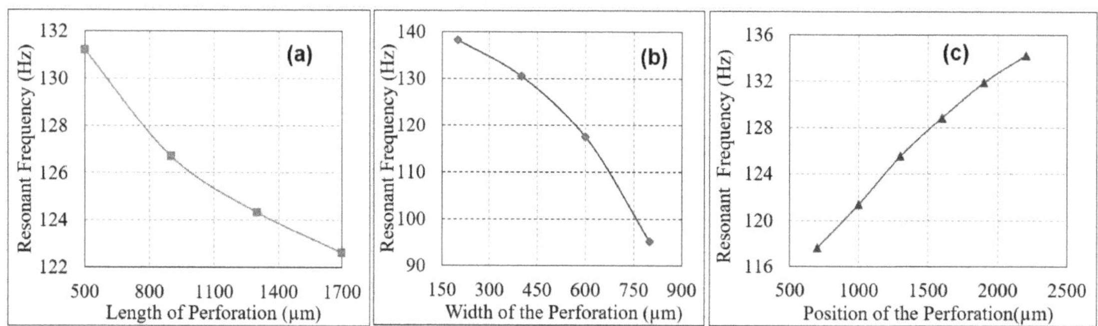

Figure 2.6: Variation in resonant frequency with (a) length of perforation (b) width of perforation (c) position of perforation from the fixed end.

smaller width. The different layer is also the same as that of the tapered cantilever structure. The length of the tapered shaped perforation is 1200 μm, and the smaller and broader width of the tapered shaped perforation is 400 μm and 500 μm, respectively. The perforation starts from 1300 μm from the fixed end, the same as the rectangular perforated cantilever structure. The proof mass is of dimension 1000 μm x 1000 μm x 850 μm. The designed cantilever structure is a tapered perforated cantilever structure as shown in Fig. 2.5(b), and the resonant frequency is 99.54 Hz.

Multi-perforation in the cantilever structure

The cantilever structure's perforation can be used to introduce discontinuity in the structure in addition to lowering the resonance frequency. Stress distribution is exacerbated by the cantilever structure's discontinuity. As mentioned in Subsection 2.3.1, the output voltage produced in the cantilever structure is exactly proportional to the cantilever's stress distribution level. In the cantilever structure, the numerous discontinuities can enhance the stress distribution more evenly. The cantilever beam can be made to have many discontinuities by adding multiple perforations. In the section that follows, the comparison of the stress distribution across all cantilevers is covered in detail.

The discussion begins with the impact of the multi-perforation on the rectangular cantilever structure. A rectangular multiperforated cantilever structure is created by adding four rectangular-shaped perforations to a rectangular cantilever structure. A distance of 50 μm separates each perforation. Each perforation has a diameter of 500 μm and a length of 250 μm. Starting around 1300 μm from the cantilever's fixed end, the first perforation occurs. As seen in Fig. 2.7 (a), the planned cantilever is known as a rectangular multi-perforated cantilever construction. The proof mass is 1000 μm x 1000 μm x 850 μm in dimension. The rectangular multi-perforated cantilever structure has a resonance frequency of 124.39 Hz.

Similarly, as illustrated in Fig. 2.7 (b), numerous holes are added to the tapered cantilever structure to create a tapered multiperforated cantilever structure. The tapered cantilever construction introduces four tapered-shaped perforations. A distance of 50 μm separates each perforation. Every tapered-shaped perforation has a length of 250 μm. Each tapered-shaped perforation has a smaller width of 400 μm and a broader width of 500 μm. The proof mass is 1000 μm x 1000 μm x 850 μm in dimension. The tapered multi-perforated cantilever structure has a resonance frequency of 98.59 Hz. This makes it possible

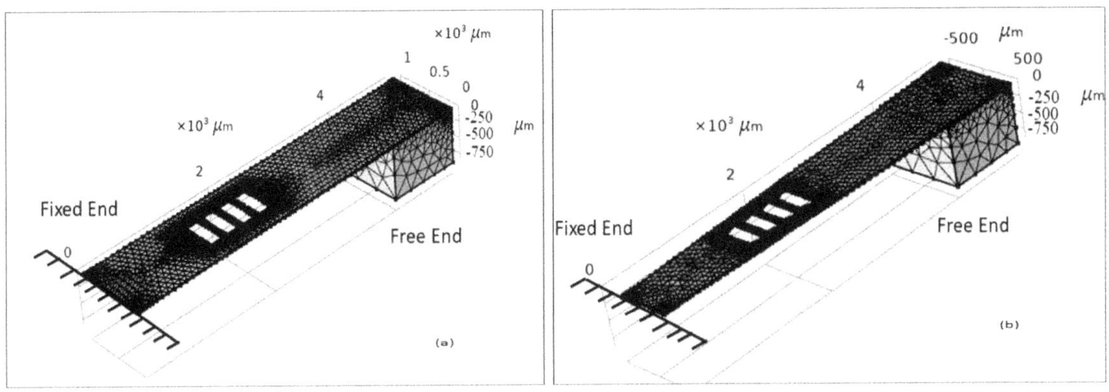

Figure 2.7: 3D-meshed (a) rectangular multi-perforated cantilever (b) tapered multi-perforated cantilever

to get the desired design frequency without having to enlarge the cantilever structure's dimensions.

In the same way, the multiple perforations are introduced in the tapered cantilever structure to form a tapered multiperforated cantilever structure as shown in Fig. 2.7 (b). The four tapered-shaped perforations are introduced in the tapered cantilever structure. Each perforation is separated by 50 μm. The length of each tapered-shaped perforation is 250 μm. The smaller width of each tapered-shaped perforation is 400 μm, and that of the wider width is 500 μm. The proof mass is of dimension 1000 μm x 1000 μm x 850 μm. The resonant frequency of the tapered multi-perforated cantilever structure is 98.59 Hz. This helps in achieving the required design frequency without increasing the dimensions of the cantilever structure. The suggested tapered multiperforated cantilever structure has a 29.3% resonant frequency reduction when compared to a rectangular cantilever structure.

2.5 Stress analysis

The discourse presented in Subsection 2.3.1 demonstrates that the cantilever structure's stress distribution directly affects the output voltage and power generated within it. Although a larger stress is preferable for higher output power and voltage, it must still stay within the material's fracture strength. When the Von Mises stress in the structure is higher than the material's Young's modulus, the material loses its elastic properties. For the cantilever construction to be mechanically stable, the maximum Von Mises stress that develops in the beam must be smaller than the material's Young's modulus. The stress produced by each structure along the cantilever structure's edge with a 1g acceleration at resonant frequency is displayed in Fig. 2.8.

The stress level in the rectangular cantilever structure is higher close to the fixed end and gradually drops as one moves away from the fixed end, as seen in Fig. 2.8. The instance of the tapering cantilever construction exhibits similar trends. It has been noted in the preceding Subsection 2.4.2 that the perforation can enhance the cantilever's stress distribution by introducing a discontinuity in the cantilever structure, in addition to lowering the resonance frequency. It can be confirmed by examining the stress distribution curve of a rectangular, tapered, perforated cantilever structure. Because there is an abrupt increase in stress at the perforation's beginning, the cantilever structure's stress distribution is more even. Because there are several places of discontinuity, the multi-perforation used in the rectangular multi-perforated and tapered multi-perforated cantilever structures further increases the stress distribution in the cantilever. Therefore, in the case of a multi-perforated cantilever construction, there are multiple peaks. Fig. 2.9, which displays a color-coded 3D depiction of the stress distribution in each cantilever structure, illustrates the same tendency. Stress is larger in the perforation and multi-perforation zone of a cantilever structure than it is at the fixed end, as is the case with rectangular and tapered cantilever structures. All of the cantilever structures' maximum stress created falls comfortably within the range of the cantilever's material's Young's modulus as given in Table 2.2. As a result, the cantilever structure has adequate stability and mechanical strength.

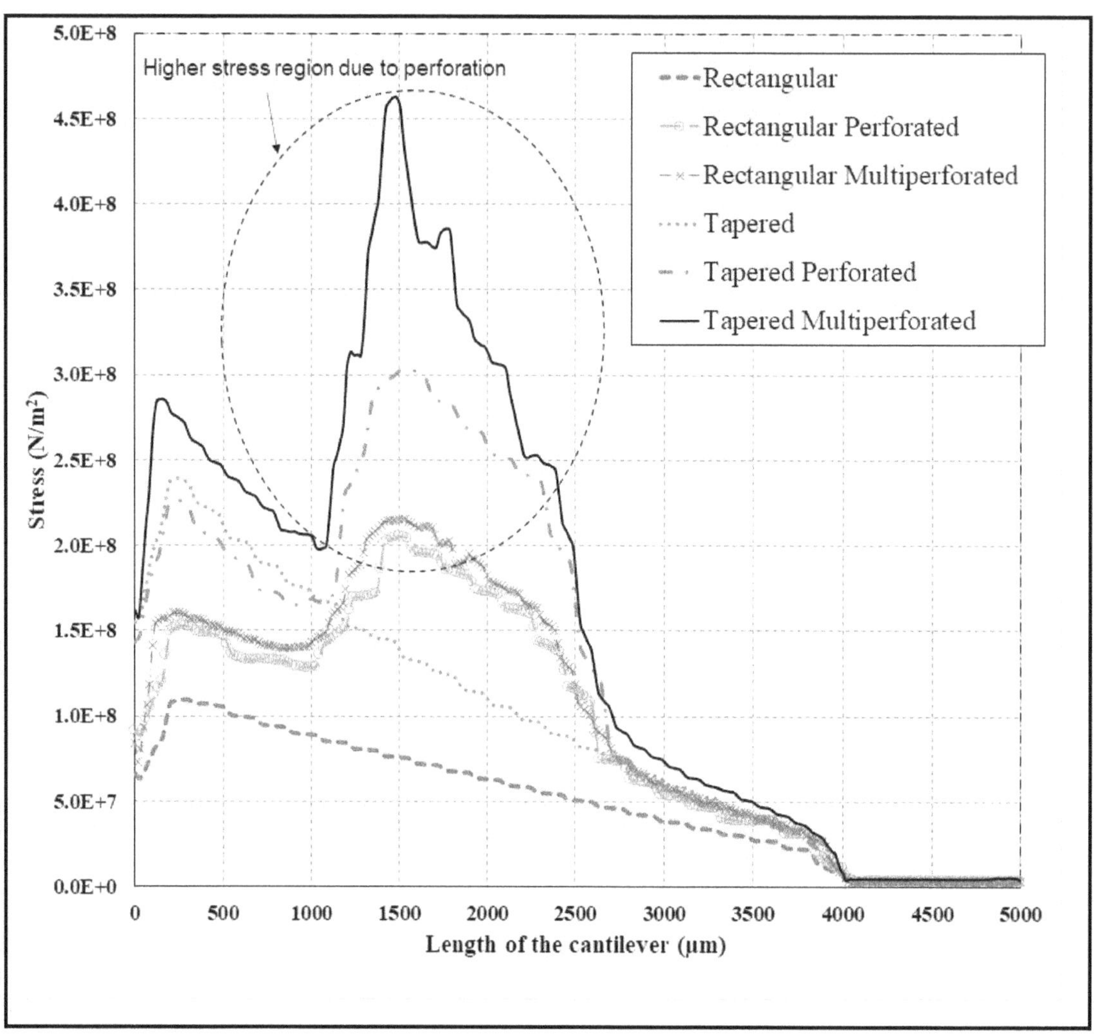

Figure 2.8: Stress distribution of different cantilever structures along the arc length of edge of cantilever structure

2.6   Electrical output of the structures

2.6.1   Output voltage of the designed structures

At the resonant frequency, [18], [20], [112], which is determined by the Eq. (2.36), the PZEH provides the maximum output voltage and output power. As covered in Subsection 2.3.1, the voltage generated by the PZEH is dependent upon the voltage coefficient, thickness of the piezoelectric material, and applied stress. To determine the time-dependent output voltage, the cantilever structure is subjected to a time-dependent analysis using the COMSOL Multiphysics software. For each structure, a sinusoidal acceleration of 1 g is applied at the resonance frequency. The transient voltage of each structure at its resonant frequency is displayed in Fig. 2.10.

The rectangular cantilever structure, rectangular perforated cantilever structure, and rectangular multiperforated cantilever structure provide peak output open-circuit voltages of 7.3 V, 11.1 V, and 12 V, respectively, at their respective resonance frequencies. At their resonant frequency, the tapered cantilever structure, tapered perforated cantilever structure, and tapered multiperforated cantilever structure provide output voltages of 12 V, 12.9 V, and 14 V, respectively. Because of the better and higher stress distribution within the structures, the perforated and multiperforated cantilever structures have higher voltages than their basic constructions. The output voltage fluctuation of each cantilever structure with stimulation frequency is displayed in Fig. 11. Table 2.3 lists all of the designs' output voltages.

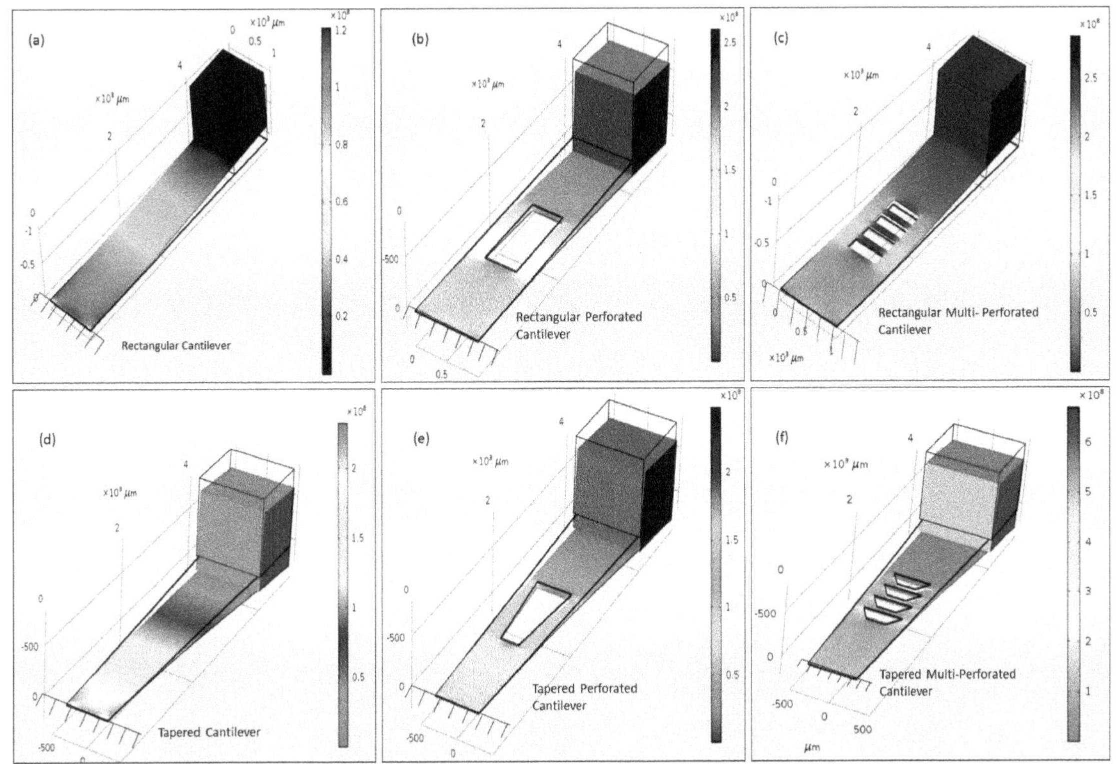

Figure 2.9: 3D-stress distribution of all cantilever structures

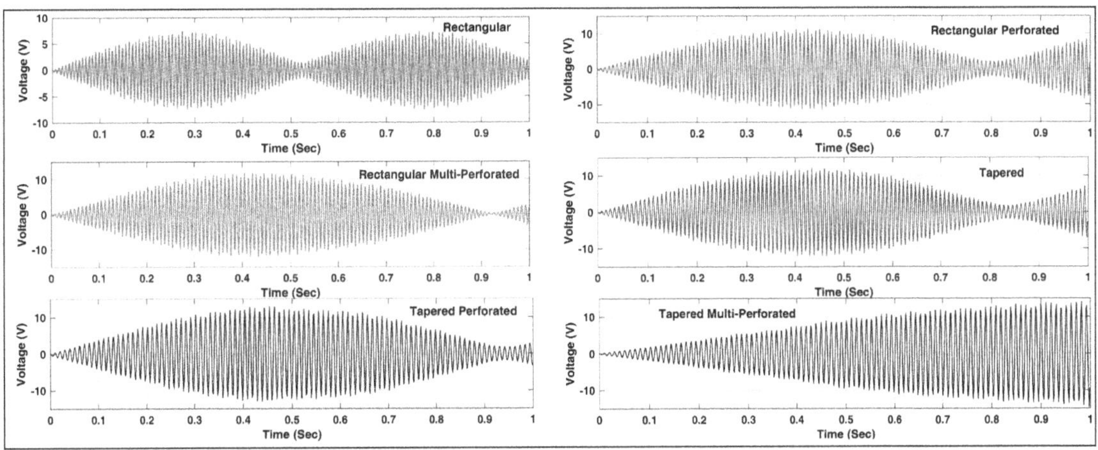

Figure 2.10: Time-dependent output voltages of all cantilever structures

2.6.2 Output power of the designed structures

The PZEH can yield its maximum output power, when these two requirements are met. The first requirement is equal excitation and resonant frequencies. The second is impedance matching, which implies that the PZEH's internal resistance (R_L) and load resistance (R_{PZ}), or ($R_L = R_{PZ}$), should match. Fig. 2.12 depicts the equivalent electrical model of the PZEH, where V_{out} represents the load voltage and $V_{o}c$ represents the open-circuit voltage produced by the PZEH. The equation for the load voltage is $V_{o}ut = (\frac{R_L}{R_L + R_{PZ}})V_{oc} = V_{oc}/2$. Equation (2.37) provides the PZEH's output power.

$$P = \frac{V_{out}^2}{R_L} = \frac{V_{oc}^2}{4R_{PZ}} \tag{2.37}$$

In order to determine the maximum power produced by the piezoelectric energy harvester, the internal resistance value must be known. The PZEH's internal resistance cannot be determined directly. Therefore, the load resistance is connected to

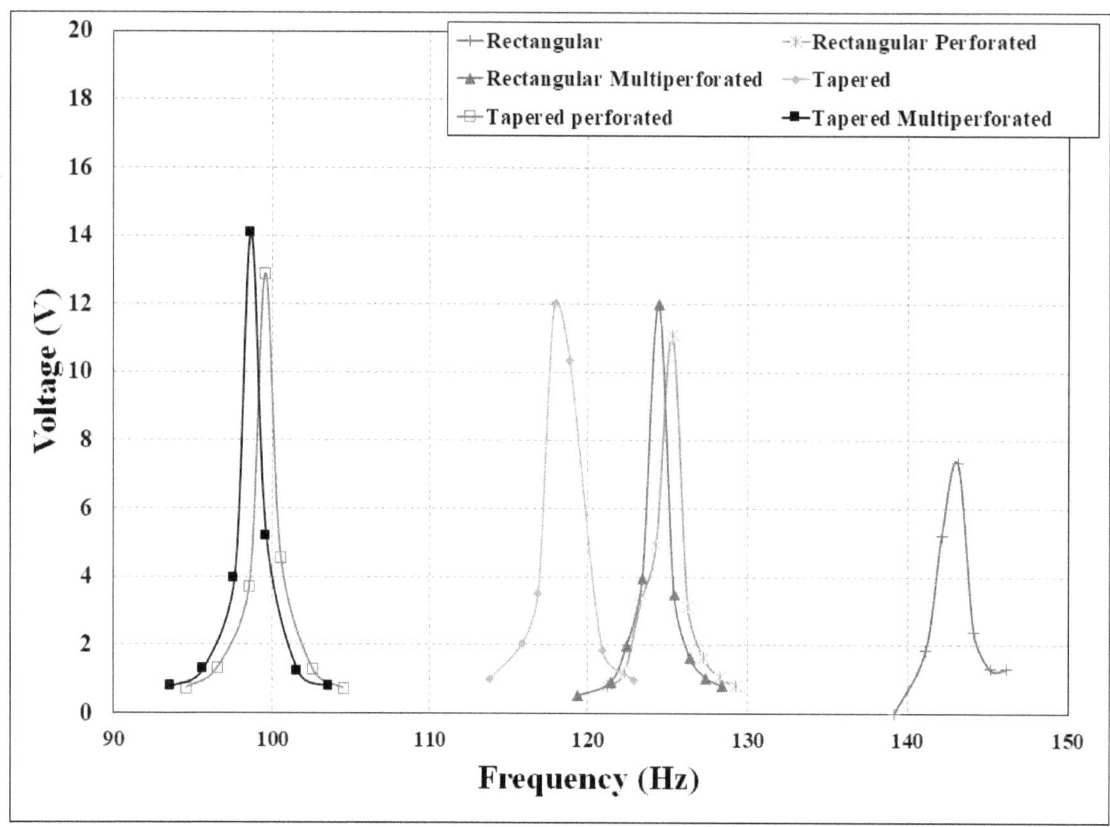

Figure 2.11: The generated output voltages of each cantilever structure at different vibration frequency

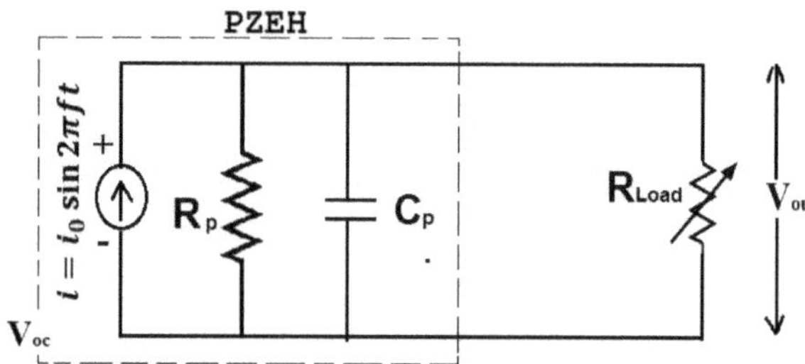

Figure 2.12: Equivalent electrical model of PZEH device

the energy harvester in order to measure the internal resistance. Next, at the cantilever structure's resonance frequency, the cantilever structure-based EH is simulated under constant load, and output power is computed by adjusting the load resistance value. The output power variation with variable load resistance is depicted in Fig. 2.13a. The maximum power theorem states that the ideal load resistance can be found at the value at which PZEH provides the most power. Given the minimal variance in the cantilever structure's cross-sectional area, the load resistance value is roughly the same for all of them. For all designs, the internal resistance of PZEH is roughly 1.6 Mohm, and this value represents the optimal load.

The output power variation of all cantilever structures with frequency at an excitation acceleration of 1g (gravitational acceleration) is displayed in Fig. 2.13b. A compilation of all the structures' output power is shown in Table 2.3. The tapered multi-perforated cantilever structure has an average output power of 7.15 μW, which is 213.59% more than the standard rectangular cantilever structure. Lastly, Table 2.4 presents a comparison between the suggested designs and the completed projects.

After determining each cantilever structure's mechanical and electrical specifications. We will then talk about how the thickness, damping coefficient, and excitation acceleration affect the cantilever's generated output power. For the sake of simplicity, only the tapered multiperforated cantilever construction has been examined in this article; nevertheless, the findings apply to other cantilever structures as well. The output power fluctuation for tapered multi-perforated cantilevers with thickness, excitation acceleration, and damping coefficient is displayed in Fig. 2.14.

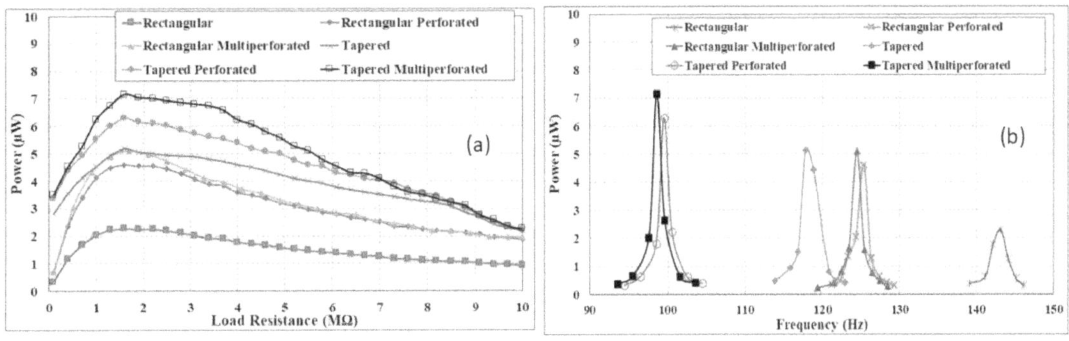

Figure 2.13: (a) The value of output power at different load resistance for all cantilever structures (b) The value of output power at different vibration frequency for all cantilever structures

Table 2.3: Comparison between different cantilever structures

Cantilever Beam	R.Freq.* (Hz)	Disp** (μm)	Voltage (V)	Power (μW)	%Increase***
Rectangular	143.16	1070	7.3	2.28	NA
Rectangular Perforated	125.25	1925	11.1	4.59	101.3%
Rectangular Multiperforated	124.39	2000	12	5.1	123.68 %
Tapered	117.87	2080	12	5.15	125.87 %
Tapered Perforated	99.54	2570	12.9	6.3	176.32 %
Tapered Multiperforated	98.59	2900	14	7.15	213.59

R.Freq.*=Resonant Frequency, Disp**=Displacement, % Increase*** = Increase in Power w.r.to Rectangular beam

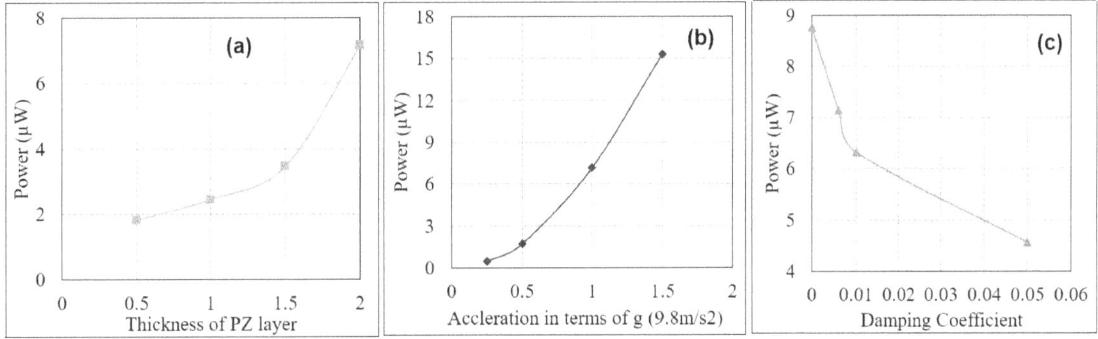

Figure 2.14: Variation of output power with (a) the thickness of piezoelectric layer, (b) excitation acceleration and (c) damping coefficient for tapered multi-perforated cantilever structure

It can be seen that as the thickness of the piezoelectric layer and excitation acceleration rise, so does the tapered multiperforated cantilever structure's output power. On the other hand, it falls when the damping coefficient rises. This indicates that increasing the thickness of the piezoelectric layer will increase the output power, but it will also cause the structure's resonant frequency to increase, as seen in Fig. 2.2, and is consistent with Eq. (2.35). Although the faster acceleration will result in more power being generated, the increased effective stress distribution could potentially weaken the structure's mechanical strength. Raising the damping coefficient will limit movement, which will lower the output power that is produced.

It is evident that the suggested structure produces the highest average output power out of all the designs and has a substantially lower resonance frequency than the majority of the other structures. It also has a better stress distribution inside the cantilever structure. A thorough breakdown of the proposed structure's fabrication stages is shown in Fig. 2.15. To build the design as illustrated in Fig. 2.15, four masks were required.

Table 2.4: Comparison of the proposed structure with the existing literatures

Ref.	Geometry	*R.Freq. (Hz)	**Accn. (m/s^2)	Voltage (V)	Power (μW)
Roundy et al. [28]	Rectangular, 1000 mm^3	120	2.5	5	375
Yu Jia et al. [113]	Circular disk membrane, Diameter – 7 mm	1572	9.8	-	2.2
Kanno et al. [114]	Rectangular, 20x3.4 mm^2	1036	10	0.097	1.1
Muralt et al. [115]	Rectangular, 0.8x1.2x0.007 mm^3	870	19.6	1.6	1.4
Beker et al. [105]	Rectangular, 4.25x4x0.595 mm^3	474	0.98	0.92	1.33
Liu et al. [40]	S-shaped, 5.2x4.2x0.407 mm^3	26	0.6	0.042	0.31
Liu et al. [56]	Rectangular, 8x5x0.41 mm^3	35.8	0.98	0.042	0.0114
Proposed work	Tapered Multiperforated, 5x1x0.8615 mm^3	98.59	9.8	14	7.15

*R.Freq. = Resonant Frequency, **Accn. = Acceleration

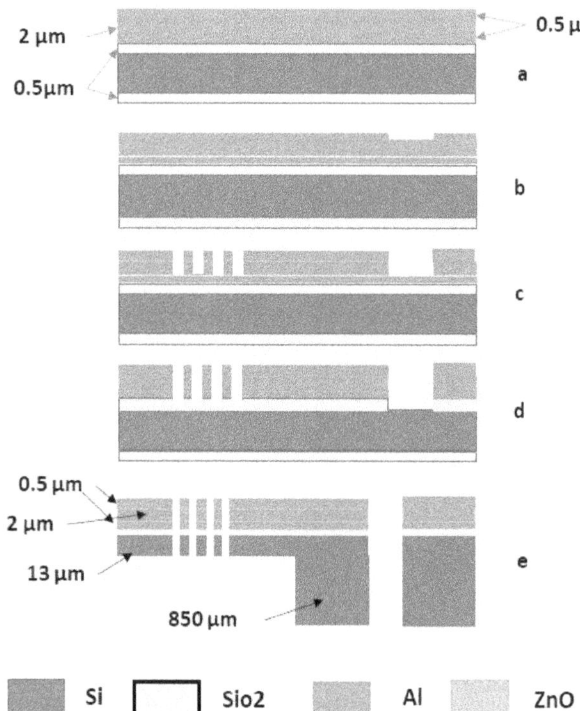

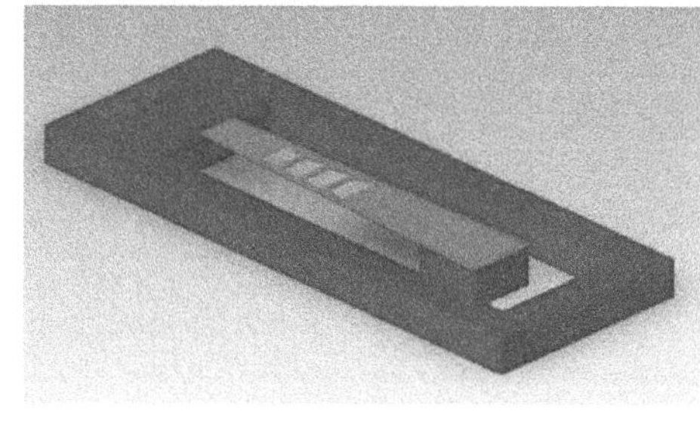

Fabrication flow chart:
(a) **Multilayer deposition**
(b) **Top electrode patterning by lift-off (mask 1)**
(c) **Bottom electrode opening via RIE (mask 2)**
(d) **Front Feature patterning of cantilever and DRIE (mask 3)**
(e) **Proof mass patterning and cantilever release via backside RIE (mask 4).**

Figure 2.15: Fabrication process of multiperforated PZEH

2.7 Summary

This chapter has covered the impact of the cantilever structure's structural alteration on its mechanical, electrical, and resonant frequency characteristics. It has been suggested that the cantilever structure benefits from perforation. COMSOL Multiphysics has been used to simulate and compare cantilever structures that are rectangular, tapered, perforated, and multi-perforated. Without enlarging the cantilever structure, the multiperforated cantilever structures create superior output voltage and power and have a better distribution of stress inside the structure. Of all the cantilever designs described, the tapered multi-perforated cantilever structure performs the best and has the lowest resonance frequency. Its average output power is 7.15 μW, and its resonance frequency is 98.59 Hz. It produces an output voltage of 14 V.

Chapter 3

Structural modification in the non-uniform piezoelectric cantilever

The design of the non-uniform PZ cantilever structure is covered in this chapter. Electricity has typically been produced using a traditional cantilever structure with consistent thickness [22]. In the conventional cantilever design, the distribution of stress and strain reaches its maximum at the fixed end and progressively diminishes towards the free end. The free end's piezoelectric layer is hence underutilised. Numerous studies attempted to alter the cantilever structure's geometry in an effort to increase PZEH's efficiency. A low resonance frequency can be achieved and improved stress distribution homogeneity through cantilever modification. This section of the chapter examines the impact of a tapered substrate thickness profile on PZEH performance. The trapezoidal cantilever configuration with homogeneous piezoelectric layer thickness and tapering substrate thickness is the suggested energy harvester. Researchers have looked into how the substrate layer thickness profile, which is tapered up and down, affects the PZEH's resonance frequency, tip mass deflection, stress distribution, voltage, and power generation capacity. The cantilever with non-uniform thickness profile and its motion, as well as other output characteristics like output voltage, tip mass deflection, and resonance frequency, are all described by the provided analytical formulation. A popular finite element analysis programme called COMSOL Multiphysics was used to design and simulate each structure. The suggested cantilever's performance has been compared to that of a rectangular cantilever construction with consistent thickness.

3.1 Mathematical analysis

The goal of this part is to construct an analytical model of the piezoelectric cantilever beam with a variable substrate thickness so that its effects on the power, generated output voltage, tip mass deflection, stress distribution, and resonant frequency can be examined. In order to construct the analytical model, we will first examine a simple cantilever beam, as seen in Fig. 2.1, which is composed of a piezoelectric layer atop a substrate layer. t_S and t_P, respectively, are the thicknesses of the substrate and piezoelectric layers.

When an external force is applied to a piezoelectric material, it has the ability to generate an electric field and vice versa. Thus, under specified mechanical stress (T) and electric field (E), Eqs. (1.4a) and (1.4b) provide the essential relationship between the mechanical strain (S) and the electric displacement (D) in piezoelectric materials.

Thus, based on the discussion in Chapter 3, it can be concluded that the applied stress, the piezoelectric coefficient, the thickness of the piezoelectric layer, and the transverse vibration of the cantilever structure all affect how much charge is generated across the PZ layer, which in turn affects how much electric voltage is developed across the PZ layer of the cantilever beam. Therefore, the cantilever structure with a larger stress distribution yields a higher voltage than the others when all other design parameters are equal.

3.1.1 Mechanical analysis

Numerous scholars examine the mechanical characterization of the cantilever vibration using various methodologies. Kirchhoff plate theory, a traditional theory of plates, is used to analyse mechanically the suggested cantilever structure with tapered substrate thickness, as illustrated in Fig. 3.1 [20], [110], [116]. The cross-section in this instance is perpendicular to the beam's axis. Lastly, FEM analysis for piezoelectric cantilever structures using COMSOL multi-physics has been used to validate the derived theory.

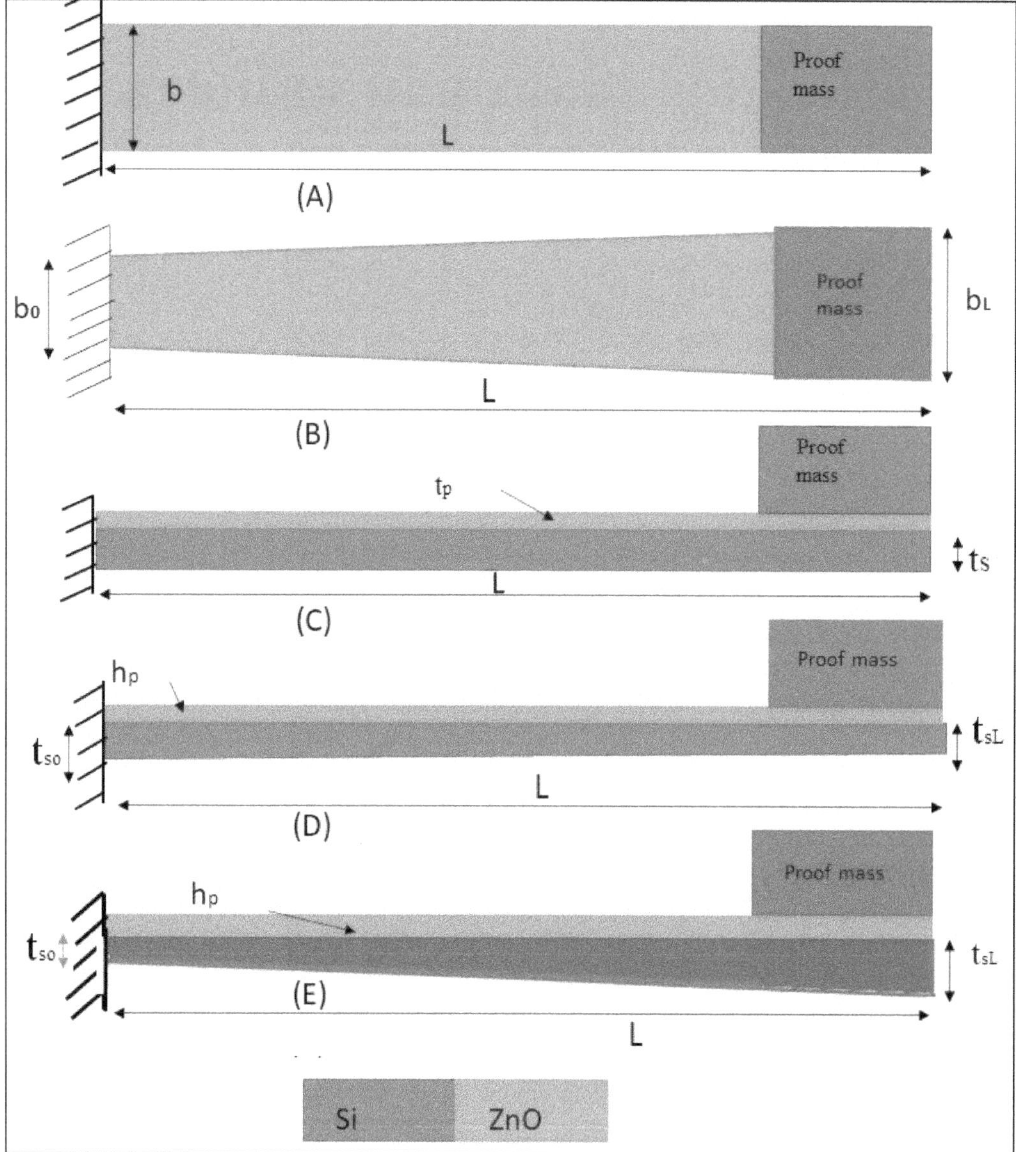

Figure 3.1: (a) Top view of rectangular cantilever (b) top view of trapezoidal cantilever (c) side view of uniform rectangular and trapezoidal cantilever (d) side view of tapered up rectangular and tapered up trapezoidal cantilever (e) side view of tapered down rectangular and tapered down trapezoidal cantilever

Equations (2.17) or (2.18) can be used to express the mechanical deviation of a rectangular cantilever plate with tapering substrate thickness in a perpendicular direction [20], [110].

The biharmonic operator in Eqs. (2.17) and (2.18) is Δ^4, which is provided in Eq. (2.19). According to Eq. (3.1), the flexural rigidity of the composite cantilever structure is D_r, while the vertical displacement of the plate is $w(x,y,t)$. The density is ρ. The external force acting on the system at any deflection $w(x,y,t)$ is denoted by $f(x,y,t)_m$.

$$D_r = \frac{Y_s t_s^3}{12(1-v_s^2)} + \frac{Y_p t_p^3}{12(1-v_p^2)}, \tag{3.1}$$

The substrate layer's and the piezoelectric layer's Young's moduli are denoted by Y_s and Y_p, respectively. The substrate and piezoelectric layer Poisson's ratios are denoted by v_s and v_p, respectively. The substrate and PZ layer thicknesses are denoted by t_s and t_p, respectively.

The cantilever structure's length is L, and its width is b. Equation (3.2) illustrates that the thickness of the substrate layer is t_s, and the thickness of the PZ layer is t_p. These values depend on the length of the cantilever.

$$t_s(x) = t_{so}\left(1 + \alpha\frac{x}{L}\right); \alpha = \left(\frac{t_{sL} - t_{so}}{t_{so}}\right) \tag{3.2}$$

The thickness of the trapezoidal cantilever beam at the fixed end is t_{so}, whereas at the free end it is t_{sL}. The cantilever's thickness tapering factor is denoted by α.

If in the Eq. (2.18), $f(x,y,t) = 0$, then it satisfy the condition of free vibration. Hence, Eq. (2.18)will be modified as equation (3.3).

$$D_r \nabla^4 w(x,y,t) + m\frac{\partial^4 w(x,y,t)}{\partial t^2} = 0, \tag{3.3}$$

Where $m = \rho_s t_s + \rho_p t_p$. The boundary limit changes from x = 0 to L along the length and from y = 0 to b along the breadth of the rectangular plate, which has length and width of L and b, respectively. Equation (2.21) can be solved using the method of separation of variables, yielding Equation (3.4).

$$w(x,y,t) = W(x,y)T(t), \tag{3.4}$$

Substituting the Eq. (3.4) in Eq. (3.3) [20],[110] we get,

$$\frac{d^2 T(t)}{dt} + \omega^2 T(t) = 0, \tag{3.5}$$

$$\nabla^4 W(x,y) - \lambda^4 W(x,y) = 0, \tag{3.6}$$

where,

$$\lambda^4 = \frac{\omega^2}{\beta^2} = \frac{m\omega^2}{D_r}, \tag{3.7}$$

Where $\beta^2 = \frac{D_r}{m}$. The plate is in sinusoidal oscillation. So, general solution of Eq. (3.5) is to be time dependent Eq. (3.8) [110].

$$T(t) = A.cos\omega t + B.sin\omega t, \tag{3.8}$$

where A and B are arbitrary constant. The solution of displacement dependent equation i.e., Eq. (3.6) can be expressed as Eq. (3.9).

$$(\nabla^4 - \lambda^4)W(x,y) = (\nabla^2 - \lambda^2)(\nabla^2 + \lambda^2)W(x,y), \tag{3.9}$$

According to the linear differential equation theory, the superimposition of Eqs. (3.10) and (3.11) will provide the complete solution of Eq. (3.9) [20], [110].

$$(\nabla^2 + \lambda^2)W(x,y) = \frac{\partial^2 W_1(x,y)}{\partial x^2} + \frac{\partial^2 W_1(x,y)}{\partial y^2} + \lambda^2 W_1(x,y), \tag{3.10}$$

$$(\nabla^2 - \lambda^2)W(x,y) = \frac{\partial^2 W_2(x,y)}{\partial x^2} + \frac{\partial^2 W_2(x,y)}{\partial y^2} - \lambda^2 W_2(x,y), \tag{3.11}$$

Now for the Eq. (3.10) by assuming the solution $W_1(x,y)$ resembles the harmonic motion, $W_1(x,y)$ [20] can be written in the form as

$$W_1(x,y) = X(x)Y(y), \tag{3.12}$$

where,

$$X(x) = c1.cos\alpha x + c2.sin\alpha x, \tag{3.13}$$

$$Y(y) = c3.cos\beta y + c4.sin\beta y, \tag{3.14}$$

The solution of equation (3.10) can be obtained using the product of Eqs. (3.13) and (3.14) as

$$W_1(x,y) = A1sin\alpha x.sin\beta y + A2sin\alpha x.cos\beta y + A3cos\alpha x.sin\beta y + A4cos\alpha x.sin\beta y, \tag{3.15}$$

In a similar manner, Eq. (3.11) can be solved, with the exception that $\iota\lambda$ is used in lieu of λ. Thus, the solution to Eq. (3.11) contains the components of the product of the sinh and cosh terms. Consequently, it is possible to solve and express Eq. (3.9) as Eq. (3.16).

$$W(x,y) = A1sin\alpha x.sin\beta y + A2sin\alpha x.cos\beta y + A3cos\alpha x.sin\beta y + A4cos\alpha x.sin\beta y$$
$$+A5sinh\alpha x.sinh\beta y + A6sinh\alpha x.cosh\beta y + A7cosh\alpha x.sinh\beta y + A8cosh\alpha x.sinh\beta y, \tag{3.16}$$

where $A1, A2, A3, A4, A5, A6, A7, A8$ are the arbitrary constants whose values depend on the initial conditions and $\lambda = \alpha^2 + \beta^2 = \theta^2 + \phi^2$. Eq. (3.7) yields the value of ω, which is represented by Eq. (3.17).

$$\omega = \lambda^2\sqrt{\frac{D_r}{m}}, \tag{3.17}$$

where the plate's border condition provides λ. The value D_r in Eq. (3.17) is derived by substituting it from Eq. (3.1) in Eq. (3.18).

$$\omega = \lambda^2\sqrt{\frac{1}{12m}\left(\frac{Y_s t_s(x)^3}{(1-v_s^2)} + \frac{Y_p t_p^3}{(1-v_p^2)}\right)}$$
$$= \lambda^2\sqrt{\frac{1}{12m}\left(\frac{Y_s}{(1-v_s^2)}\left(t_{so}\left(1+\alpha\frac{x}{L}\right)\right)^3 + \frac{Y_p t_p^3}{(1-v_p^2)}\right)} \tag{3.18}$$

The non-uniform cantilever structure will transform into the uniform cantilever structure if the tapering factor $\alpha = 0$. It is evident that the cantilever beam's frequency is dependent on the thickness tapering factor as determined by Eq. (3.18).

3.2 Design of cantilever structures

This section applies the finite element method (FEM) to verify the theory stated in the previous section. A variety of cantilever constructions, including rectangular and trapezoidal cantilevers with tapering substrate thickness and uniform substrate thickness, have been built and examined. In COMSOL Multiphysics, every planned beam configuration is simulated at an excitation acceleration of 1g ($9.8\ ms^{-2}$). All of the cantilever structures were designed using Si and ZnO as the substrates and PZ layers.

First, an analysis and design were done for a rectangular cantilever beam with a homogeneous thickness. Next, a trapezoidal cantilever with a consistent thickness has been created. Once the uniform thickness basic cantilever was established, a cantilever with tapered substrate thickness was created. Analysis has been done on the impact of tapered substrate thickness on the PZEH's generated output voltage, output power, stress distribution, resonance frequency, and tip mass deflection.

3.2.1 Uniform rectangular cantilever

Initially, a unimorph rectangular cantilever with a uniform substrate thickness of 10000 μm in length, 1000 μm in breadth, and 30 μm in total thickness was created. The thickness of the zinc oxide (ZnO) layer (t_p) is 2 μm, while the thickness of the silicon (Si) substrate (t_s) is 28 μm. In order to lower the resonant frequency, a Si-based solid proof mass with dimensions of $(1 \times 1 \times 0.85)\ mm^3$ has been attached to the cantilever's free end. Fig. 3.1 ((A) and (C)) displays the top and side views of the uniform rectangular cantilever structure that has been designed, respectively.

Both the theoretical and simulation methods are used to calculate the natural frequency of the uniform rectangular cantilever, which is designed in COMSOL Multiphysics. The natural frequency computed for the uniform rectangular cantilever structure closely matches the theoretical value. The uniform rectangular cantilever constructed has a simulated natural frequency value of 122.87 Hz, with a percentage error of 2.48 % compared to the theoretical value. Table 3.1 presents a comprehensive tabulation of the resonant frequency comparison between theoretical and simulated for all cantilever structures.

3.2.2 Tapering of cantilever structure

To lower the resonant frequency and improve PZEH performance, numerous researchers have experimented with various structural modification methods [18], [20], [31], [35], [49], [108]. By lessening the stiffness of a cantilever, the low resonant frequency and improved PZEH performance can be attained. By altering the cantilever beam's changeable substrate thickness and cantilever construction, the stiffness can be decreased.

A. Design of uniform trapezoidal cantilever

From the foregoing mathematical study shown in Subsection 3.1.1, it is evident that the cantilever structure's shape affects its natural frequency. Initially, a trapezoidal cantilever structure with consistent thickness is created by modifying the rectangular cantilever structure. The uniform rectangular cantilever structure with ZnO at the top of the Si substrate layer and the uniform trapezoidal cantilever structure are built similarly. Fig. 3.1 ((B) and (C)) displays the top and side views of the uniform trapezoidal cantilever structure that has been designed, respectively. The uniform trapezoidal cantilever structure and the rectangular cantilever structure share the same fabrication area. The trapezoidal cantilever has the same length as a rectangular cantilever, with a width of 1000 μm at the free end (b_L) and 600 μm at the fixed end (b_O). The ZnO layer (t_p) is 2 μm thick, while the Si substrate layer (t_S) is 28 μm thick. At the free end of the trapezoidal cantilever is affixed the Si based proof mass of dimension $(1000 \times 1000 \times 850)$ μm^3. The uniform trapezoidal cantilever's natural frequency of 101.17 Hz closely matches the predicted value. According to the theory under discussion, the uniform trapezoidal cantilever structure's resonant frequency is lower than the uniform rectangular cantilever's natural frequency. 1.18 % is the percentage error between the simulated and theoretical values of the resonant frequency.

B. Tapered thickness in the cantilever

After designing the cantilever with uniform thickness, the cantilever with non-uniform substrate thickness is discussed. Both tapered up and tapered down substrate thickness profile have been discussed here. In the tapered up cantilever structure, the thickness is more at the fixed end than at the free end whereas, in the tapered down cantilever structure, the thickness of the substrate is less at the fixed end than at the free end. The details design of the cantilever with a non-uniform thickness profile is discussed below.

Tapered up configuration   In both rectangular and trapezoidal cantilever structures, the substrate thickness is first introduced in a tapered up shape. The rectangular cantilever construction is the first to use the tapered up design. The tapered up rectangular cantilever structure has the same length as the cantilever mentioned before. The Si substrate layer has a width of 1000 μm, a thickness of 28 μm at the fixed end and 18 μm at the free end (t_{SL}). The ZnO layer (t_p) has a thickness of 2 μm. The dimensions of the Si-based proof mass are identical to those of previous cantilever structures. The tapered up rectangular cantilever structure's top view and side view are displayed in Fig. 3.1 ((A) and (D)), respectively. The intended tapered up rectangular cantilever has a natural frequency of 108.37 Hz, with a 3.2 % deviance from the theoretical value.

The trapezoidal cantilever structure has a lower resonance frequency than the rectangular cantilever structure, as was covered in the section before this one. In order to further lower the resonance frequency, the trapezoidal cantilever construction has incorporated a tapered up thickness profile. The uniform trapezoidal cantilever structure and the tapered up trapezoidal cantilever structure have the same length and width. The Si layer (t_{SO}) has a thickness of 18 μm at the free end and 28 μm at the fixed end. ZnO is maintained at the same thickness as conventional cantilever constructions. The evidence mass's dimensions and location are identical. Fig. 3.1 ((B) and (D)) displays the top and side views of the planned tapered up trapezoidal cantilever structure, respectively.

Table 3.1: Comparison of resonant frequency of different cantilever structures using analytical and simulated model

Cantilever Structures	Dimension	Analytical R.Freq. (Hz)	Simulated R.Freq. (Hz)	Absolute Error
Uniform Rectangular	$L = 10$ mm, $b = 1$ mm, $t_s = 28\ \mu m$, $t_p = 2\ \mu m$	126	122.87	-2.48 %
Tapered Up Rectangular	$L = 10$ mm, $b=1$ mm, $t_{SO} = 28\ \mu m$, $t_{SL} = 18\ \mu m$, $t_p = 2\ \mu m$	105	108.37	3.2 %
Tapered Down Rectangular	$L = 10$ mm, $b = 1$ mm, $t_{SO} = 18\ \mu m$, $t_{SL} = 28\ \mu m$, $t_p = 2\ \mu m$	72.6	77.63	6.92 %
Uniform Trapezoidal	$L = 10$ mm, $b_O = 0.6$ mm, $b_L = 1$ mm, $t_S = 28\ \mu m$, $t_p = 2\ \mu m$	99.3	101.17	1.18 %
Tapered Up Trapezoidal	$L = 10$ mm, $b_O = 0.6$ mm, $b_L = 1$ mm, $t_{SO} = 28\ \mu m$, $t_{SL} = 18\ \mu m$, $t_p = 2\ \mu m$	83.3	89	6.84 %
Tapered Down Trapezoidal	$L = 10$ mm, $b_O = 0.6$ mm, $b_L = 1$ mm, $t_{SO} = 18\ \mu m$, $t_{SL} = 28\ \mu m$, $t_p = 2\ \mu m$	59	62.41	5.77 %

R.Freq. = Resonant Frequency

Tapered down configuration   It's time to create the cantilever structure with a tapered down configuration after creating the cantilever beam with a tapered up configuration and examining its impact on the resonant frequency. Initially, a tapered down rectangular cantilever with the same width and length as the uniform rectangular cantilever is designed. ZnO (t_p) has a thickness of 2 μm, while the Si substrate layer has a thickness of 18 μm at the fixed end and 28 μm at the free end (t_{SL}). The proof mass's dimensions and location at the free end are identical to those of other cantilever structures. The rectangular cantilever beam that is tapered down has a resonance frequency of 77.63 Hz, which is 6.92% off from the theoretical value. Relative to the planned tapered down rectangular cantilever construction, Fig. 3.1 ((A) and (E)) displays the top and side views.

Last but not least, the tapered down trapezoidal cantilever structure is designed using the tapered down configuration. The uniform trapezoidal and tapered up trapezoidal cantilevers have the same length and width as the tapered down cantilever. The Si substrate layer has a thickness of 18 μm at the fixed end (t_{SO}) and 28 μm at the free end (t_{SL}). The ZnO layer (t_p) has a thickness of 2 μm. The proof mass's location and dimensions match those of previous cantilever structures. The tapered down trapezoidal cantilever has a resonance frequency of 62.41 Hz. The discrepancy between the simulated and theoretical resonant frequency values is 5.77%.

Fig. 3.1 ((B) and (E)) displays the top and side views of the planned tapered down trapezoidal cantilever structure, respectively.

Following the design of every cantilever structure, Table 3.1 tabulates the comparison between the simulated and analytical resonant frequency of every cantilever structure.

3.3   Mechanical output of the cantilever structure

3.3.1   Deflection of the proof mass

One of the most crucial parameters that essentially determines the strain distribution inside the cantilever construction is the proof mass deflection, which is understood from Equations. Refeqn:StrainX1, Refeqn:StrainY1, Refeqn:StrainXY1). For every cantilever construction, the proof mass deflection is computed using the transient solver approach at various frequencies. When the excitation frequency and the planned cantilever's resonant frequency coincide, the cantilever structure's proof mass deflection reaches its maximum. The PZEH can provide the maximum output voltage and power in these conditions. Figure 3.2 presents a comparison of each cantilever beam's proof mass deflection. Fig. 3.2 shows that each cantilever structure's peak deflection occurs at the resonant frequency. The cantilever beams with the following peak displacements: 1.93 mm, 2.25

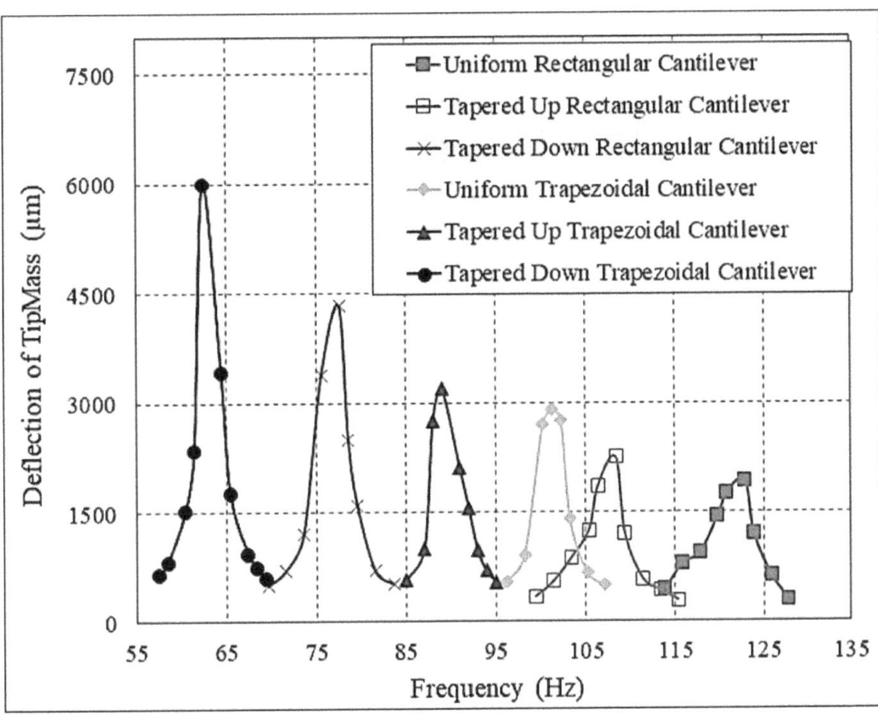

Figure 3.2: Deflection of the cantilever beams

mm, 4.3 mm, 2.9 mm, 3.2 mm, and 6 mm for uniform rectangular, tapered up rectangular, tapered down rectangular, uniform trapezoidal, and tapered up trapezoidal.

3.3.2 Stress distribution

As can be seen from the subsection 2.3.1a, the cantilever structure's stress distribution directly affects the output voltage and power. Although a larger stress is preferable for higher output voltage and power, it must be less than the material's fracture strength. When the structure's von-mises stress exceeds its Young's modulus, the material loses its elastic properties. For the cantilever construction to be mechanically stable, the maximum von-mises stress that develops in the beam must be smaller than the material's Young's modulus. The stress distribution for each cantilever structure with a 1 g excitation acceleration is displayed in Fig. 3.3.

Figure 3.3 illustrates that for both uniform rectangular and uniform trapezoidal cantilevers, the stress peaks at the fixed end and progressively diminishes towards the free end. Compared to a uniform rectangular cantilever, a uniform trapezoidal cantilever has a more even distribution of stress. A similar pattern is seen in the tapered up trapezoidal and rectangular cantilevers, but the stress distribution in these cases is more evenly distributed than in the comparable basic cantilever. Compared to uniform rectangular and tapered up rectangular cantilevers, the stress distribution of the tapered down rectangular cantilever has performed better. Of all the cantilever constructions that have been covered here, the tapered down trapezoidal cantilever has the best stress distribution. Compared to the standard uniform rectangular cantilever, the suggested tapered down trapezoidal cantilever has a peak stress that is roughly 3.55 times higher.

3.4 Electrical output of the cantilever structures

3.4.1 Output voltage of the designed structures

Equation (3.18) yields the highest output voltage produced by PZEH at the resonant frequency. Equations (2.13), (2.14), and (2.15) yield the generated output voltage, which is dependent on the applied stress, piezoelectric charge, voltage coefficient, and PZ layer thickness. Using the time-dependent analysis feature of the COMSOL multiphysics software, the voltage produced by each planned PZEH is determined. At their individual resonance frequencies, all of the planned structures are aroused at

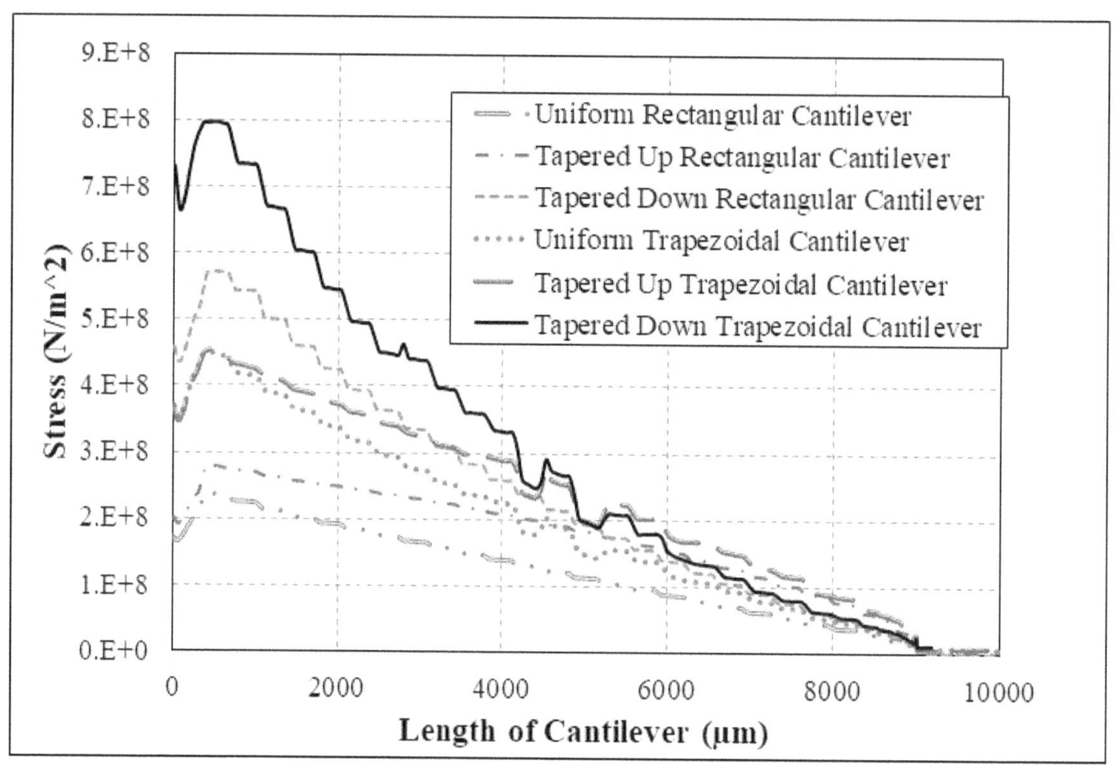

Figure 3.3: Stress distribution within the cantilever beams

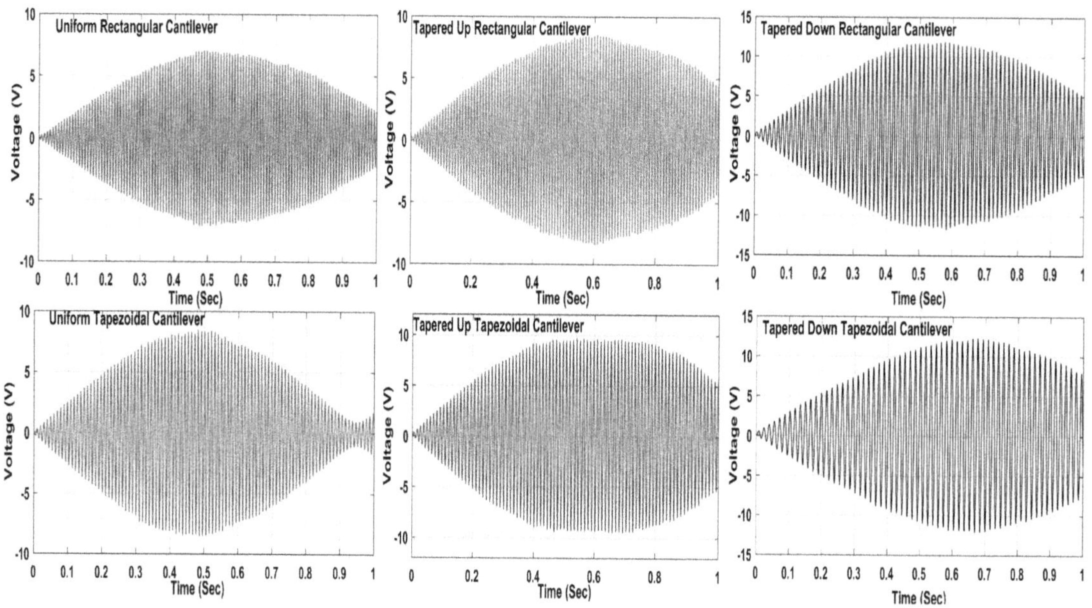

Figure 3.4: Transient output voltage of all cantilever structures

an acceleration of 1g ($= 9.8\ ms^{-2}$). Every proposed cantilever's transient voltage at each natural frequency is displayed in Fig. 3.4. At their respective resonant frequencies, the uniform rectangular, tapered up rectangular, and tapered down rectangular cantilevers provide peak output open circuit voltages of 7 V, 8.5 V, and 11.8 V, respectively. At their resonant frequency, the output voltage produced by the tapered up trapezoidal, tapered down trapezoidal, and uniform trapezoidal cantilevers is 9.7 V, 12.5 V, and 9.7 V, respectively. For every cantilever at a 1g acceleration, the output voltage variation with frequency is displayed in Fig. 3.5.

The higher voltage generated by the tapered down cantilever structures than the corresponding uniform and tapered up

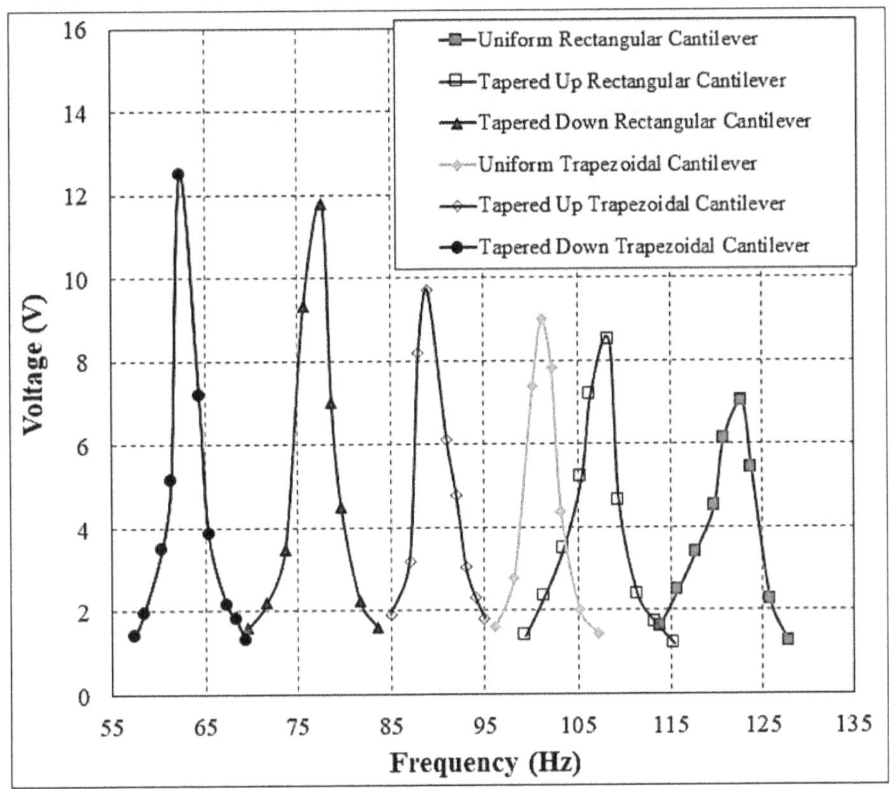

Figure 3.5: Variation of output voltage with frequency for all cantilevers

cantilever is because of the better stress distribution within the cantilever structure.

3.4.2 Output power of the designed structures

If the excitation frequency coincides with the resonant frequency and the internal resistance (R_L) of the PZEH is equal to the load resistance (R_{pz}), that is, ($R_L = R_{pz}$), the PZEH can produce its maximum power. An electrical equivalent model of a piezoelectric cantilever can be expressed as follows: an equivalent current source I_p, clamping capacitance C_p, and internal resistance R_{pz}. Fig. 2.12 depicts this electrical equivalent model of a piezoelectric cantilever plate.

The PZEH's maximum power generation cannot be determined without the knowledge of its internal resistance value. The PZ device's internal resistance cannot be directly calculated. So, to indirectly compute the internal impedance, a known load resistance is connected to the EH. Next, the PZEH is simulated at a constant load at the cantilever's resonant frequency, and the output power is computed by adjusting the load resistance values. Fig. 3.6 illustrates how output power changes as load resistance changes. The PZEH produces the most power at the ideal load resistance, which is equal to the internal impedance, according to the maximum power theorem. Because the cantilever's cross-sectional area varies very little, the load resistance value is roughly the same for all cantilever structures. The cantilever beam as a whole has an internal resistance of about 2 Mohm.

At an excitation acceleration of 1g, the power generated by various PZEH at different frequencies is assessed using the simulated value of internal resistance. The generated average power graph is displayed in Fig. 3.7, plotted against frequency. The suggested tapered up trapezoidal cantilever has an average output power of 7 μW, which is 293.79% more than the standard uniform rectangular cantilever.

Table 3.2 contains a tabulation of all the computed output parameters for all cantilever structures. In the end, Table 3.3 presents a comparison between the suggested study and the existing literature.

The construction of a tapered down trapezoidal cantilever structure involves challenging processes. Therefore, Fig 3.8 illustrates the potential fabrication procedures for the stair-shaped trapezoidal cantilever structure. To build the design as depicted in Fig 3.8, eight masks were required. The dimensions of the tapered down trapezoidal cantilever structure and the staircase-shaped trapezoidal cantilever structure are the same. By simulating the structure, the associated distinct parameter is

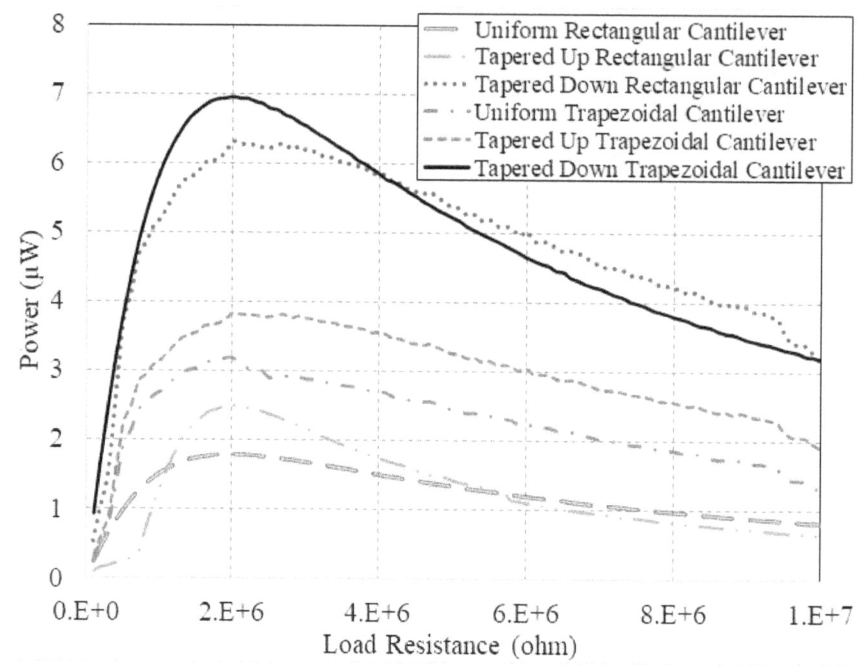

Figure 3.6: Variation of power with load resistance

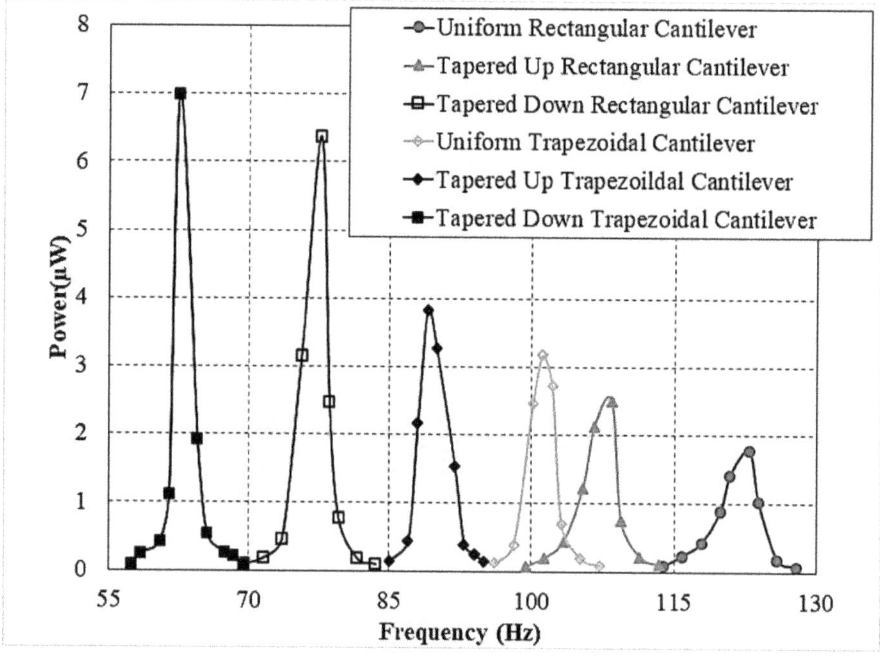

Figure 3.7: Variation of output power with frequency

computed. A peak output voltage of 12.6 V can be produced at the resonance frequency of 62.12 Hz. It produces 7.1 μW of output power. Fig. 3.9 compares the output voltage and power produced by the tapered down trapezoidal cantilever with the staircase-shaped trapezoidal cantilever. The staircase trapezoidal cantilever's electrical output parameter and the tapering down trapezoidal cantilever's structure closely match each other.

Table 3.2: Comparison between different PZEH

Cantilever	Natural Freq* (Hz)	Defn.** (mm)	Voltage (V)	Average Power (μW)
Uniform Rectangular	122.87	1.93	7	1.78
Tapered Up Rectangular	108.37	2.25	8.5	2.5
Tapered Down Rectangular	77.63	4.33	11.8	6.3
Uniform Trapezoidal	101.17	2.9	9	3.18
Tapered Up Trapezoidal	89	3.2	9.7	3.83
Tapered Down Trapezoidal	62.41	6	12.5	7

Freq* = Frequency;

Defn.** = Deflection of the tip mass

Table 3.3: Comparison of the proposed work with available literatures

Reference	Material and Dimension	R.Freq.	Output Parameter	Remarks
[16] 2005	PZT, Volume - 1 cm^3	120 Hz	Power- 120 μW	Tapering of the cantilever structure increases the power density.
[45] 2005	PZT, length - 5 cm	55 Hz	Power - 27.5 mW	Tapering of rectangular cantilever at free end increases the strain distribution along the length.
[46] 2015	PZT-5H, 0.35 $\times 0.01 \times 0.0006$ m^3	541.87 Hz	Voltage- 3.2 V	Truncation can improve strain distribution.
[48] 2013	PZT, $50.8 \times 31.8 \times 0.5$ mm^3	4.98 Hz	Normalized Power- 0.0096 (Ws^4/m^2)	Quadratic Shaped cantilever generates twice energy than rectangular cantilever.
[50] 2015	PVDF, 40 mm $\times$ 14 mm $\times$ 170 μm	30.7 Hz	Voltage 4.72 V, Power- 8.59 μW	Multistep thickness profile can reduce resonant frequency and improves performance.
[54] 2021	PZT-5H, 2.578 cm^3	99.80 Hz	Power- 1.4 mW	Tapered substrate thickness gives more uniform stress in than conventional cantilever beams. Dimension is large.
This work	ZnO, 10 mm $\times$ 1 mm $\times$ 30 μm	62.41 Hz	Voltage-12.5 V, Power-7 μW	Tapered substrate thickness reduces the resonant frequency, improves stress distribution and generates more output voltage and power.

3.5 Summary

This chapter has covered the impact of the tapered substrate thickness on the output voltage, power, tip-mass deflection, resonance frequency, and stress distribution inside the cantilever structure. It is clear from this that variations in the thickness and shape of the cantilever framework can affect the cantilever's inherent frequency. The cantilever structure's stress distribution determines the voltage produced by the PZEH. The cantilever structure's stress distribution is enhanced by the substrate layer's tapering thickness. Compared to both tapered up and simple uniform cantilever structures, the tapered down cantilever construction has a superior distribution of stress. The optimal stress distribution is found in the tapered down trapezoidal cantilever construction. The minimum resonant frequency of 62.41 Hz is attained by the tapered down trapezoidal cantilever, which is 48.83 % lower than that of the uniform rectangular cantilever. Out of all the cantilever structures, the suggested tapered down trapezoidal cantilever structure produces the highest output voltage and power. At the resonant frequency of 62.41 Hz, it produces an average output power of 7 μW and a max output voltage of 12.5 V.

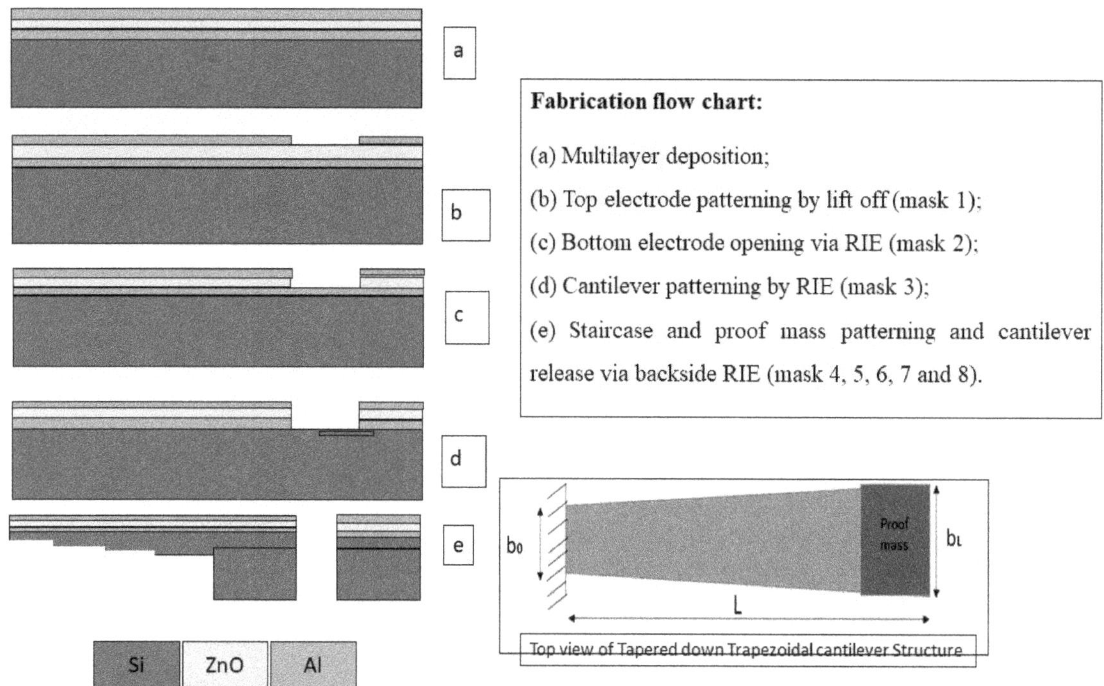

Figure 3.8: Fabrication process of cantilever of non uniform substrate thickness cantilever

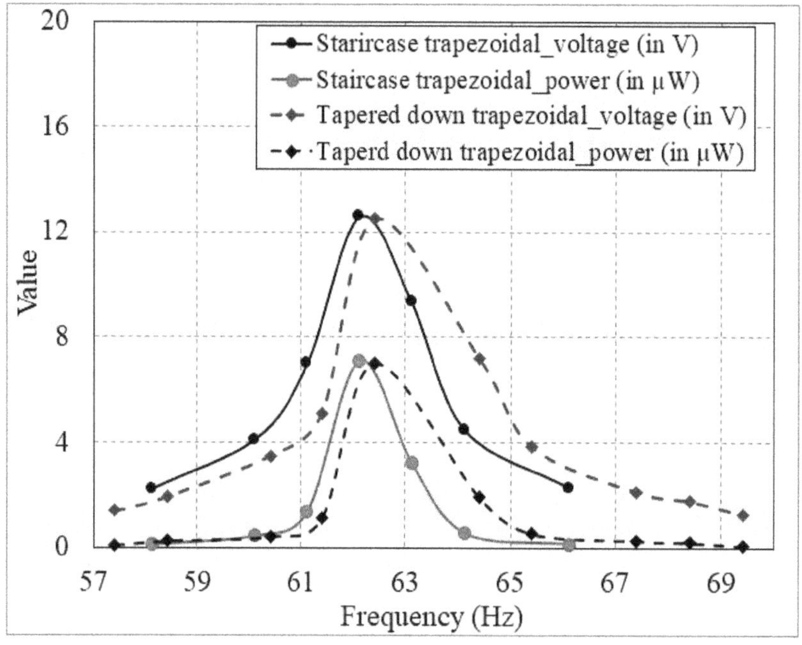

Figure 3.9: Comparison between the electrical output of staircase trapezoidal cantilever and tapered down trapezoidal cantilever structure

Chapter 4

L-shaped piezoelectric energy harvester for low frequency application

The creation of tiny, low-power electronic devices for implanted medical devices (IMDs) is the result of a recent advancement in the field of semiconductor devices. military hardware, wireless sensor nodes (WSN) [28] [22] [108] [111] [20] [111]. To power these devices, standard batteries are used. These batteries need to be periodically recharged or replaced due to their limited lifespan. Certain gadgets are utilised in inaccessible areas such within machinery, in isolated spots, or inside the human body, like in pacemakers. It becomes challenging to replace the batteries in these devices. A prime example of this is a machine health monitoring system, in which sensor nodes are installed in difficult-to-reach locations like induction motors or turbines. Therefore, the gadgets that have an integrated energy harvesting (EH) technology to replenish the battery are in great demand. The best energy harvester to power these microdevices is vibration-based [108][22]. Vibration energy harvesters are perfect for low power micro devices because they harness the unused vibration energy from the surrounding environment to produce electrical energy. Due to its straightforward design and increased electrical energy output, the piezoelectric energy harvester (PZEH) is preferred over electromagnetic EH [24] and electrostatic [117]. The PZEH produces electrical energy by utilising ambient vibration instead of an external voltage source. Micro Electro Mechanical Systems (MEMS) and CMOS technology make it simple to implement.

Because it is simple to build and implement, the cantilever-based design is most frequently employed in PZEH based on MEMS [20][116]. One end of the cantilever beam is fixed, and the other is free to vibrate. The application of load causes the cantilever beam to flex. When the load is removed, it reverts to its initial shape and keeps vibrating because of the material's elasticity and inertia. The cantilever beam bends, producing an alternating output voltage. The cantilever beam has the maximum deflection when the resonant frequency of the intended structure (f_piezo) is equal to the source frequency (f_source) $i.e. f_piezo = f_source$. In this situation, the cantilever beam generates the highest output voltage and, thus, the most output power. Low frequency vibration is present in our surroundings [118][29]. The MEMS-based energy harvester has demonstrated significant success in producing a significant voltage at low frequencies, making it suitable for a variety of applications. Initially, researchers worked on the addition of the proof mass to lessen the resonance frequency [2]. Afterwards, scientists attempted to alter the cantilever structure's design in order to attain a lower resonance frequency [28][22] [108] [111] [20] [18].

To enhance the PZEH's performance, we have suggested an L-shaped cantilever construction in this chapter. The L-shaped contributes to the cantilever structure's homogeneous stress distribution in addition to helping to lower the resonant frequency. Each cantilever beam's output voltage, power, and stress distribution have been measured. At a resonance frequency of 79.59 Hz, the L-shaped cantilever beam produces a maximum output voltage of 11.6 V.

4.1 DESIGN AND ANALYSIS

This chapter focuses on designing a cantilever beam for the PZEH that maintains the fabricated length within 5 mm while achieving a low resonance frequency. As little as 0.5 μm of thin film deposition is possible on the substrate using the current thin film deposition technology. The PZ layer in this article has a thickness of 2.5 μm, while the silicon substrate has a thickness of 13 μm. These values may be enough to support the cantilever structure mechanically. The Si layer is covered by a layer of ZnO.

Zinc oxide (ZnO) is the PZ material used in this chapter to design the PZEH. As covered in Chapter 2, lead zirconate titanate (PZT) has a higher piezoelectric coefficient (d_{31}) than the majority of other known PZ materials. PZT is inappropriate for this investigation since it contains lead.

4.1.1 Mathematical Analysis

When external tension is applied to the PZ layer's surface, an electric field is created within the layer and vice versa. According to Eqs. (1.5a) and (1.5b), respectively, the strain (S) and electric displacement (D) under the effect of mechanical stress (T) and electrical field (E) have a basic relationship. According to Eqs. (1.5a) and (1.5b), the device is operating in mode 31, which involves applying stress and strain in the X direction and generating an electric field in the Z direction.

Equation given below provides the cantilever beam's vibrational frequency as

$$\frac{D_r}{m}\frac{\partial^4 w(x,t)}{\partial x^4} + \frac{\partial^2 w(x,t)}{\partial t^2} = f(x,t) \tag{4.1}$$

First, the bending strain formula, which is provided as, can be used to estimate the total strain SP at the middle of the PZ layer.

$$S(x,t) = -t_{pc}\frac{\partial^2 w(x,t)}{\partial x^2} \tag{4.2}$$

The centre portion of the PZ layer's net stress is provided by

$$T_P = Y_P\left(-t_{pc}\frac{\partial^2 w(x,t)}{\partial x^2}\right) - d_{31}Y_P E \tag{4.3}$$

Equation (1.5b) can be used to estimate the electric flux density within the PZ layer of the piezoelectric cantilever by using the net stress value from the previous equation.

$$D = d_{31}\left[Y_P\left(-t_{pc}\frac{\partial^2 w(x,t)}{\partial x^2}\right) - d_{31}Y_P E\right] + \varepsilon_{33}^T E \tag{4.4a}$$

$$= d_{31}\left[-t_{pc}\left(\frac{\partial^2 w(x,t)}{\partial x^2}\right) + \left(\frac{\varepsilon_{33}^T E}{d_{31}} - d_{31}Y_P\right)E\right] \tag{4.4b}$$

Here $\left(\frac{\varepsilon_{33}^T E}{d_{31}} - d_{31}Y_P\right) = \varepsilon_{33}^s$ and $E = V(t)/t_p$.

The produced output voltage across the PZ layer under attention is denoted by V(t). The charge produced by the PZ layer as a result of the applied stress is as follows:

$$q = \int_0^L d_{31}\left[-t_{pc}\left(\frac{\partial^2 w(x,t)}{\partial x^2}\right) + \varepsilon_{33}^s V(t)/t_p\right]dx \tag{4.5}$$

$I = \frac{\partial q}{\partial t}$ represents the total current generated in the PZ layer. According to Ohm's Law, the output voltage is provided by $V(t) = I(t)R$ if R is the beam's internal resistance.

$$V(t) = R\left[\int_0^L d_{31}\left(-t_{pc}\left(\frac{\partial^2 w(x,t)}{\partial x^2 \partial t}\right) + \varepsilon_{33}^s\frac{\partial V(t)}{t_p \partial t}\right)dx\right] \tag{4.6}$$

4.1.2   Design of the cantilever structure

Designing the cantilever construction is based on the resonant frequency formula [29], which is provided by,

$$\omega = (\beta l)^2 \sqrt{\frac{0.236 D_r}{(l - l_m/2)^3 (0.236 mbl + \Delta m)}} \qquad (4.7)$$

where $D_r = b \times \frac{Y_s^2 t_s^2 + Y_P^2 t_P^2 + 2Y_s Y_P t_s t_P (2t_s^2 + 2t_P^2 + 3t_s t_P)}{12(Y_s t_s + Y_P t_P)}$ and $m = \rho_P t_P + \rho_s t_s$ and Δm is the mass of the proof mass.

A popular FEM analysis programme called COMSOL Multiphysics is used to build and simulate the L-shaped PZ cantilever structure. Solid mechanics is used for the mechanical analysis of the beam, and the electrostatics physics module in COMSOL Multiphysics is used for the electrical modelling. The planned structure is meshed using standard meshing techniques. The planned beam arrangement accelerates at a rate of 9.8 metres per square second (1 g).

As seen in figure 4.1, the L-shaped cantilever is built using Si as the substrate layer and ZnO as the PZ material. Si-based proof mass, attached at the structure's free end [6], is used. The PZ layer measures 2.5 µm in thickness, while the silicon substrate has a thickness of 13 µm. Table 4.1 provides the cantilever structure's detail dimensions. Table 4.2 lists the various mechanical properties of the materials utilised in the cantilever structure's design. The intended L-shaped cantilever structure has a resonance frequency of 79.5 Hz.

Table 4.1: Dimension of the cantilever

Parameter	Description	Value
L	Length of the cantilever	5000 (µm)
W	Breadth of the cantilever	1000 (µm)
hp	Thickness of PZ layer	2.5 (µm)
hs	Thickness of Si layer	13 (µm)
Proof mass	Dimension of proof mass	1000x1000x850 (µm3)

Table 4.2: Mechanical property of different material

Properties	Zinc Oxide	Silicon
Modulus of elasticity (GPa)	210	170
Density of the materials (Kg/m3)	5680	2329
Poisson Ratio	0.33	0.29

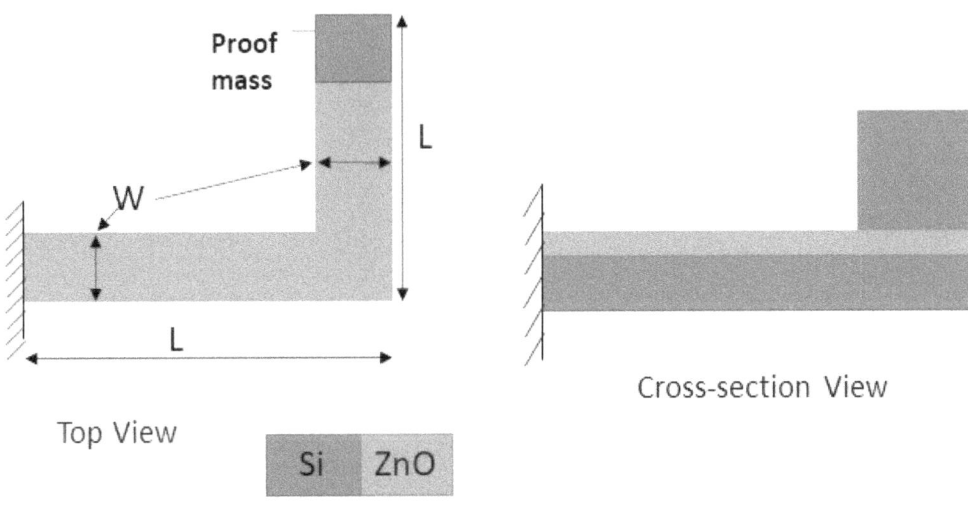

Figure 4.1: Top and Cross-section view of L-shaped cantilever structure

4.2 SIMULATION AND RESULTS

4.2.1 Mechanical Analysis

The end mass deflection of the cantilever structure is one of the most essential characteristics which fundamentally decides the stress and strain distribution within the cantilever structure, which can be understood from equations (4.2) and (4.3). For every cantilever construction, the end mass deflection is computed using the transient solver approach at various frequencies. When the excitation frequency matches the resonance frequency of a cantilever that is designed, the deflection of the cantilever structure's end mass reaches its maximum. The PZEH can provide the maximum output voltage and power in these conditions. The deflection of the cantilever beam's end mass is depicted in Figure 4.2. A PZ structure has a peak deflection of 4820 μm at a frequency of 79.5 Hz.

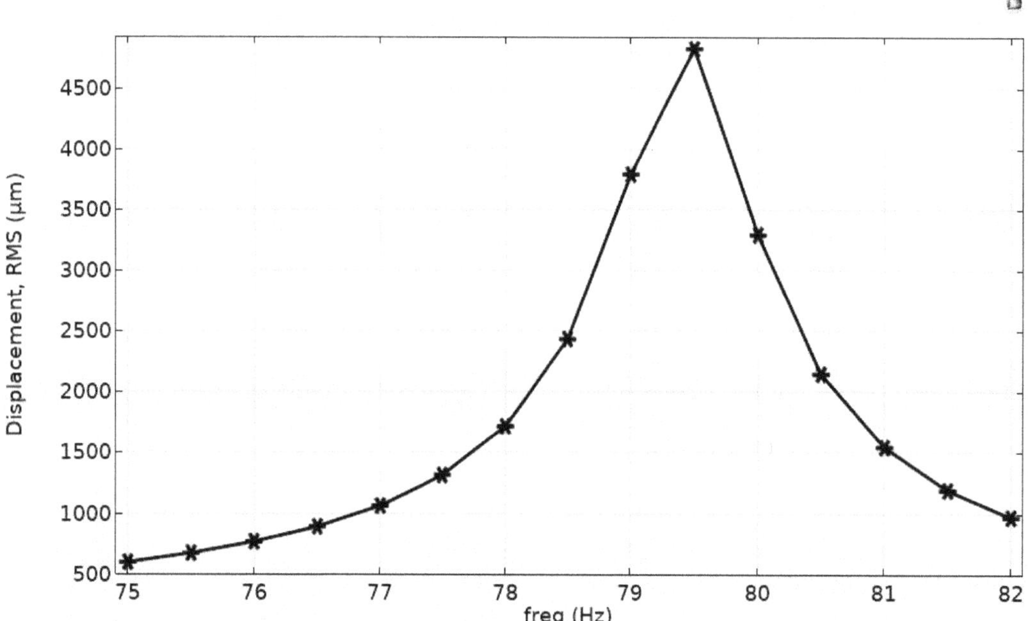

Figure 4.2: Deflection of the end mass of the L-shaped cantilever beam

The section above makes clear that the output power and voltage of the cantilever structure are directly impacted by the distribution of stress inside it. Although a larger stress is preferable for higher output voltage and power, it must be less than the material's fracture strength. When the structure's von mises stress exceeds its Young's modulus, the material loses its elastic properties. Therefore, for appropriate mechanical stability, the maximum von-mises stress created in the PZ structure must to be less than the material's Young's modulus. At an excitation acceleration of 1g, the distribution of stress throughout the cantilever structures' arc-length is depicted in Figure 4.3. Figure 4.3 illustrates that the maximum stress is well within the permissible level.

4.2.2 Electrical Analysis

Equation (10) yields the resonance frequency, which is the highest output voltage produced by PZEH. The voltage coefficient, applied stress, piezoelectric charge, and PZ layer thickness all affect the generated output voltage. The time-dependent analysis feature in the COMSOL Multiphysics software is used to determine the voltage produced by the designed PZEH. The suggested configurations are simulated using an excitation acceleration of 1 g. The transient voltage of the suggested L-shaped structure is depicted in Figure 4.4. Figure 4.5 displays the output voltage value at various frequencies. The L-shaped cantilever construction generates a peak voltage of 11.6 V.

If the excitation frequency is the same as the resonant frequency and the internal resistance (R_L) of the PZEH is equal to the load resistance (R_{pz}), that is, ($R_L = R_{pz}$), then the PZEH can produce its maximum power. The output power produced by the PZEH is determined by equation $P = (V_{OC}^2)/R_{PZ}$.

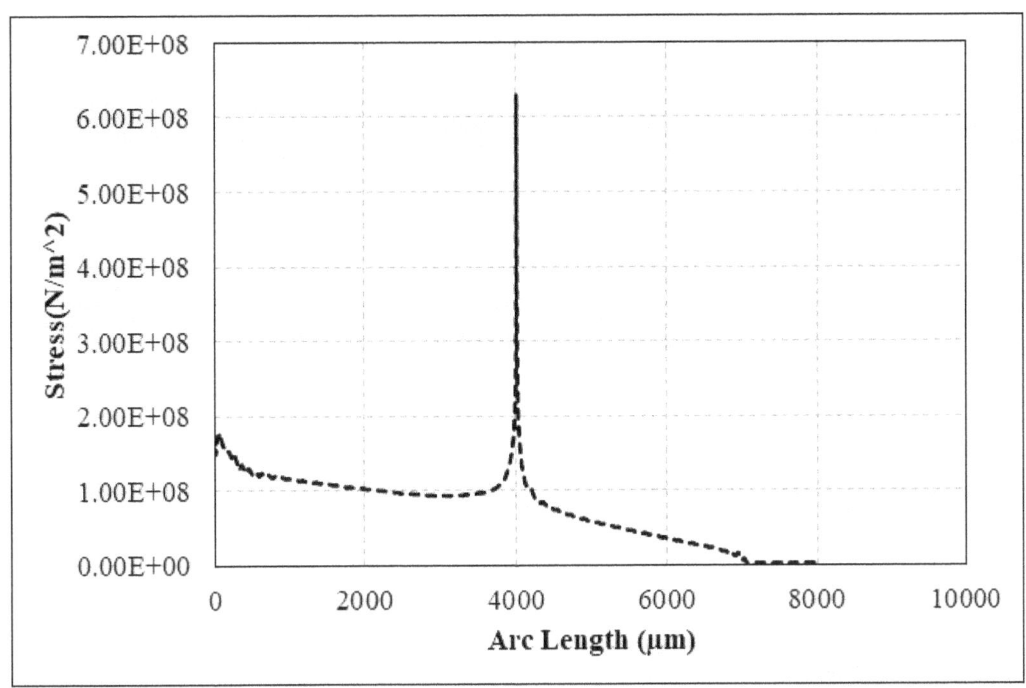

Figure 4.3: Stress distribution of the L-shaped cantilever beam

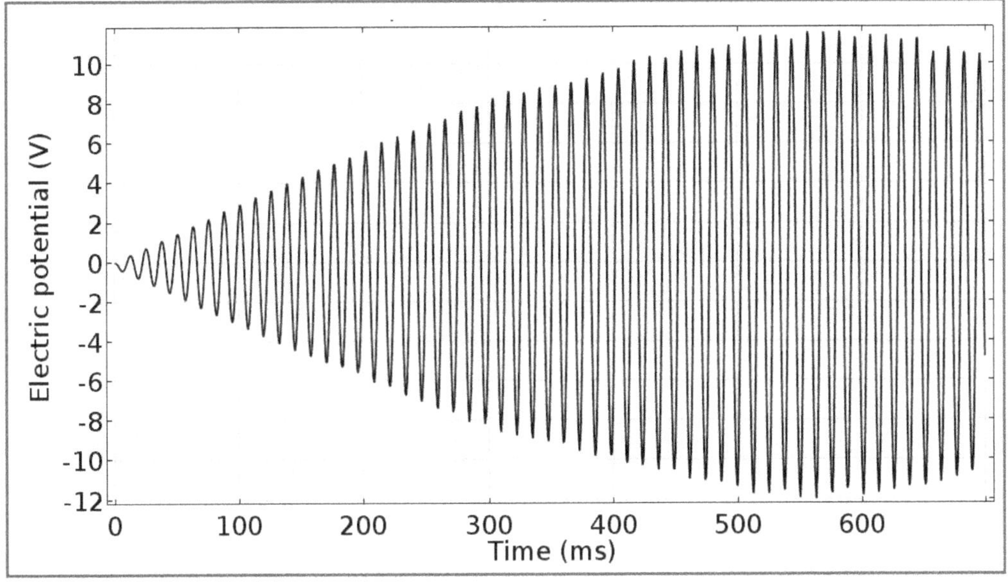

Figure 4.4: Transient voltage of the L-shaped cantilever structure.

The PZ device's internal resistance cannot be directly calculated. In order to indirectly compute the internal impedance, an external resistance with a known value is connected to the EH. At the fixed resonance frequency, the PZEH is subjected to a steady load. Next, the output power is calculated by simulating the structure by adjusting the external resistance. As seen in Figure 4.5, a graph is plotted for the generated output power at various external load variations. The PZEH produces the most power at the ideal load resistance, according to the maximum power theorem. The load resistance and internal impedance have the same value. 3.5 $M\Omega$ is the ideal load resistance, according to Figure 4.5.

Following the determination of the ideal load, the output power is computed at various frequencies. Figure 6 illustrates how the output power value is computed at various frequencies. Based on Figure 4.6, it is evident that the output reaches its maximum power of 10.8 µW at 79.5 Hz.

In Table 4.3, the planned cantilever's detail summary is provided. A table 4.4 compares this work with the body of existing

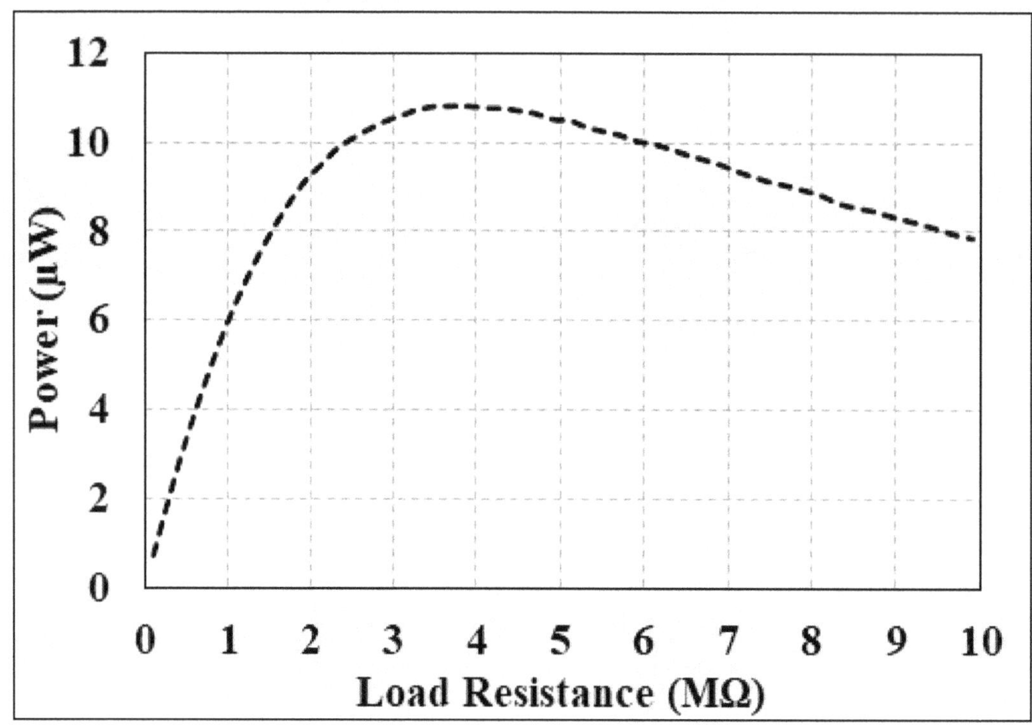

Figure 4.5: Value of output power at different load resistance

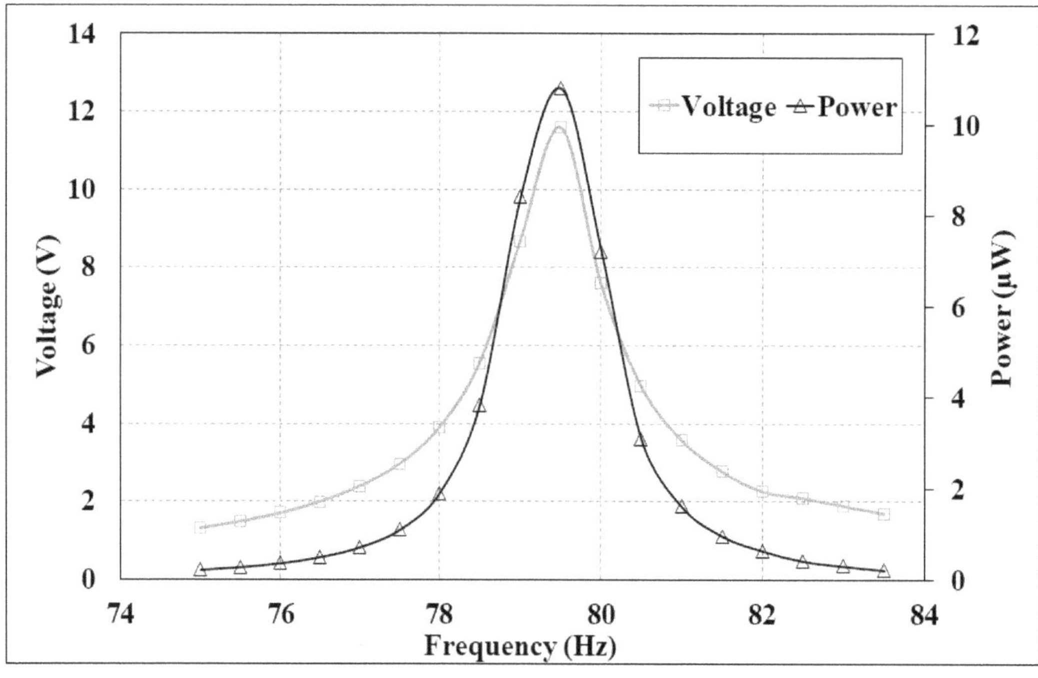

Figure 4.6: Value of output voltage and power at different frequency

literature.

The explanation above makes clear that any low power wireless sensor or device can be powered by the L-shaped piezo-electric energy harvester, which produces the necessary output voltage and power.

Table 4.3: Summary of the output parameter of L-shaped cantilever

Parameter	Value
Resonant Frequency	79.5 Hz
Peak deflection	4820 μm
Peak output voltage	11.6 V
Optimum load	3.5 Mohm
Average output Power	10.8 μW

Table 4.4: Comparison of proposed structure with the existing literatures

Ref. year	Structure	Resonant Frequency (Hz)	Electrical output
Roundy et al. (2004) [28]	Rectangular, 1 cm^3	120	Voltage-5 V, Power -375 μW
Yu Jia et al. (2015) [113]	Circular disk, Diameter – 7 mm	1572	Power - 2.2 μW
Isaku kanno et al. (2012) [114]	Rectangular, 20 x 3.4 mm^2	1036	Voltage-0.097 V, Power -1.1 μW
Muralt et al (2009) [115]	Rectangular, 0.8x1.2x0.007 mm^3	870	Voltage-1.6 V, Power -1.4 μW
Hua Yu et.al. (2014) [119]	Rectangular, 11 x 12.4 mm^2	234.5 Hz	Voltage- 7.0 Power- 66.75 μW
Ansari et.al. (2015) [107]	Fan folded structure 1x1x1 cm^3	170 Hz	Power 2.12 μW
This work	L-shaped, 5x5 mm^2	79.5	Voltage-11.6 V, Power -10.8 μW

4.3 Summary

The L-shaped PZ cantilever beam is intended for PZEH applications that require low frequencies. Low power gadgets' batteries can be recharged using the mechanism that was developed for them. The wireless sensor node for the machine monitoring system is mostly included in this. The EH is within 5 mm of its size. A voltage of 11.6 V is generated at a frequency of 79.5 Hz when the suggested structure is simulated with a 1g acceleration. At its resonance frequency, the suggested L-shaped PZEH generates an output power of 10.8 μW.

Chapter 5

Design of spiral cantilever

The size and power consumption of electronic devices are being significantly reduced by the development of VLSI technology. Most of these gadgets run on batteries, and it's challenging to reduce the size of a conventional battery without compromising its longevity. Because of the short battery life, low-power battery-operated devices have a limited lifespan. As a result, these batteries require routine recharging or replacement. When an energy harvester is included with these low-power devices, the devices' lifespan can be increased. As a result, the integration of energy harvesters is gaining traction as a research topic in industries that require low power electronic devices, including wireless communication, medicinal, military, and consumer electronics. Especially with medical implanted devices such as pacemakers because replacing the battery involves extra surgery to the patients. The most appropriate energy harvester (EH) for micropower devices is one that operates on vibration. In the vicinity of the resonance frequency, the piezoelectric energy harvester operates effectively [20]. One such use of PZEH is the replacement or recharge of the pacemaker's battery. Since Ni-Cd pacemaker batteries have a limited lifespan, they must be changed on a regular basis [120]. To get around this, a number of researchers [89], [90], [95], [103], [104] attempted to power the pacemaker by drawing electrical energy from the body.

The goal of this research is to create an energy harvester that is minimally dimensional and compatible with current pacemakers, making it an easy integration. This chapter will cover the creation of a spiral-shaped PZEH that uses a pacemaker's cardiac vibration to power its battery.

5.1 Design constraints and objectives

Recharging the pacemaker's battery is the aim of the suggested PZEH. The human heart's vibration was measured in the time domain by Kanai et al. [109], as Figure 5.1 illustrates. An impulse is the form that the heartbeat takes. As a result, the frequency spectrum of the heartbeat can be very varied. The heartbeat's waveform is very amplitude across a broad frequency range. The majority of high amplitude frequencies are less than 50 Hz, as seen in Fig. 5.1b [98], [99], and [107]. Thus, getting the planned structure's resonance frequency below 50 Hz is the primary design constraint on the PZEH for the pacemaker.

The dimensions of a modern pacemaker are around 1 cm^3, according to [99], [104], and [121]. Consequently, keeping the PZEH's size as small as feasible—at least less than 1 cm^3—is another restriction throughout design.

5.2 Design and analysis

Research has shown that when cantilever length increases, the resonant frequency of the beam drops [49], [116]. However, by making the structure less compact, an increase in length results in an increase in the PZEH's size. As a result, a cantilever with a rectangular spiral shape is suggested. The cantilever beam's compactness is preserved while its length is efficiently increased by the spiral design. The spiral structure's resonant frequency is lowered as a result of this decrease in the spring constant caused by the effective length increase. As seen in Figs. 5.2(a, b, c, d, and e), the five distinct rectangular spiral-shaped cantilever PZEHs are built with silicon (Si) as the substrate material and ZnO as the piezoelectric material in all of the cantilevers. COMSOL Multiphysics is used to design all spiral cantilever structures with a silicon substrate (100 orientation).

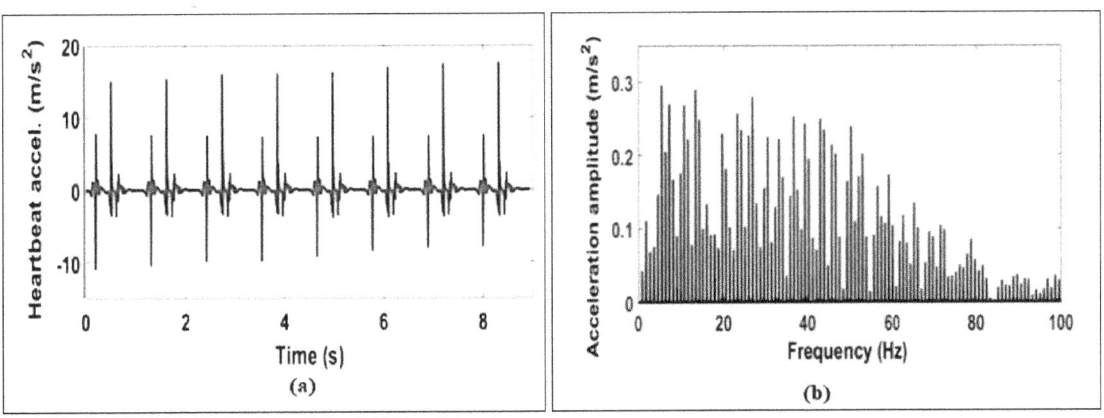

Figure 5.1: (a) Normal heartbeat vibrations in the time domain [18], [98], [99] (b) Fourier transform of a normal heartbeat [18], [98], [99]

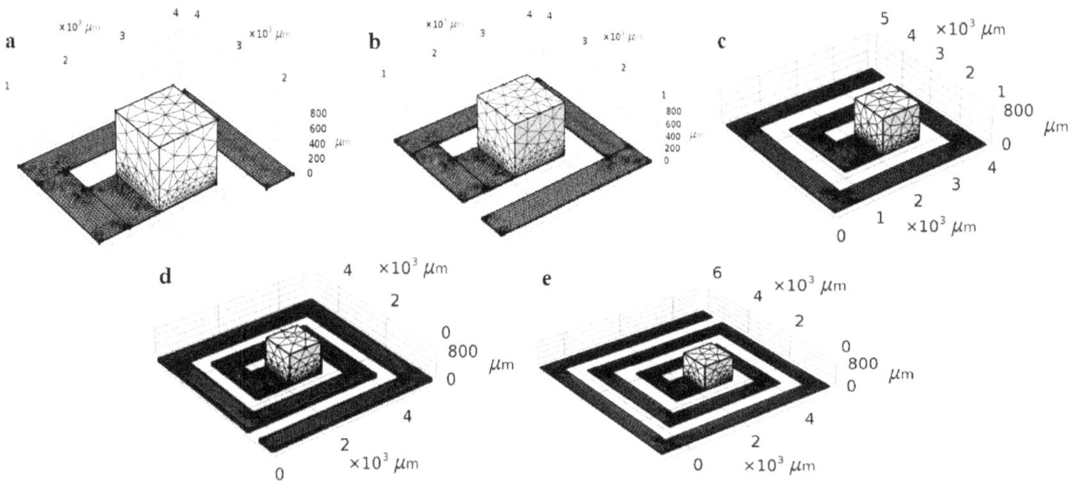

Figure 5.2: Meshed structure of (a) 1.25 turns spiral (b) 1.5 turns spiral (c) 2 turns spiral (d) 2.5 turns spiral (e) 3 turns spiral

The thin-film ZnO utilised as the piezoelectric material in the cantilever design has a (002) crystal orientation [122]. The higher value of the piezoelectric coefficient (d_{31}), which in turn results in the superior piezoelectric behaviour of the thin film ZnO, is caused by the greater grain size and reduced surface roughness. Every spiral cantilever structure has the Si-proof mass at its middle. 1.25 turn, 1.5 turn, 2 turn, 2.5 turn, and 3 turn spiral cantilever constructions have lengths and widths of 2 mm, 3 mm, 4 mm, 5 mm, and 6 mm, respectively. Every spiral has arms that are 0.5 mm wide and have a 0.5 mm gap between them. The arm that is attached to the proof mass has a width of 1 mm. The spiral construction contains varying amounts of the piezoelectric substance ZnO. ZnO is two μm thick, while the Si beam is twelve μm thick. The spiral cantilever's outer arm is fixed. For all three structures, the proof mass dimensions are $1 \times 1 \times 0.85 \ mm^3$.

Chapter 2 already covered the various mechanical characteristics of the materials utilised in the spiral cantilever structure design.

5.3 Mechanical output of the structure

The resonant frequency of each planned structure is determined by the application of eigenvalue analysis. As illustrated in Fig. 5.3, it has been found that the resonant frequency of the spiral structure drops as the spiral's number of turns increases. The spiral cantilever's effective length will grow as the number of turns increases, which will reduce the cantilever's effective stiffness without compromising the structure's compactness. The spiral cantilever's resonance frequency will drop as the stiffness decreases. The spiral cantilever with 1.25 turns, 1.5 turns, 2 turns, 2.5 turns, and 3 turns has a resonance frequency of 217.11 Hz, 125.08 Hz, 45.8 Hz, 67.9 Hz, and 30.61 Hz, in that order. Because the spiral cantilever with 1.25 and 1.5 turns has a resonance frequency that is significantly higher than the pacemaker's target frequency. That being said, the 1.25 turns and 1.5 turns spiral cantilevers will not be discussed. We'll talk about the spiral cantilever with two, three, and 2.5 turns in more detail.

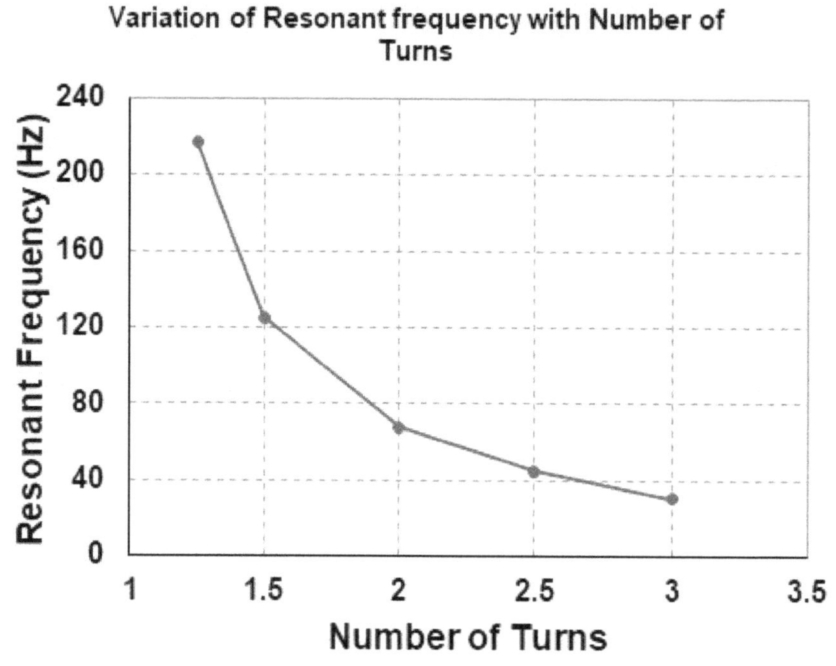

Figure 5.3: Variation of resonant frequency with the number of turns in spiral cantilever structure

One of the most crucial factors determining the distribution of stress and strain inside the cantilever structure is the end mass deflection, which is determined by the parameters found in Eqs. (2.8a), (2.8b), and (2.8c). For every cantilever construction, the end mass deflection is computed using the transient solver approach at various frequencies. When the excitation frequency and the planned cantilever's resonant frequency coincide, the cantilever structure's end mass deflection reaches its maximum. The PZEH can produce its maximum output voltage and power in these circumstances. Fig. 5.4 displays the peak displacement for each of the three types of cantilever beams: two-turn, 2.5-turn, and three-turn spiral cantilever structures at various frequencies. At their respective resonance frequencies, the highest displacement of the cantilever beams with two, three, and four turns spirals is 8.5 mm, 9 mm, and 10.5 mm, respectively.

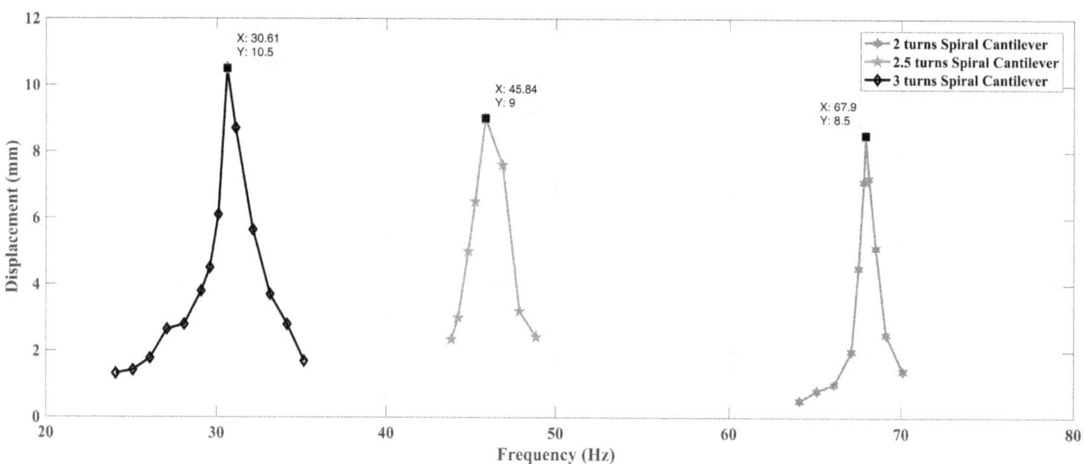

Figure 5.4: Peak displacement of the spiral structures with frequency

As can be shown from Chapter 2 of Section 2.3.1a, the cantilever structure's stress distribution directly affects the output voltage and power. Although a larger stress is preferable for higher output voltage and power, it must be less than the material's fracture strength. When the structure's von-mises stress exceeds its Young's modulus, the material loses its elastic properties.

Therefore, for appropriate mechanical stability, the maximum von-mises stress created in the cantilever beam must be less than the material's Young's modulus. For each of the three spiral cantilever beams, the strain distribution and matching stress distribution are displayed over the arc length in Figs. 5.5, 5.6, and 5.7. Figures 5.5, 5.6, and 5.7 demonstrate the abrupt increase in stress and strain values at the spiral cantilever's corner point. It demonstrates how the cantilever beam's stress distribution is improved and the corner point provides the point of discontinuity. It contributes to raising the cantilever beam's output voltage.

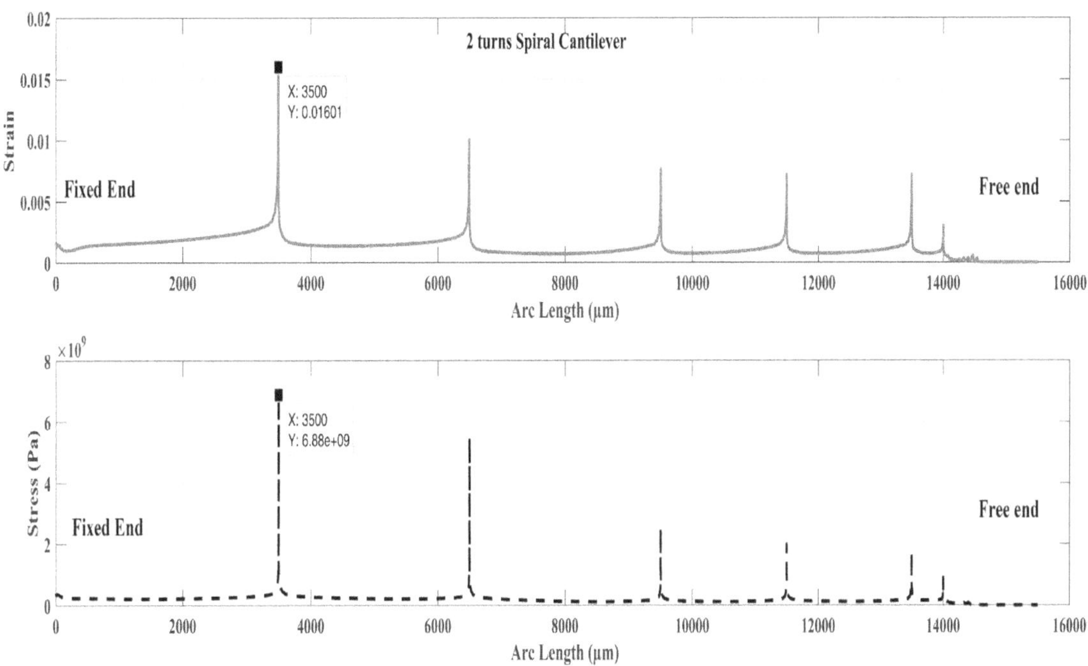

Figure 5.5: Variation of the strain and stress distribution with the arc length of the 2-turn spiral cantilever beam at resonant frequency

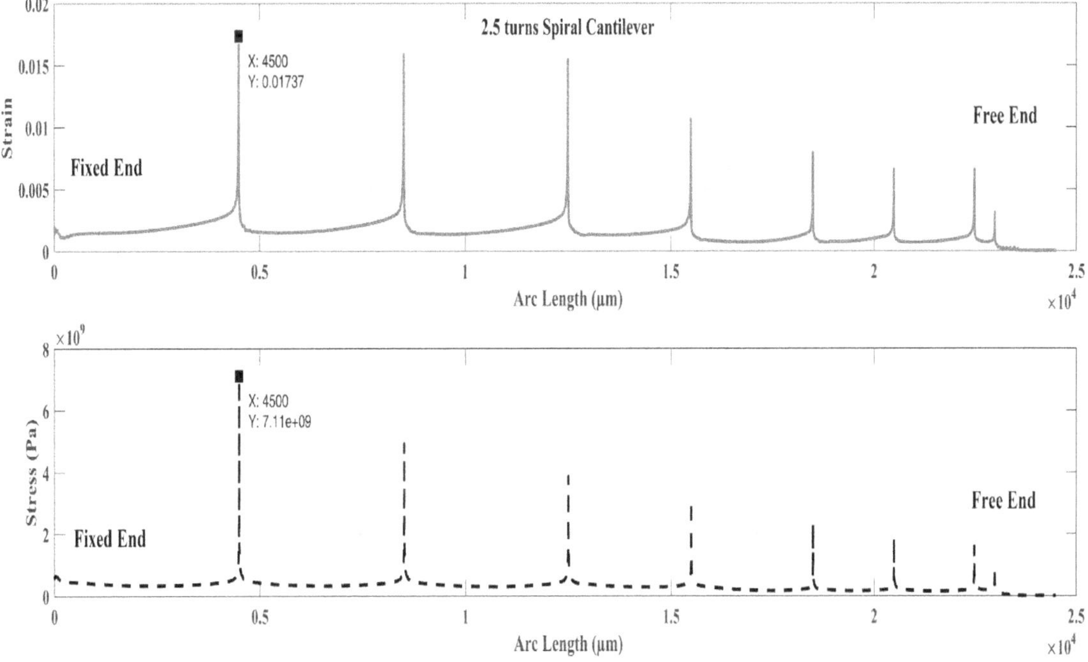

Figure 5.6: Variation of the strain and stress distribution with the arc length of the 2.5-turn spiral cantilever beam at resonant frequency

The average stress distribution in the cantilever beam is closely related to the output voltage, as demonstrated by Eq. (2.13).

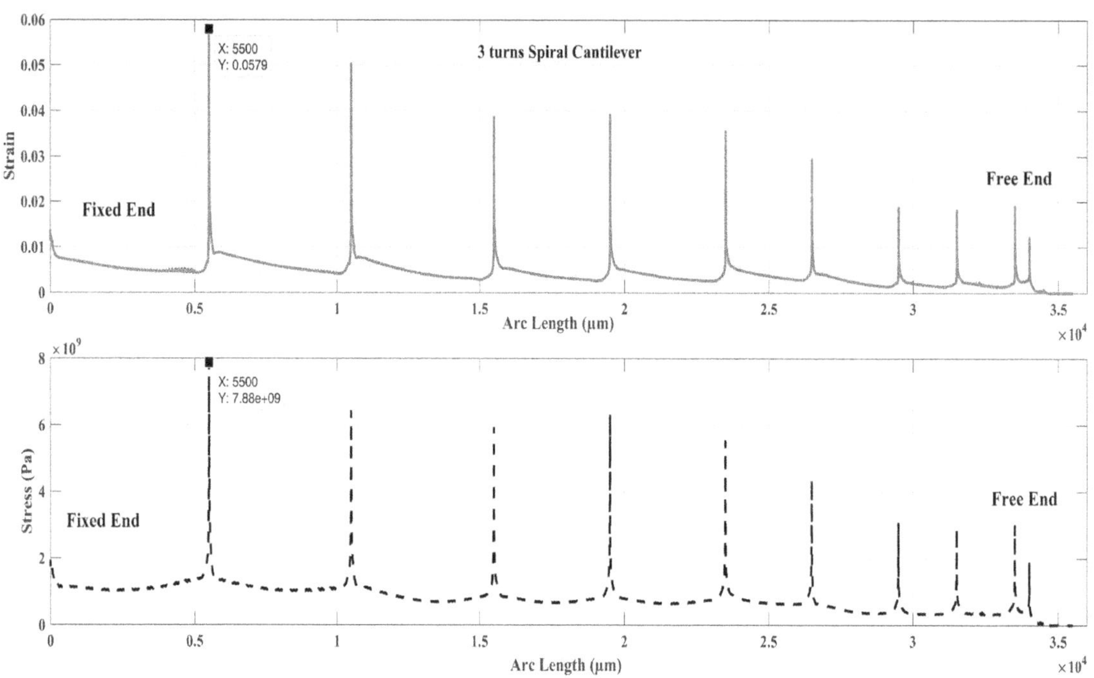

Figure 5.7: Variation of the strain and stress distribution with the arc length of the 3-turn spiral cantilever beam at resonant frequency

The fluctuation of the maximum stress with frequency is depicted in Fig. 5.8. When designing a spiral cantilever, the maximum stress in the cantilever should be less than the Young's modulus of the materials employed. If the stress level exceeds the appropriate Young's modulus, the material will lose its elastic properties and the cantilever's mechanical strength will be jeopardised. Fig. 5.8 demonstrates that the stress level is substantially below Young's modulus of the Si and ZnO. Consequently, the mechanical strength of all three spiral cantilever beams is adequate.

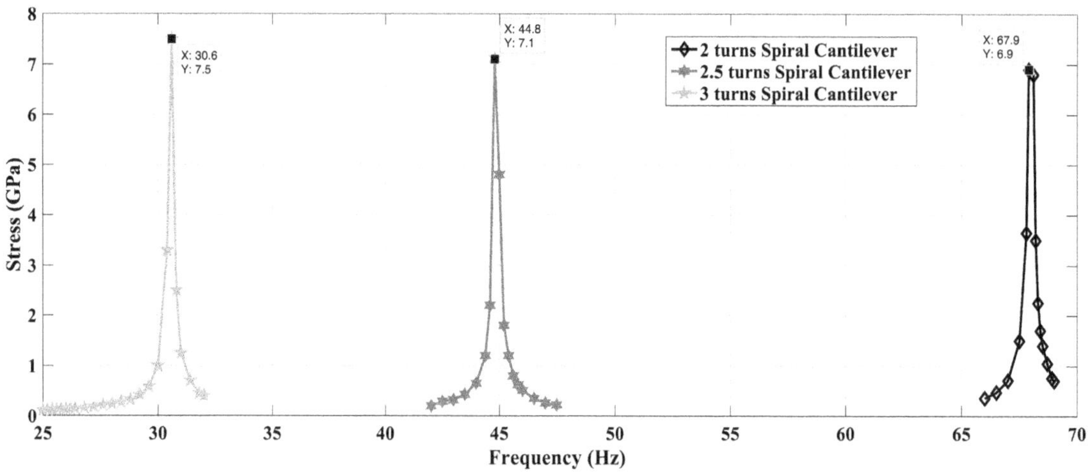

Figure 5.8: Variation of stress with frequency for all spiral cantilever structures

5.4 Electrical output of structures

5.4.1 Output voltage of designed structure

Equation (5.1) provides the highest output voltage and output power at the resonant frequency, which is where the PZEH is found.

$$\omega = \sqrt{\frac{K}{m}} \tag{5.1}$$

where m is the cantilever structure's mass and K denotes the stiffness of the structure. As covered in Subsection 2.3.1a's Chapter 2, the voltage generated by the PZEH is dependent on the thickness of the piezoelectric material, the voltage coefficient, and the applied stress.

To determine the time-dependent output voltage, COMSOL Multiphysics is used to do a time-dependent study of the structure. The spiral cantilever beams with two turns, three turns, and four turns have corresponding resonance frequencies of 67.9 Hz, 44.8 Hz, and 30.6 Hz. At each spiral structure's individual resonance frequency, a sinusoidal acceleration of 1g is applied. Fig. 5.9 shows the time-dependent output voltage of both the spiral cantilever structure. For the 2 turns, 2.5 turns, and 3 turns spiral cantilever structures, the peak output open-circuit voltage generated at the resonant frequency is 3.1 V, 3.2 V, and 4 V, respectively. Figure 5.10 illustrates how the output voltage of each spiral cantilevers.

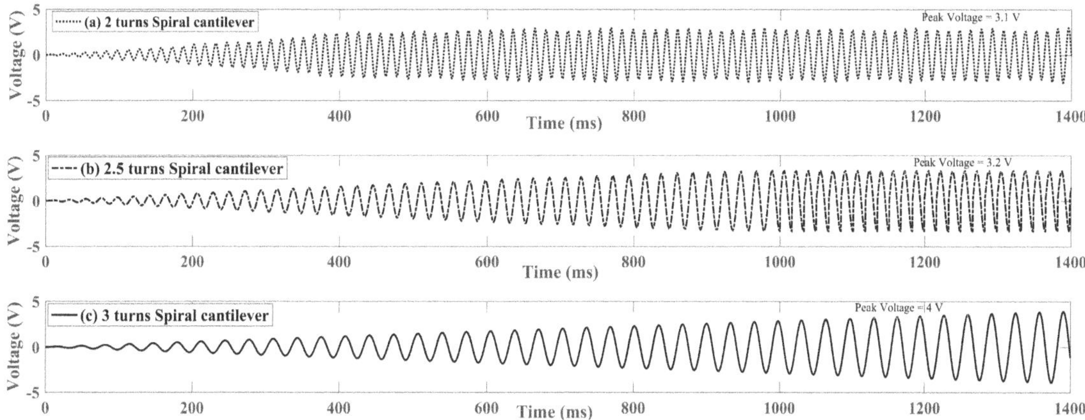

Figure 5.9: Time-dependent output voltage (a) 2 turns spiral cantilever structure (b) 2.5 turns spiral cantilever structure (c) 3 turns spiral cantilever structure

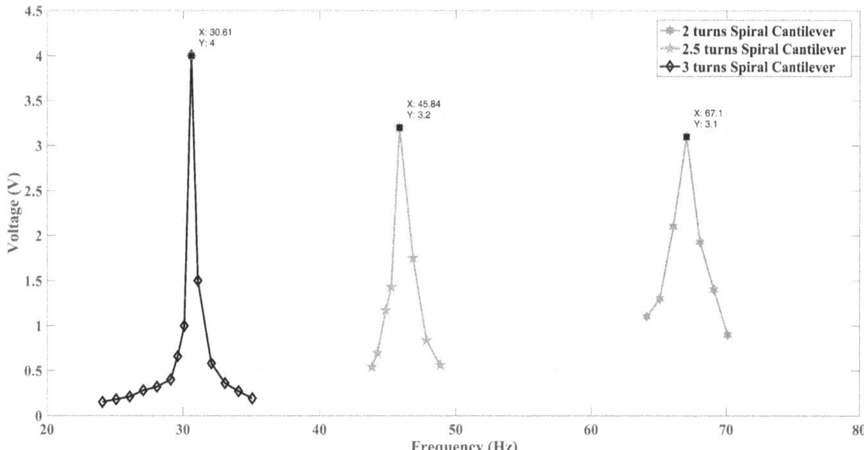

Figure 5.10: Variation of output voltage with frequency for all spiral cantilever structures

5.4.2 Output Power of designed Structures

When the energy harvester's internal resistance, load resistance, and resonance frequency are all identical, the PZEH produces its highest output power. The electrical equivalent of the PZEH is depicted in Fig. 2.12. Eq. provides the voltage at the load resistance (5.2).

$$V_{out} = \frac{V_{PZ}}{R_{PZ} + R_L} R_L \tag{5.2}$$

where the open circuit voltage of the PZEH is denoted by V_{PZ}, the output voltage across R_L is denoted by V_{out}, and the internal and external load resistances are denoted by R_{PZ} and R_L, respectively. When R_{PZ} and R_L are equal, the PZEH yields the maximum power, which is provided by Eqn. (5.3).

$$P = \frac{V_{out}^2}{R_L} = \frac{V_{oc}^2}{4R_{PZ}} \tag{5.3}$$

With knowledge of the total internal resistance, the PZEH's maximum power may be computed. The internal resistance cannot be calculated directly. Knowing the ideal load that is connected to the PZEH and yields the highest output power can be used to calculate the internal resistance. The output power of the spiral cantilever beam is determined by the fluctuating load resistance when it is simulated at a constant load at the resonance frequency. The relationship between the output power and the load resistance is depicted in Fig. 5.11. The ideal load resistance is the load resistance at which the spiral cantilever produces the most output power. The optimum load resistance is the internal resistance of all three-spiral cantilever, illustrated in Table 5.1.

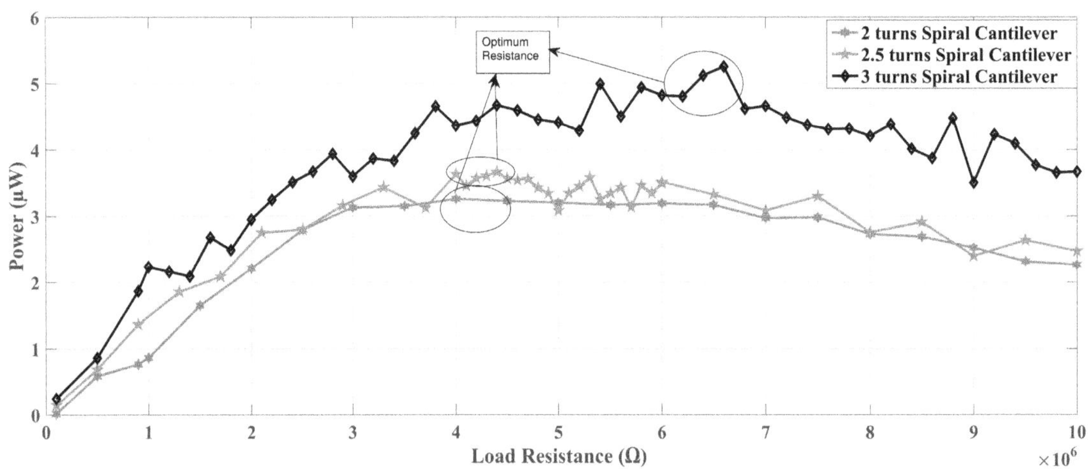

Figure 5.11: Variation of output power with load resistance for all spiral cantilever structures

Table 5.1: Comparison of a different parameter of all structures

Structures	Resonant frequency (Hz)	Internal resistance ($M\Omega$)	Output voltage @1g (V)	Output Power @1g (μW)
2 turns Spiral	67.9	4	3.1	3.25
2.5 turns Spiral	45.8	4.3	3.2	3.44
3 turns Spiral	30.6	6.2	4	5.3

At the ideal load, the output power of each of the three spiral cantilever constructions is computed. The output power variation of all spiral cantilevers with frequency at an excitation acceleration is depicted in Fig. 5.12, with the acceleration due to gravity, $g = 9.8 m/s^2$), as the unit of measurement. Figure 5.13 illustrates how the output power of various spiral cantilever beams increases as the excitation acceleration increases. A compilation of the three spiral structures' output powers is shown in Table 5.1. Lastly, Table 5.2 presents a comparison between the suggested structure and the body of current literature.

Fig. 5.14 illustrates the probable fabrication procedures of the proposed structure in detail. To create the design as depicted in Fig. 5.14, four masks were required.

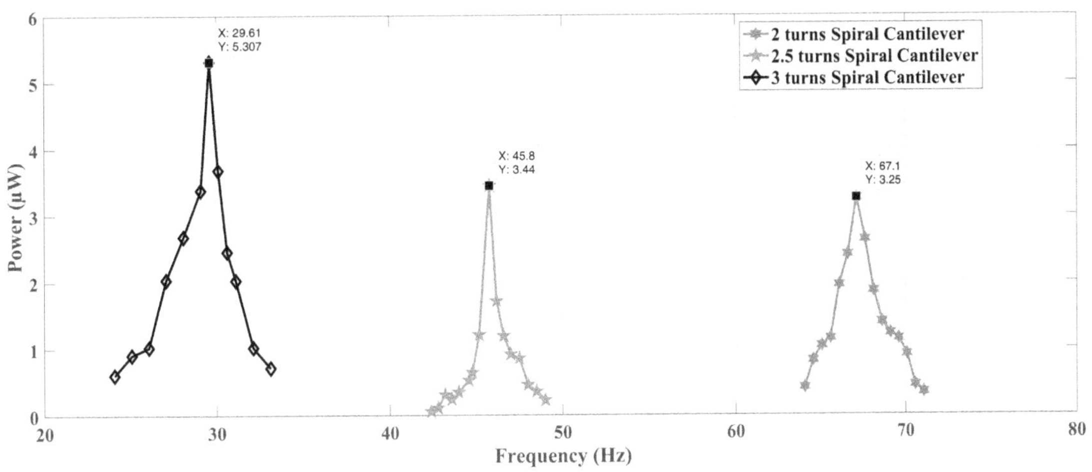

Figure 5.12: Variation of output power with frequency for all spiral cantilever structures

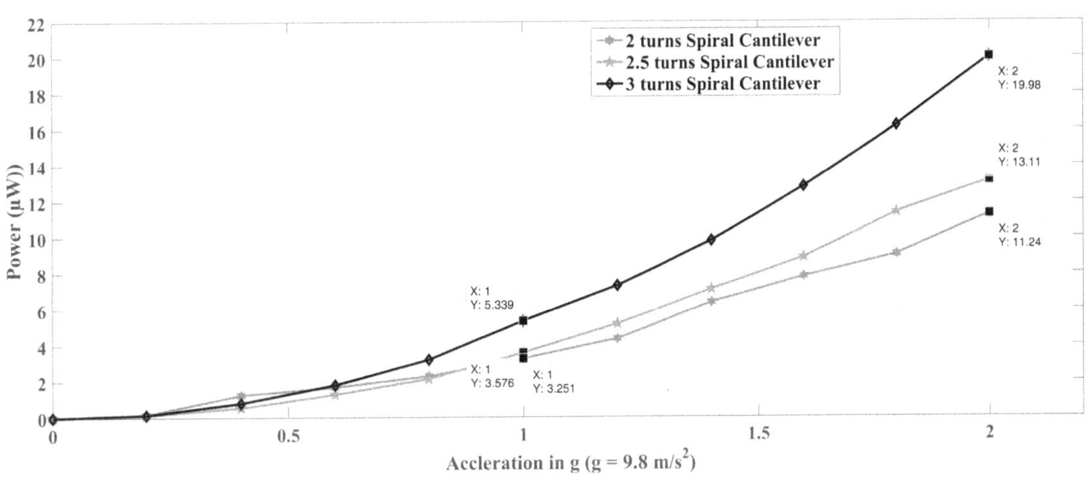

Figure 5.13: Variation of output power with excitation acceleration

5.5   Summary

This chapter describes the design and simulation of a spiral-shaped piezoelectric energy harvester for pacemakers. The pacemaker's battery is meant to be recharged by the system in order to extend its lifespan. The harvester's dimensions are within the range of the current pacemaker that is accessible. A comparison is made between the suggested structure and various spiral cantilevers beams with varying dimensions. It is discovered that the suggested cantilever beam produces the output power required for a modern pacemaker and has the lowest resonance frequency. $6 \times 6 \times 0.85 \ mm^3$ is the dimension of the piezoelectric energy harvester's proposed structure. At an excitation acceleration of 1g, it produces an output open-circuit voltage peaking at 4 V at the resonance frequency of 30.6 Hz. The peak output power generated by the structure is 5.3 μW at the resonant frequency.

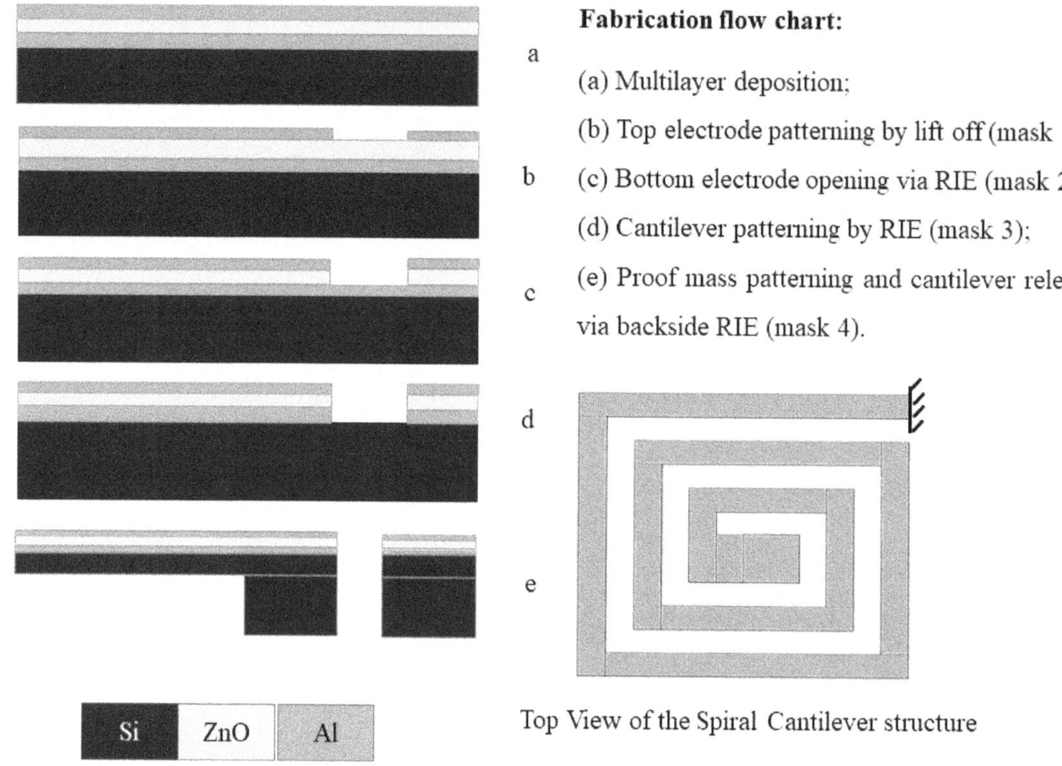

Figure 5.14: Possible fabrication steps of the spiral cantilever structure

Table 5.2: Comparison of a proposed work with available literatures

Ref.	Geometry and Material	*R.Freq. (Hz)	Electrical output	Remarks
Ansari et al. [107]	Fan folded structure $1 \times 1 \times 1$ cm^3, PSI-5A 4E piezo sheets	170 Hz	Power 2.12 μW	Very high frequency
Ansari et al. [99]	Fan folded geometry, $2 \times 0.5 \times 1$ cm^3, PZT	15.79 Hz	Power 16.25 μW	PZT is used and 18.4g tip mass is too heavy for the energy harvester.
Rufer et al. [101]	Rectangular, $40 \times 5 \times 0.38$ mm^3, PZT	15 Hz	Voltage 1.5-4 V, Power 6 -18 μW	PZT is used and Impractical geometrical dimension for pacemaker
Jay et al. [102]	Rectangular, $32 \times 12.19 \times 0.194$ mm^3, PVDF	47 Hz	Voltage 25 V	Large dimension
Jackson et al. [103]	Rectangular, $8 \times 4 \times 0.00046$ mm^3, AlN	28.5 Hz	Power 2.92 μW	Reliability issue with the cantilever
This work	Spiral $6 \times 6 \times 0.85$ mm^3, ZnO	30.6 Hz	Voltage 4 V, Power 5.3 μW	Biocompatible material is used and the dimension and frequency is within the permitted standard of modern pacemaker.

*R.Freq.- Resonant frequency

Chapter 6

Bandwidth enhancement using multi-plate structure

The technique of extracting energy from environmentally friendly power sources is known as energy harvesting (EH) or energy scavenging. This energy can be used immediately or stored for use at a later time. Transistors now have many times more capacity and consume significantly less power thanks to the recent decades' fast advancements in semiconductor manufacturing technology. Low-power electronic gadgets can be readily powered by the energy harvesters. Thus, one way to think of the energy harvesters is as an additional means of self-powering these gadgets. These are especially helpful in cases when the equipment—such as wireless sensor nodes [16], [22], or implanted devices [18], [108]—is situated in an inaccessible location. It does away with the necessity for limited-life power sources, such as batteries, which must be changed on a finite basis. Harvesting electrical energy from available ambient vibrations is one of the key energy harvesting techniques [19], [22], [44], [85]. Piezoelectric energy harvesters are used in this process. These cantilever structures, known as piezoelectric energy harvesters, are composed of a thin layer of piezoelectric material placed on a substrate, such as silicon. An output voltage is produced in the piezoelectric layer when the cantilever shakes as a result of external vibration. After that, the output voltage is processed to provide the battery with electricity. Micro-electro-mechanical systems (MEMS) technology is used in the implementation of these PZEH to minimise their physical dimensions. The capacity to work with vibrations that are non-periodic and vary across a wide frequency range is one of the design goals of these energy harvesters. For optimal performance, the PZ harvesters should keep their resonant frequency at the same as their vibration frequency. It produces the greatest amount of tension, which causes the biggest output voltage to be produced. Low frequency vibrations are commonly observed in our surroundings [118]. MEMS-based energy harvesters have been successful in harvesting considerable voltage levels [57] from these low-frequency vibrations [123] and hence considered to be suitable for diverse applications [1], [4], [5], [6], [12], [124], [125]It has been noted that these single beam systems with cantilevers cannot function across a large frequency range. Wideband energy harvesters must therefore be designed for deployment in a variety of settings and applications. Several models have been proposed for the wideband energy harvesters [55], [56], [57]. However, a thorough examination of these parallel multibeam constructions was not accessible.

The phenomena that takes place in the multibeam cantilever array connected in parallel to one another is mostly explained in this chapter. The goal of illuminating this phenomenon is to recognise how one beam affects the other nearby beams in a multi-beam/multi-plate construction. This is significant when determining the overall bandwidth and resonant frequencies of the entire structure. However, it is generally accepted that a wider beam is necessary to boost the EHs' output power. As a result, the structures get closer to the parallel-connected multi-plate array. A coupling effect is the result of one plate's vibration influencing that of its adjoining plate. An analytical model of this coupling effect has been created in this chapter. Therefore, the multi-plate structure's finite element study has confirmed the coupling effect's impact.

6.1 Coupling effects between multi-plate structure

The resonant frequency of a basic elastic beam or plate that is vibrating exhibits maximum displacement at a specific frequency. A layer of piezoelectric material is put on top of a substrate to create a piezoelectric beam or plate. A piezoelectric beam or plate has a different resonance frequency than an elastic beam or plate. A piezoelectric beam or plate vibrates because it generates charge inside of it. This charge then influences the beam or plate's vibration, changing its resonant frequency [49]. When multiple beams or plates are connected in parallel, the issue becomes more complicated.In this case, the output and vibration of adjacent beams or plates are influenced by the vibration of a single beam or plate. The "coupling effect" helps to explain this dependence between the nearby beams or plates. As previously mentioned, PZ plates are frequently taken into consideration in place of PZ beams in order to boost the output power of PZ-based EH. As a result, an analytical model for the coupling effect between PZ plates connected in parallel has been created. To explain this phenomenon, a parallel connection between two piezoelectric cantilever plates, Plates 1 and 2, has been studied (Fig. 6.1). Due to the buildup of charge at its electrodes, Plate 1 will first vibrate and produce an electric field. Because both plates are linked, this electric field appears as an external field across Plate 2. Plate 2 experiences strain as a result of this external field, which modifies both its vibration and electric output.

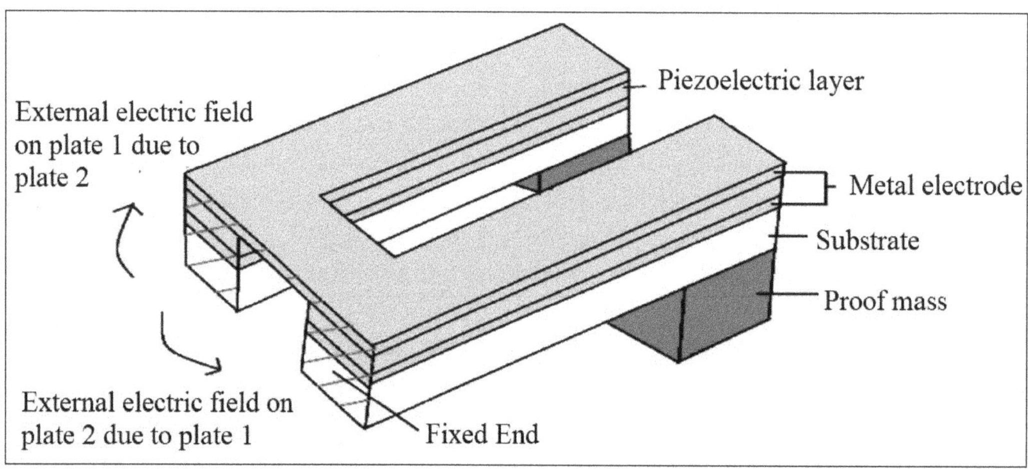

Figure 6.1: Schematic diagram illustrating coupling effect occurring in two-plate cantilever structure

In a similar manner, Plate 1's electrical output is impacted by the electric field produced in Plate 2. Therefore, the output of both plates determines the composite structure's final production. Assuming that the Kirchhoff plate theory governs the vibrations of the two plates, this effect may also be studied in terms of their mechanical behaviour [20], [110]. By maintaining the externally applied pressure loading on the plate at a non-zero value determined by the external force resulting from the adjacent plate, their behaviour may be examined. In the following sections of this chapter, this coupling effect is modelled mathematically.

6.2 Mathematical analysis

The development of the analytical model for the multi-plate piezoelectric cantilever's coupling effect has been the main goal of this part. In order to construct the analytical model, we will first examine a simplified cantilever plate, as seen in Fig. 2.1, which is composed of a piezoelectric layer atop a substrate layer. The substrate layer thickness is t_S, while the piezoelectric layer thickness is t_P. As seen in Fig. 6.1, it should be emphasised that the practical device has electrodes on both surfaces of the piezoelectric material. However, as the metal electrode's thickness is often quite tiny, its impacts on the cantilever plate's vibration may be disregarded. Therefore, the cantilever plate presented in Fig. 2.1 does not take these electrodes into account.

To understand the relationship between the electric field and the external force acting on the piezoelectric layer in the piezoelectric material, one can refer to Equations (1.4a) and (1.4b), respectively.

Stress is applied along the x, y, and x-y planes in the transverse displacement of the rectangular plate-type piezoelectric cantilever. Equations show the link between the generated electric field, induced strain, and applied stress. (2.3a, 2.3b, 2.3c)

[20].

Eqs. (2.5) and (2.6a, 2.6b, 2.6c) provide the position of the neutral axis and the bending strain developed in three planes, respectively, as they are covered in Chapter 2, Section 2.3.1a.

6.2.1 Electrical analysis of the multi-plate structure

An actuator-sensor model made up of multi-plate cantilever structures with layers of both the substrate and the piezoelectric material in each has been taken into consideration for the accurate study of the coupling effect. It is first assumed that there would be no external electric field acting on Plates 1 and 2, and that they will simply be vibrating.

The total strain S_P at the middle of the piezoelectric layer is provided in Eqs. (2.7a, 2.7b, 2.7c).

To obtain the value of total stress in the middle of the PZ layer, which is given in Eqs. (2.8a, 2.8b, and 2.8c), substitute the value of total strain (S_p) in Eqs. (2.3a, 2.3b, 2.3c) from Eqs. (2.7a, 2.7b, 2.7c).

The electrical displacement along the z direction is produced by the tension applied in the x, y, and xy planes, and is evaluated independently. Similar to this, a separate calculation is made for the charge induced in the PZ plate. First, an estimate of the charge that the stress in the x plane has caused in the piezoelectric layer is made.

To obtain the value of the electric flux density in the PZ layer, which is represented by Eq. (2.9), substitute the value of T_P in the x plane (T_{pxx}) in Eq. (1.5a) from Eq. (2.8a).

Assuming that the plates are vibrating independently of one another and that there is no external electric field acting on them, the electric field E is assumed to be zero. Consequently, D_{zx}, the electric flux density, is now shown as

$$D_{zx} = -d_{31}t_{pc}\frac{Y_p}{1-v^2}\left[\frac{\partial^2 w(x,y,t)}{\partial x^2} + v\frac{\partial^2 w(x,y,t)}{\partial y^2}\right] \tag{6.1}$$

In this instance, the charge created within the plate can be acquired through the integration of the electric displacement D_{zx} across the plate's area. The phrase that results is

$$q_{zx,single}(t) = d_{31}\frac{-Y_p.t_{pc}}{1-v^2}\int_0^L\int_0^b[(\frac{\partial^2 w(x,y,t)}{\partial x^2}) + v(\frac{\partial^2 w(x,y,t)}{\partial y^2})]dxdy \tag{6.2}$$

where the plate's length is L and its width is b. This is the charge produced by a single plate vibrating on its own without the application of an external electric field. There will now be an external electric field $E = (V(t))/t_p$ that appears against Plate 1 when Plate 2 vibrates in tandem with Plate 1. Next, by integrating Eq. (refC5eqn:chargePZ), which is represented by Eq. (refC5eqn:chargePZ1), the charge produced in the plate as a result of this external field may be found.

$$Q_{zx,Total}(t) = q_{zx,single}(t) + d_{31}\int_0^L\int_0^b[(\varepsilon_{33}^T - d_{31}Y_p)E]dxdy$$
$$= q_{zx,single}(t) + d_{31}\int_0^L\int_0^b\left[\varepsilon_{11}^s\frac{V(t)}{t_P}\right]dxdy \tag{6.3}$$

Where $(\varepsilon_{33}^T - d_{31}Y_p) = \varepsilon_{31}^s$, $E = (V(t))/t_p$, t_p is the thickness of the piezoelectric layer, $V(t)$ is the voltage created in the piezoelectric layer.

According to Eq. (refC5eqn:current), the total current generated in this plate in the presence of the external field of the adjoining plate is therefore $I_{zx}(t) = frac{partial Q_{zx,Total}(t)}{partial t}$. If R is the PZ plate's internal resistance, then $V_1(t) = I(t) \times R$, or Eq. (6.5), represents the voltage created in the piezoelectric plate. This is in accordance with Ohm's law.

$$I_{zx}(t) = \frac{\partial q_{zx,single}(t)}{\partial t} + d_{31}\int_0^L\int_0^b\left[\frac{\varepsilon_{31}^s}{t_p}\frac{\partial V(t)}{\partial t}\right]dxdy \tag{6.4}$$

$$V_1(t) = -R\left[\frac{\partial q_{zx,single}(t)}{\partial t} + d_{31}\int_0^L\int_0^b\left[\frac{\varepsilon_{31}^s}{t_p}\frac{\partial V(t)}{\partial t}\right]dxdy\right] \tag{6.5}$$

Similar to Eq. (6.6) and (6.7), respectively, Eqs. (2.8b) and (2.8c) may be used to find the voltage generated by the stress T_{pyy} and T_{pxy}.

$$V_2(t) = -R\left[\frac{\partial q_{zy,single}(t)}{\partial t} + d_{32}\int_0^L \int_0^b \left[\frac{\varepsilon_{32}^s}{t_p}\frac{\partial V(t)}{\partial t}\right]dxdy\right] \tag{6.6}$$

$$V_3(t) = -R\left[\frac{\partial q_{zxy,single}(t)}{\partial t} + (d_{31}+d_{32})\int_0^L \int_0^b \left[\frac{(\varepsilon_{31}^s+\varepsilon_{32}^s)}{t_p}\frac{\partial V(t)}{\partial t}\right]dxdy\right] \tag{6.7}$$

The net voltage created across the cantilever plate's piezoelectric layer is $V_4(t) = V_1(t)+V_2(t)+V_3(t)$, as found in Eq. (6.8), which is the result of adding the values of Eqs. (6.5), (6.6), and (6.7).

$$V_4(t) = -R\left[-3\frac{\partial q_{zxy,single}(t)}{\partial t} + \int_0^L \int_0^b \left(\left[\frac{d_{31}\varepsilon_{31}^s}{t_p}\frac{\partial V(t)}{\partial t}\right] + d_{32}\left[\frac{\varepsilon_{32}^s}{t_p}\frac{\partial V(t)}{\partial t}\right]\right.\right.$$
$$\left.\left. +(d_{31}+d_{32})\left[\frac{(\varepsilon_{31}^s+\varepsilon_{32}^s)}{t_p}\frac{\partial V(t)}{\partial t}\right]\right)dxdy\right] \tag{6.8}$$

The governing equation of the electrical circuit of the system is in the form of Eq. (6.9).

$$V(t) - \frac{1}{C_i}\int i(t)dt - V_4(t) - iR_L = 0 \tag{6.9}$$

The internal capacitance of the piezoelectric plate is C_i, where $C_i = (\varepsilon_o\varepsilon_p A)/t_p$, and the load resistance is R_L. The current in the system is denoted by i(t). where the relative permittivity of the PZ plate and the air permittivity are denoted by $\varepsilon_o, \varepsilon_p$. In the same way that $V(t)$ was originally thought to be the excitation of the first plate, this voltage $V_4(t)$ generated in the plate is now connected to the adjoining plate and functions as a source of excitation of the neighbouring plate. Therefore, it is possible to see how interdependent the beams are. As a result, the two plates experience this electric feedback continuously in the same way as previously mentioned.

It can be seen from the above-discussed equations that the charge produced by a piezoelectric plate vibrating in the other cantilever plate's external electric field is different from that produced by the plate vibrating in the absence of any external field by a factor of $(d_{31}\varepsilon_{31}^s + d_{32}\varepsilon_{32}^s + (d_{31}+d_{32})(\varepsilon_{31}^s+\varepsilon_{32}^s))\frac{V(t)}{t_p}bL$. This indicates that when the multi-plate cantilever structure vibrates alone, the charge it generates will differ from that of the single-plate structure. This is dependent on the external voltage's phase because of the nearby plate's vibration. In a linked multi-plate system, the plate generates more charge (and hence greater voltage) when its vertical displacement and the externally applied voltage are in phase, as opposed to when it is vibrating alone. Similarly, when the externally provided voltage is opposite to the phase of the plate displacement, the plate generates less charge and, consequently, less voltage.

6.2.2 Mechanical analysis of the multi-plate structure

A variety of techniques are employed to analyse plate structure mechanical vibration. In this case, the cantilever is a thin plate construction with comparable length and width and a much smaller thickness than either of the two dimensions. So, the mechanical behaviour of the vibrating cantilever plates has been described by the Kirchhoff plate theory [20], [110]. Lastly, FEM analysis in COMSOL Multiphysics has been used to verify the derived theory [126]. According to the Kirchhoff plate theory, the equation of motion of the cantilever plate displacement in the transverse direction is stated in Eq. (2.17) or Eq. (2.18) [20], [110].

The biharmonic operator in Eqs. (2.17) and (2.18) is Δ^4, which is provided in Eq. (2.19). The vertical displacement of the plate is denoted by $w(x,y,t)$, the density is ρ, and the flexural rigidity is D_r, as found in Eq. (2.20). The external force acting on the rectangular plate is denoted by $f(x,y,t)$.

When there is no external loading on a free vibrating plate, $f(x,y,t)$ is assumed to be zero. However, in the multi-plate piezoelectric cantilever construction, as covered in Section 6.1, the vibration of one plate influences the vibration of its neighbouring plates. Mathematically, this can be explained by assuming that just one plate is vibrating initially. To see how Plate 1's vibration affects Plate 2, it is assumed that Plate 1 is vibrating on its own. There will be some voltage across Plate 1 as a result of its oscillation. Because of the inverse PZ effect, an internal force will develop inside Plate 2 as the produced voltage is applied across it. The internal force on Plate 2 will result in the development of the internal pressure f(x,y,t), which is equivalent to the internal force per unit area. The electrical force operating on the Plate 2 can be expressed as $E(t).Q_Total(t)$, where $Q_Total(t)$

is the total charge in Plate 2 and E(t) is the electric field in Plate 2 as a result of the voltage generated in Plate 1.

The Kirchhoff plate equation becomes $\frac{(V_1(t)Q_{Total}(t))}{(t_p.b.L)}$ when the external pressure $f(x,y,t)$ loading on Plate 2 is represented.

$$D_r\nabla^4 w(x,y,t)+\rho t_p\frac{\partial^4 w(x,y,t)}{\partial t^2} = \frac{(V_1(t)Q_{Total}(t))}{(t_p bL)} \tag{6.10}$$

To solve this differential equation in terms of w(x,y,t), the standard method is applied. By first assuming that the differential equation's R.H.S. is 0, or the case of free vibrations, the complementary function for this differential equation can be determined.

In Section 2.3.1b, the derivation of free vibration of the piezoelectric cantilever plate is solved. Equation (6.11) describes the resonant frequency resulting from the free vibration of the PZ cantilever construction.

$$\omega = \lambda^2\sqrt{\frac{D_r}{\rho t_p}} \tag{6.11}$$

Where λ is given by the boundary condition of the plate.

Currently, Eq. (2.17) or Eq. (2.18) will be taken into consideration in order to discover the entire solution of displacement of the rectangular piezoelectric plate cantilever under the effect of the external electrical force due to Plate 2 [20].

$$D_r\nabla^4 w(x,y,t)+\rho t_p\frac{\partial^4 w(x,y,t)}{\partial t^2} = f(x,y,t) \tag{6.12}$$

Eq. 6.13 is obtained by assuming the vertical displacement of the plate.

$$w(x,y,t) = \sum_{m=1}^{\infty}\sum_{n=1}^{\infty} w_{mn}(x,y)T_{mn}(t) \tag{6.13}$$

wherein $w_{mn}(x,y) = B_{1mn}\sin\frac{m\pi x}{L}\sin\frac{n\pi y}{b}$; $m,n = 1,2,3$, and so on. The normal modes are normalised according to the normalisation condition which is given as Eq. (6.14).

$$\int_0^L\int_0^b \rho t_p w_{mn}^2 dxdy = 1 \tag{6.14}$$

$B_{1mn} = \frac{2}{\sqrt{\rho t_p Lb}}$ is the result. The normalisation condition in Eq. (6.13) can be used to obtain the equation of generalised coordinates $T_{mn}(t)$ by substituting it into Eq. (2.18).

$$\frac{\partial^2 T_{mn}(t)}{\partial t^2}+\omega_{mn}^2 T_{mn}(t) = N_{mn}(t); m,n = 1,2,3.., \tag{6.15}$$

Where $N_{mn}(t)$ is the generalized force and the natural frequency ω_{mn} is given by,

$$N_{mn}(t) = \int_0^L\int_0^b w_{mn}(x,y)f(x,y,t)dxdy \tag{6.16}$$

$$\omega_{mn} = \pi^2(\sqrt{\frac{D_r}{\rho t_p}})\left[\left(\frac{m}{L}\right)^2+\left(\frac{n}{b}\right)^2\right]; m,n = 1,2.., \tag{6.17}$$

The solution of Eq. (6.15) can be expressed as Eq. (6.18),

$$T_{mn}(t) = T_{mn}(0)\cos\omega_{mn}t+\frac{1}{\omega_{mn}}\frac{\partial T_{mn}(t)}{\partial t}\sin\omega_{mn}t+\frac{1}{\omega_{mn}}\int_0^t N_{mn}(t)\sin\omega_{mn}(t-\tau)d\tau, \tag{6.18}$$

The final solution of the rectangular plate vibration under magnetic force is given by Eq. (6.19).

$$W(x,y,t) = \sum_{m=1}^{\infty} \sum_{n=1}^{\infty} T_{mn}(0) \sin\frac{m\pi x}{L} \sin\frac{n\pi y}{b} \cos\omega_{mn}t$$

$$+ \sum_{m=1}^{\infty} \sum_{n=1}^{\infty} \frac{\partial T_{mn}(0)}{\partial t} \frac{1}{\omega_{mn}} \sin\frac{m\pi x}{L} \sin\frac{n\pi y}{b} \sin\omega_{mn}t \qquad (6.19)$$

$$+ \sum_{m=1}^{\infty} \sum_{n=1}^{\infty} \frac{1}{\omega_{mn}} \sin\frac{m\pi x}{L} \sin\frac{n\pi y}{b} \int_{0}^{t} T_{mn}(\tau)\sin[\omega_{mn}(t-\tau)]d\tau$$

Therefore, it is evident from the preceding deduction that Plate 2's natural frequency and angular velocity differ from those of the free vibration situation. This is because of Plate 1's coupling effect. Because of Plate 2's vibration, a comparable coupling effect is seen on Plate 1. Thus, the preceding mathematical study of the multiple cantilever plates in parallel connection leads to two important conclusions.

1. When a single plate vibrates on its own, the output voltage is different from the voltage created by each plate in the multi-plate arrangement.

2. When multiple parallel plates are present, the resonance frequencies of the individual plates shift from those of the plate vibrating alone, that is, without any external impact.

The simulations and observed findings for various single and multi-plate structures will now be discussed in the next section.

6.3 Simulations and results

6.3.1 Single plate structure

Initially, a solitary rectangular cantilever plate measuring 5000 μm in length, 1000 μm in breadth, and 17.26 μm in total thickness is designed. The Silicon substrate layer had a thickness of 14.53 μm and Zinc Oxide (ZnO) piezoelectric layer had a thickness of 2.73 μm. A solid proof mass with a cubic structure measuring one millimetre on each side was fastened to the cantilever plate's free end. The building is known as Plate 1. Fig. 6.2 displays the assembled plate.

The substrate and PZ layer have the same density and Young's modulus as those found in Chapter 2.

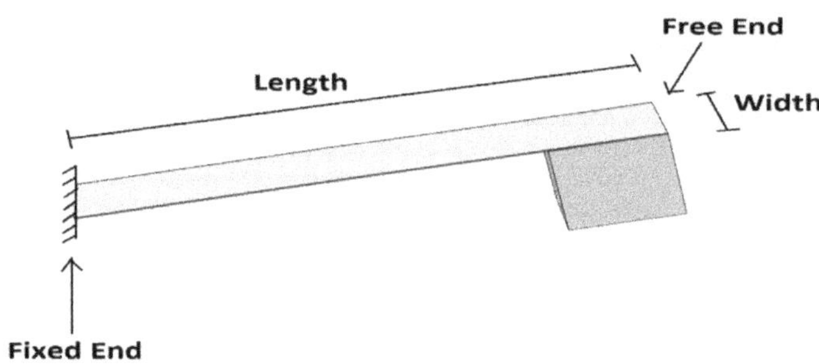

Figure 6.2: Diagram of a single cantilever plate structure with a cubic proof mass

The design of Plate 1 is followed by the eigenfrequency analysis. 143 Hz is the resonance frequency that was found. Subsequently, transient analysis is carried out with a sinusoidal body load of 1 g in amplitude, while adjusting the applied load frequency across the resonant frequency. The observed values of Plate 1's output power and peak voltage at various frequencies have been recorded. The values are displayed in Fig. 4 and documented in Table 6.1, accordingly.

Fig. 6.4 displays the displacement and output voltage vs time shown for the Plate 1 vibrating free end at its resonant frequency of 143 Hz.

 Output peak voltage and power generated by Plate 1 at different frequencies

Frequency (Hz)	Peak voltage (V)	Power Generated (μW)
133	1.8	0.19
138	2.8	0.48
140	4.7	1.2
142	11.2	7.3
143	12.4	7.9
150	3.2	0.2

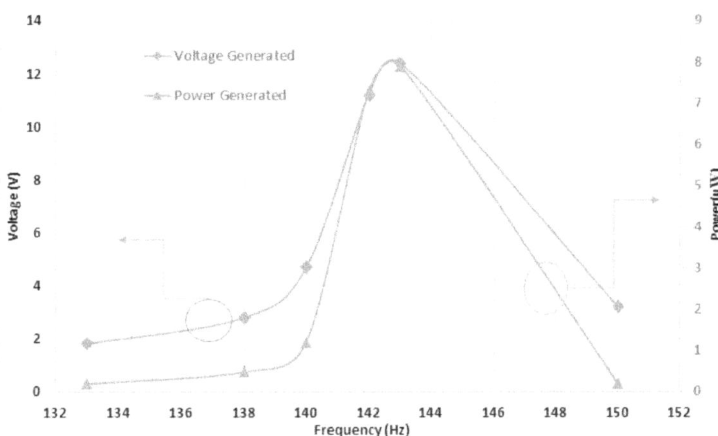

Figure 6.3: Output voltage and power generated by Plate 1 at different frequencies

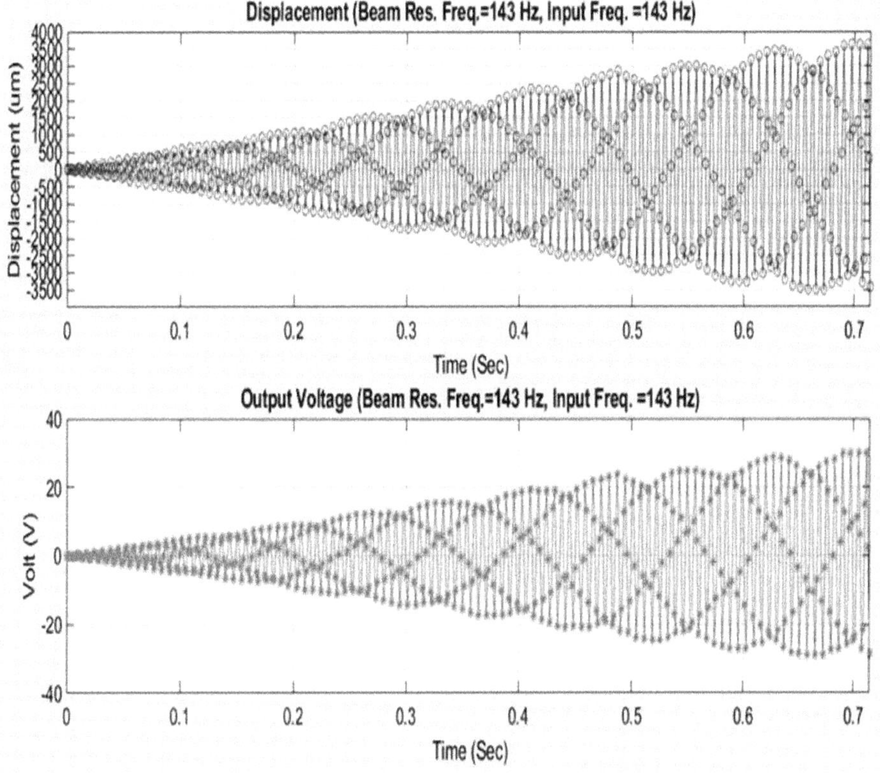

Figure 6.4: Plot of displacement and output voltage for Plate 1 vibrating at its resonant frequency (143 Hz)

It can be seen that with time, both the displacement and the output voltage continue to rise. The plate is vibrating at its resonance frequency, which is why this is happening. The same contour of the displacement and output voltage charts is another noteworthy aspect. This demonstrates that the movement of the plate and the voltage it generates are directly related. A charge is produced inside the plate as a result of the displacement. In Eq. (6.2), this is shown. The plate's internal current is then generated by this charge. An output voltage is produced across the PZ layer of the plate by this current flow in the internal resistance and capacitance of the PZ material.

Therefore, an electrical equivalent model that consists of an equivalent current source I_p, clamping capacitance C_p, and internal resistance R_p can be used to describe a piezoelectric plate. In this case, the current and vibration velocity are proportionate. Fig. 6.5 illustrates this electrical equivalent model of a piezoelectric cantilever plate. The coupled multi-plate structure had to be designed using a number of single plate constructions with various resonance frequencies. Here are the simulation findings up to a connected four-plate structure. Thus, for the purpose of discussion, four single plates with various resonant frequencies are required.

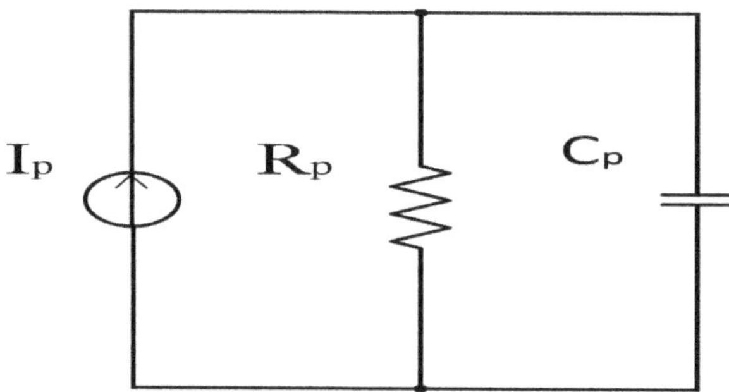

Figure 6.5: Electrical equivalent model of a PZ cantilever structure

The only difference between these plates' designs was the length of Plate 1, with all other measurements and material characteristics remaining unchanged. The various rectangular plates are referred to as Plate 2, Plate 3, and Plate 4 correspondingly. Their respective lengths are 5100 μm, 5045 μm, and 5150 μm. These plates were discovered to have resonance frequencies of 138 Hz, 140 Hz, and 136 Hz, in that order. All four of the simulation's plates have the following specifications: length, width, thickness, and resonance frequency, which are listed in Table 6.2 columns (B), (C), (D), and (E), respectively. In order to have a comprehensive understanding of the vibration behaviour of the plates, all of the plates' displacement and output voltage data are recorded at a specific frequency.

Since it roughly represents the mean of the resonant frequencies of all the plates, the frequency of 140 Hz was selected as that particular value. Thus, in order to have a better understanding, the transient analysis of the various cantilever plate structures at 140 Hz will be examined going forward. Plate 1's simulation result at 140 Hz frequency is displayed in Fig. 6.6. It is evident from Fig. 6.6 that beating happens at a time of around 0.4 seconds, meaning that the resonant frequency is approximately $\left(140 \pm \frac{1}{4}\right)$ Hz. This is consistent with Plate 1's resonant frequency of 143 Hz.

Table 6.2: Dimensions and resonant frequencies of different plates used in simulation

Plate (A)	Length (μm)	Width (μm)	Thickness (μm)	Resonant Frequency (Hz)
Plate 1	5000	1000	17.26	143
Plate 2	5100	1000	17.26	138
Plate 3	5045	1000	17.26	140
Plate 4	5150	1000	17.26	136

The design and simulation of connected multi-plate structures, such as coupled two-, three-, and four-plate structures, will be covered in the section that follows the simulation of the single plate structures.

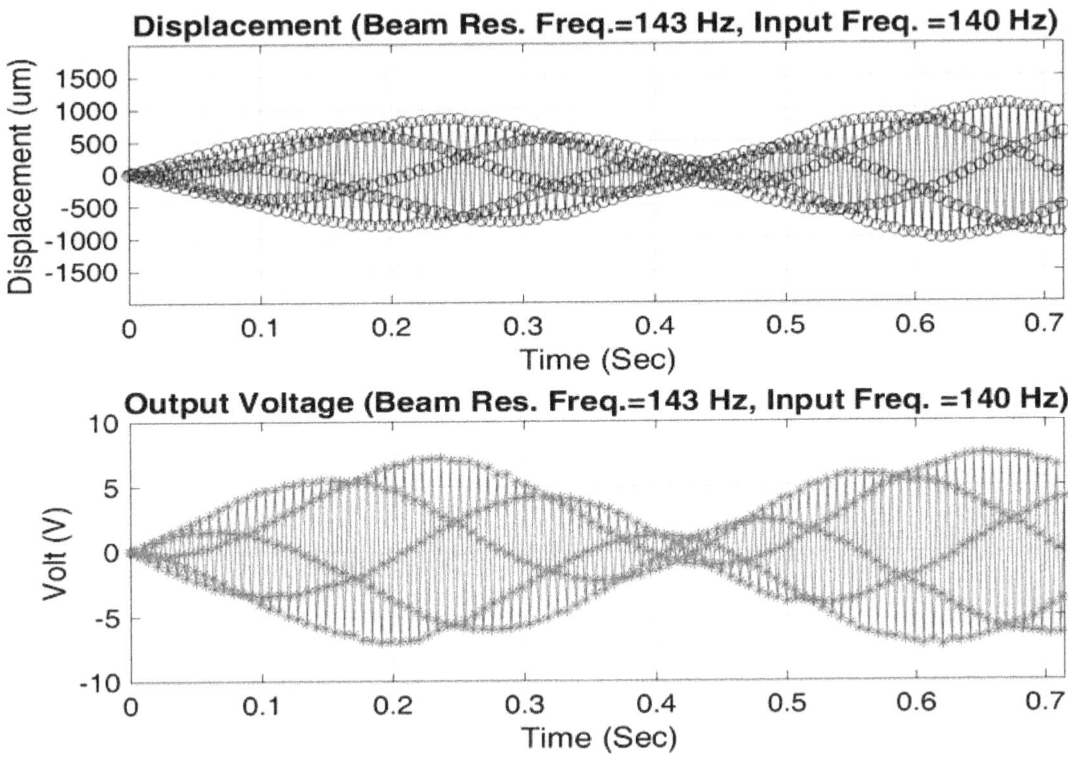

Figure 6.6: Plot of displacement and output voltage for Plate 1 at 140 Hz

6.3.2   Coupled two plate structure

A coupled double plate structure made up of Plates 1 and 2 is constructed after taking note of the simulated characteristics of the single plate structures. The bottom electrodes in this linked structure are thought to be at ground potential, whereas the top electrodes of both plates are joined by a metal layer—in this example, aluminium. Fig. 6.7 illustrates the twin plate structure that was developed. It is necessary to talk about the equivalent circuit model of the connected two-plate structure before moving on to its simulation. Fig. 6.5 already displays the electrical equivalent model of a single piezoelectric plate. There are two single plates in a coupled two-plate structure: Plate 1 and Plate 2. Their electrodes are linked to one another in parallel. Therefore, a parallel combination of two current sources, two capacitors, and two resistors can likewise be used to approximate the electrical equivalent of the connected plate construction. Fig. 6.8 displays a similar circuit model. Thus, an equivalent current source (equal to the sum of the current sources for the individual plates), an equivalent capacitor (equal to the sum of the values of the capacitors for individual plates connected in parallel), and an equivalent resistor (equal to the reciprocal of the sum of the reciprocal of resistance) make up the electrical equivalent circuit model of the coupled plate.

After talking about the electrical equivalent circuit model, we will now talk about the linked two-plate structure simulation. Comparable to the single plate structure simulation. Peak voltage and produced power values are observed while simulating the connected two-plate system at various frequencies. The results of the simulation are depicted in Fig. 6.9 and reported in Table 6.3. It can be seen that each plate's max output voltage value is close to its resonance frequency, which is 143 Hz for Plate 1 and 138 Hz for Plate 2, respectively.

A decrease in output voltage is noticeable when the connected two-plate structure vibrates at 140 Hz. (6.7) and (6.8) provide an explanation for this decline. In a multi-plate arrangement, as was previously said, the charge produced by a plate vibrating alone is dependent upon the electric field produced by the next plate. The two plates will generate an electric field in the opposite direction if their displacements are in opposing phases. Consequently, the voltage created by the connected two-plate configuration will be in the opposite phase.

The connected two-plate structure's displacement and output voltage are both seen to be oscillating at 140 Hz. Fig. 6.10 displays the outcome. The displacements of the two plates are largely out of phase with one another, as is evident. A charge

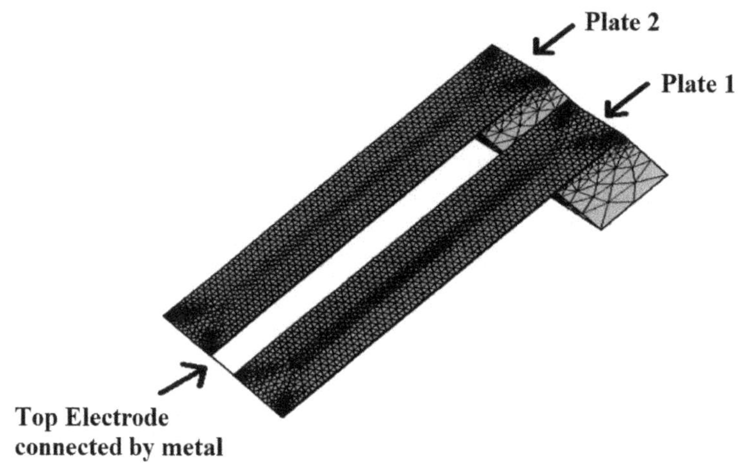

Figure 6.7: Diagram of the designed two-plate structure

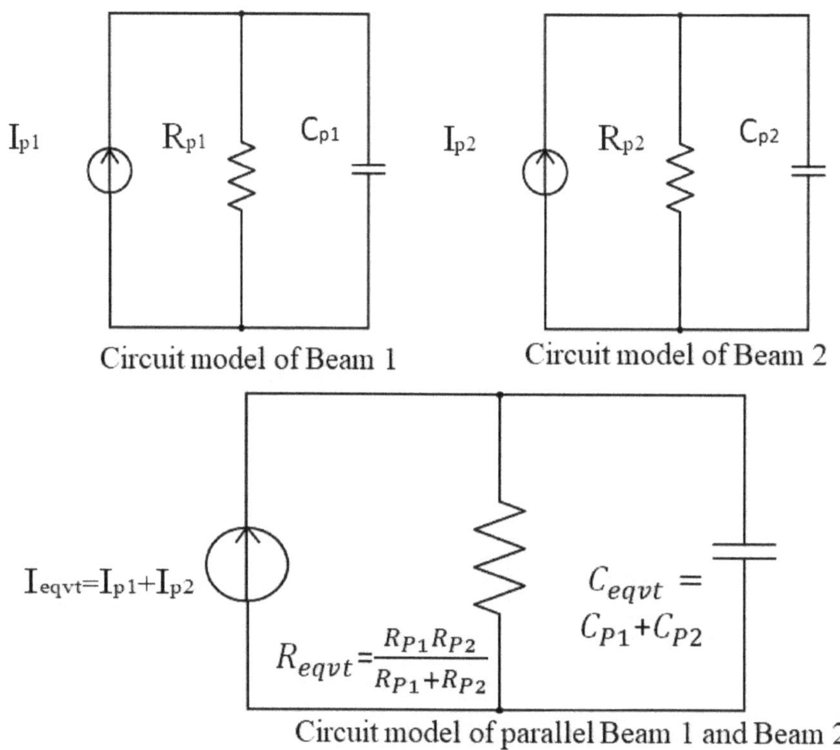

Figure 6.8: Electrical equivalent circuit model for coupled two plate structure

of opposite polarity is induced in both plates when one of the plates deviates towards the positive maxima and the other plate deviates towards the negative maxima. Consequently, at that moment, the current produced in both plates is in the opposite phase. As seen in Fig. 6.8, the equivalent current in the connected two-plate arrangement is the total of the current in both plates. The output voltage of the coupled two-plate structure decreases when currents in the opposite phase are added because the coupled two-plate structure's effective current is reduced. It is evident from Fig. 6.10 that the output voltage and combined displacement have the same contour. The study of the connected two-plate structure's analogous circuit model makes this clear. An comparable single plate is used to depict the parallel combination of plates. As a result, the total displacement of the two plates will resemble a single plate and have a profile identical to the output voltage.

We will now verify the theory derived from Eqs. (6.7) and (6.8), which states that the output voltage of a single vibrating plate alone is not the same as the voltage generated by a plate in a multi-plate structure. Plotting the voltage produced by Plates 1 and 2 when they vibrate independently and the output voltage of the connected two-plate construction at a specific frequency

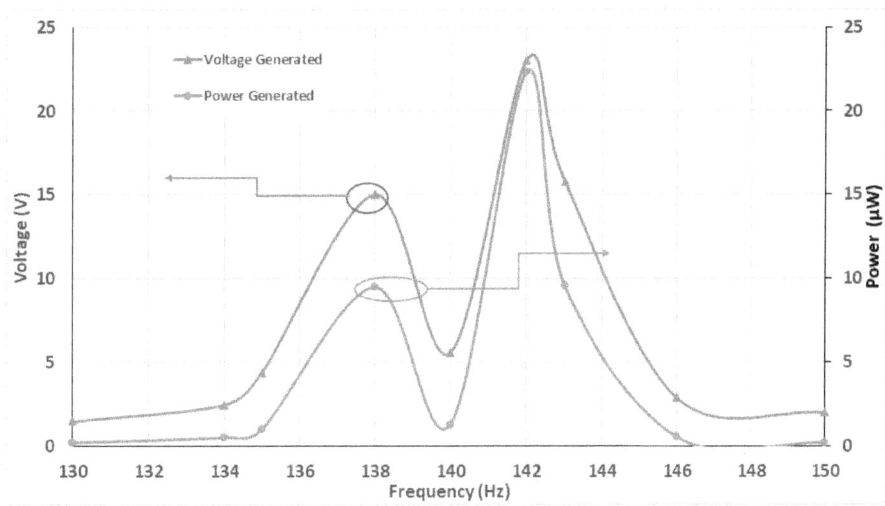

Figure 6.9: Output voltage and power generated by coupled two-plate structure at different frequencies

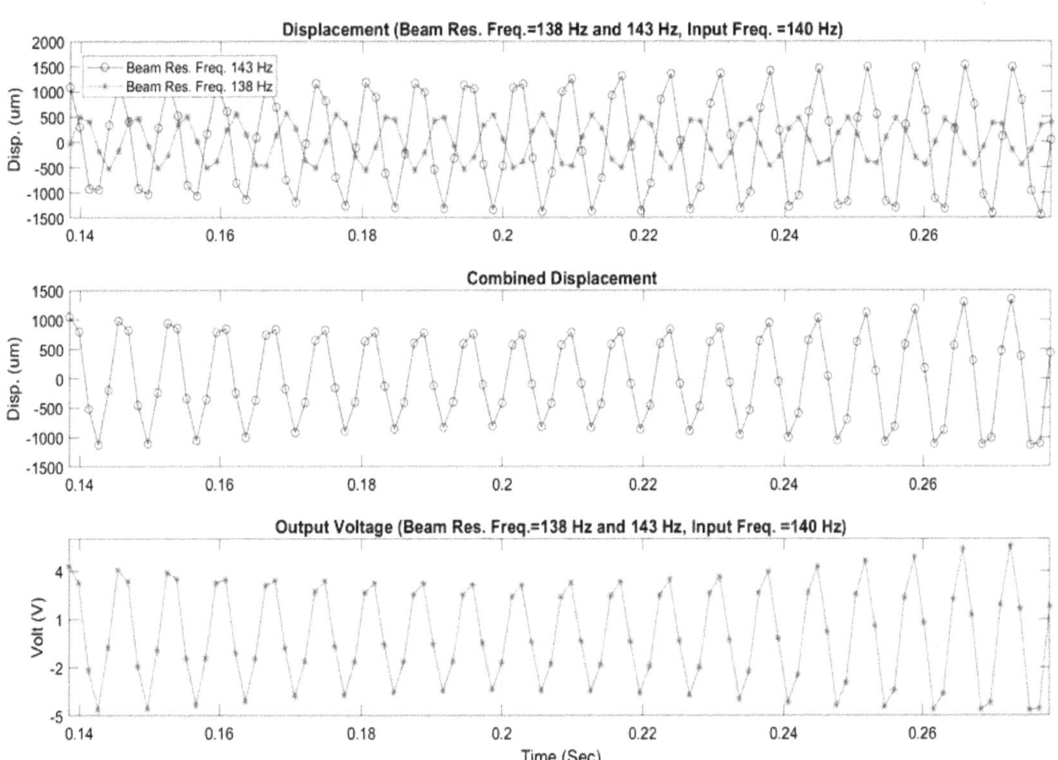

Figure 6.10: Plot of displacement and output voltage for coupled two-plate structure vibrating at 140 Hz

can both show this.

Plotting the corresponding voltage produced by the single plates vibrating independently and the output voltage of the connected two-plate structure vibrating at 140 Hz are both visible. Fig. 6.11 illustrates this.

6.3.3 Coupled three plate structure

Plate 3 is used with Plates 1 and 2 to build a connected three-plate structure. Table 6.2 already contains information on Plate 3's dimensions and resonance frequency. Similar to the coupled two-plate construction, the top electrodes of these three plates

Table 6.3: Output voltage and power generated by coupled two plate structure comprising of Plate 1 and Plate 2 at different frequencies

Frequency (Hz)	Peak voltage (V)	Power Generated (μW)
130	1.5	0.21
134	2.5	0.52
135	4.4	1
138	15	9.5
140	5.6	1.3
142	23	22.3
143	15.8	9.6
146	2.9	0.56
150	2	0.2

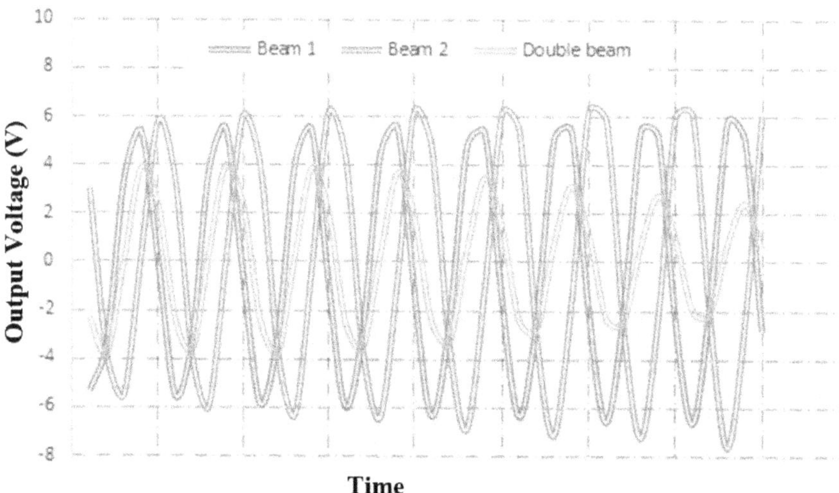

Figure 6.11: Voltage generated by single plate and coupled two- plate structures

were joined by a metal layer.

At various frequencies, the coupled three-plate structure's transient study was carried out. Table 6.4 contains the output voltage and generated power values at various frequencies, which are plotted in Fig. 6.12. It is evident from Fig. 6.12 that the highest voltage happens at an intermediate frequency of 142 Hz. This relates to the fact that the three plates' movement occurs in the same phase at this frequency.

This coupled three-plate structure's displacement and output voltage at 140 Hz are observed similarly to that of a coupled two-plate and one-plate construction. This will help us understand the three plates' vibrations at this frequency better. Fig. 6.13 displays the output voltage and observed displacement.

Table 6.4: Output voltage and power generated by coupled three plate structure comprising of Plate 1, Plate 2 and Plate 3 at different frequencies

Frequency (Hz)	Peak voltage (V)	Power Generated (μW)
130	1.85	1.70
137	16.5	4.13
138	5.37	1.47
140	12.55	6.25
142	17.13	12.5
143	8.25	4.25
146	3.74	0.62
150	1.64	0.12

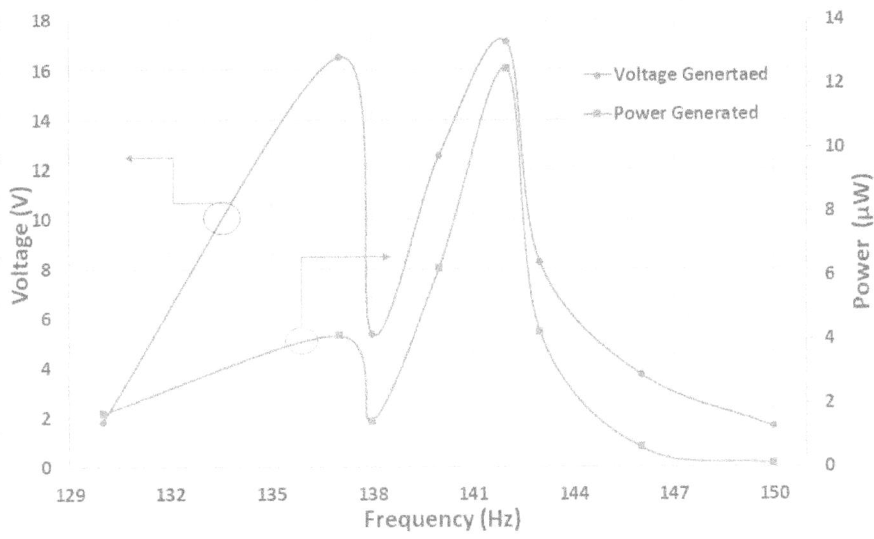

Figure 6.12: Output voltage and power generated by coupled three plate structure at different frequencies

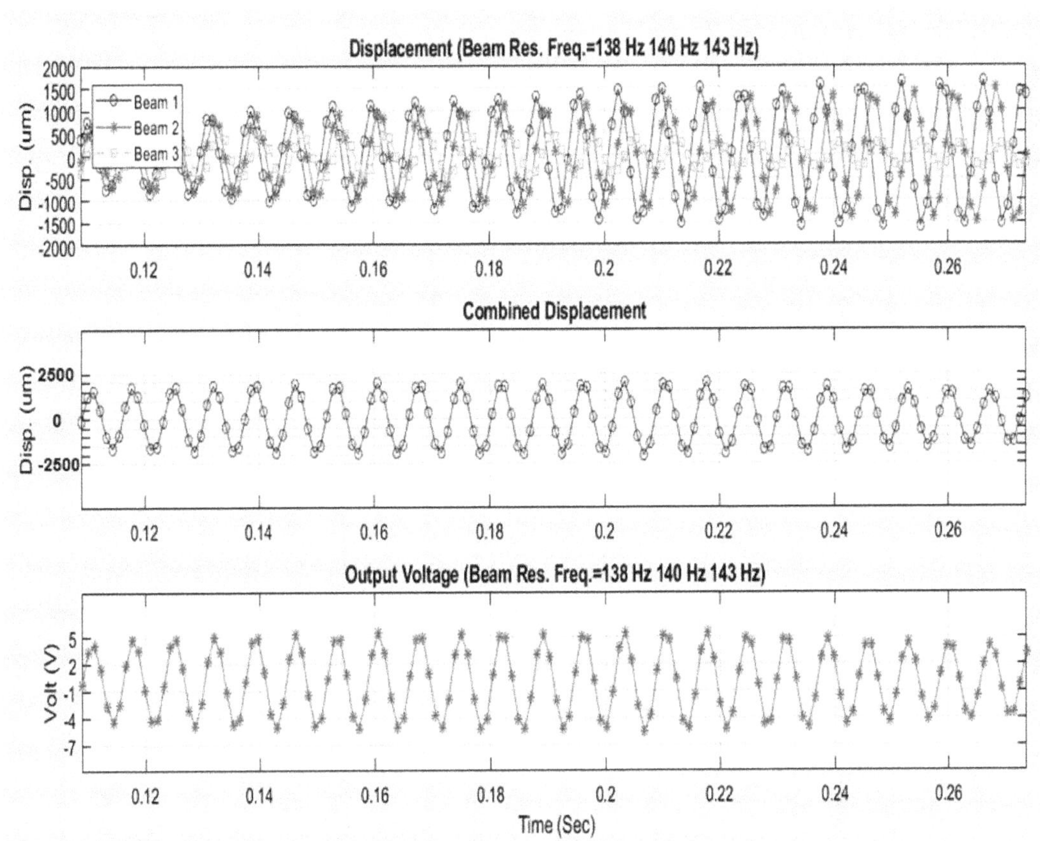

Figure 6.13: Plot of displacement and output voltage for coupled three-plate structure vibrating at 140 Hz

It is clearly visible that the three plates' displacements are typically in the same phase. The net displacement is considerable because the displacements in the same phase are added together. Because of the high degree of net displacement, a high output voltage is observed at this frequency. This conduct appears to be at odds with what is seen in the case of a connected two-plate structure. In the connected two-plate system, Plate 1 and Plate 2 displacements occurred at 140 Hz in opposing phases. However, Fig. 6.12 makes it evident that in the connected three-plate configuration, all three plates are in the same phase. In this case, the addition of Plate 3 to the multi-plate structure also influences Plates 1 and 2's individual displacements. This provides more proof of the plates' coupling effect.

We will now talk about the design and simulation of connected four-plate structures.

6.3.4 Coupled four plate structure

The coupled four-plate structure is designed similarly to the coupled multi-plate structures that were designed earlier. Here, Plate 4 has been incorporated into the design in addition to Plates 1, 2, and 3. Table 6.2 contains information about plate 4's size and resonance frequency. Similar to a coupled two-plate construction, the top electrodes of the four plates were joined by a metal layer.

Table 6.5: Output voltage and power generated by coupled four plate structure comprising of Plate 1, Plate 2, Plate 3 and Plate 4 at different frequencies

Frequency (Hz)	Peak voltage (V)	Power Generated (μW)
132	1.5	0.16
135	3.36	0.62
138	6.9	3.2
139	5.37	1.2
140	4.2	0.87
142	5.06	1.29
143	8.25	22.7
146	6.12	2.48
150	2.81	0.43

Different sets of output voltage at different frequencies are obtained from the transient analysis of the connected four-plate structure. Table 6.5 contains the output voltage and generated power values at various frequencies, which are plotted in Fig. 6.14.

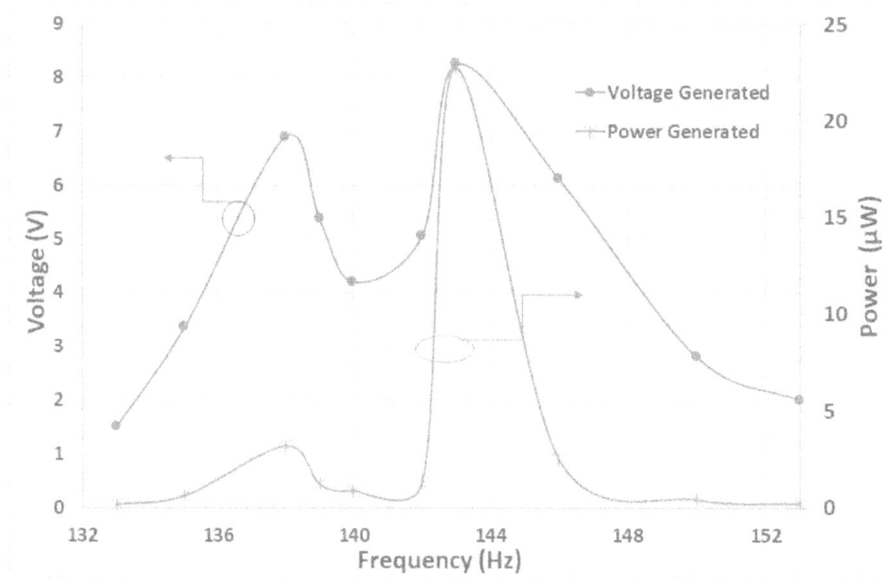

Figure 6.14: Output voltage and power generated by coupled four plate structure at different frequencies

It is clear from Fig. 6.14 that 143 Hz is when the 8.25 V peak voltage occurs. At 140 Hz, there is a dip in the output voltage profile. Given that the plates are vibrating in the opposite phase, this suggests that the structure's net displacement should be smaller. Following the examination of the connected four-plate structure's vibration at 140 Hz, this may be confirmed. Fig. 6.15 displays the observed displacement and output voltage.

Plates 1 and 2 vibrate in the same phase, while Plates 3 and 4 vibrate in the opposite phase, as seen in Fig. 6.15. Thus, at some time instants, the net displacement decreases and even becomes negligibly little. The low output voltage at this fre-

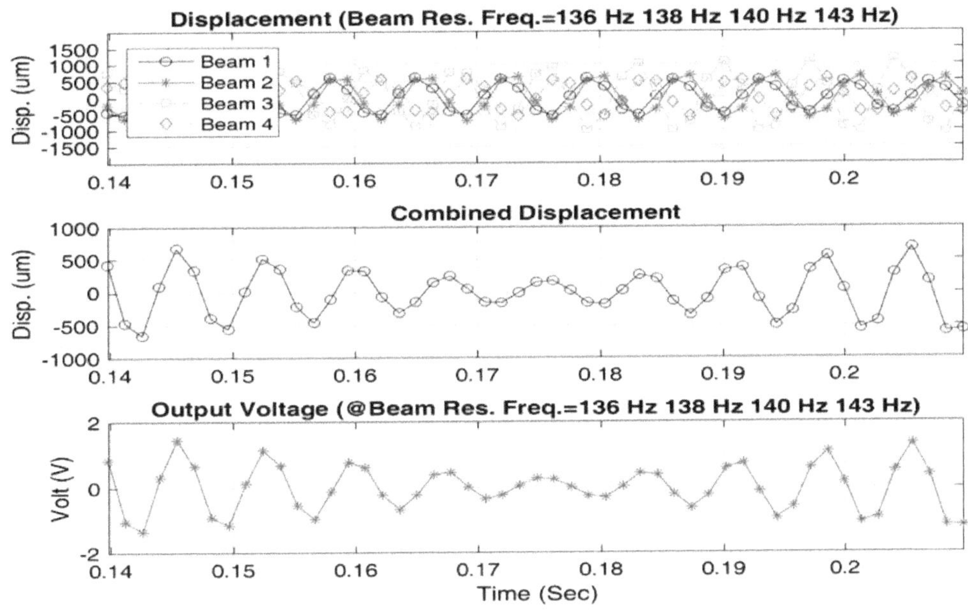

Figure 6.15: Plot of displacement and output voltage for coupled four-plate structure vibrating at 140 Hz

quency is caused by the separate plates' out-of-phase oscillations. This situation is comparable to that of the coupled two-plate construction.

It is evident by looking at the displacement of several multi-plate constructions at 140 Hz that different multi-plate configurations shake the same plate in different ways. In a multi-plate structure, a plate's behaviour is determined by its surrounding plates. In one type of multi-plate construction, two plates vibrating at a certain frequency and phase might vibrate in the opposite phase in another type of multi-plate structure.

The output voltage produced by the multi-plate structures is represented on the same frequency scale following individual analysis of the various single-plate and multi-plate structures. This provides insight into the various connected multi-plate architectures' operational bandwidth. Fig. 6.16 displays the output voltage of single and multi-plate designs at various frequencies.

In this case, it has been assumed that the operating bandwidth is the range of frequencies at which the output voltage exceeds 2 V. The bandwidth of Plate 1 and the connected two-plate construction are 15 Hz and 17 Hz, respectively, as can be shown. The bandwidth of a connected three-plate structure is eighteen hertz (Hz). Compared to other connected multi-plate structures, the coupled four-plate structure has a substantially wider bandwidth of 20 Hz. As a result, it can be seen that a multi-plate structure's operating bandwidth improves as the number of plates grows. It is important to keep in mind, nevertheless, that the various plates need to have resonant frequencies that allow the finished device to generate noticeably high voltage across a broad frequency range. In a multi-plate construction, this can be accomplished by recognising the impact that one plate has on its adjacent plates. Therefore, the coupling effect between the plates should be considered while choosing the plates for a multi-plate construction. In a linked multi-plate system, improper selection of the resonant frequencies of the plates may result in a large drop in the output voltage at certain frequencies. It is not possible to employ these multi-plate structures as wideband energy harvesting structures. Lastly, Table 6.6 presents a comparison between the suggested structure and the body of current research.

Fig. 6.17 illustrates the possible fabrication procedures of the proposed structure in detail. To build the design as depicted in Fig. 6.17, four masks were needed.

After discussing and confirming the suggested theory for the coupling effect among the multi-plate structure, simulation results of several solo and linked multi-plate structures were examined. We will now talk about a few significant applications of this idea in the next section.

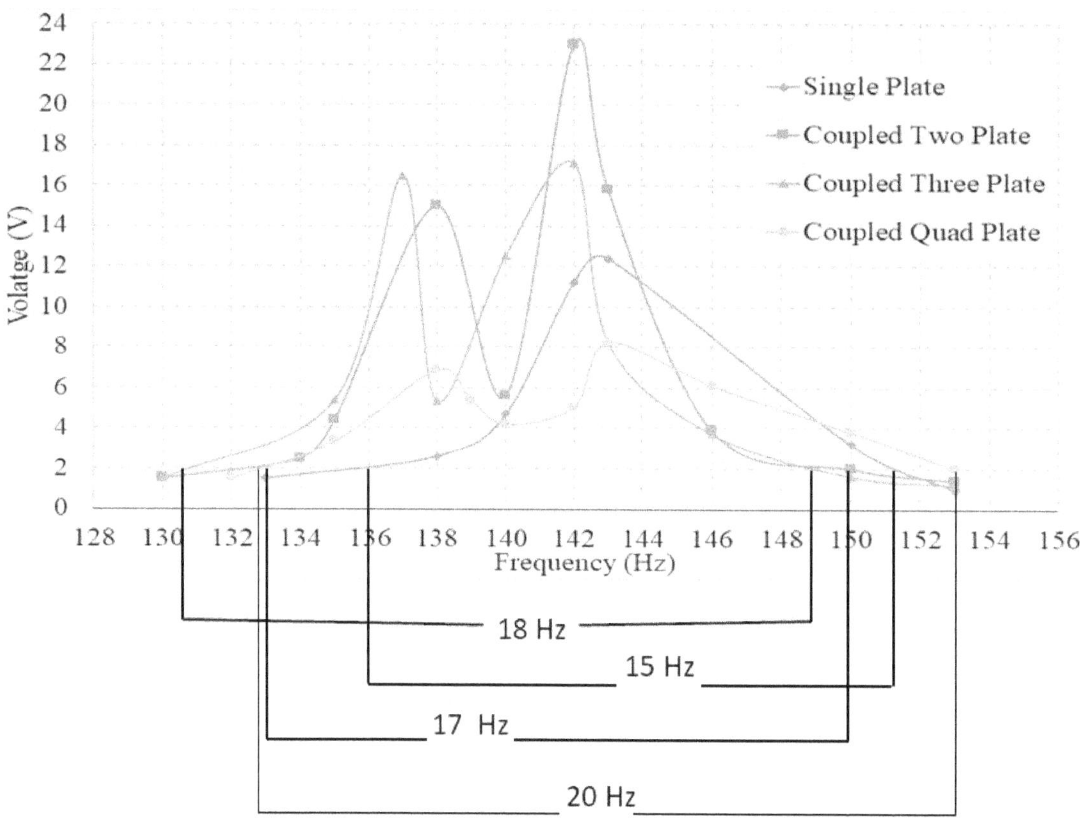

Figure 6.16: Output voltage of Plate 1, coupled two plate structure, coupled three plate structure and coupled four plate structure at different frequencies

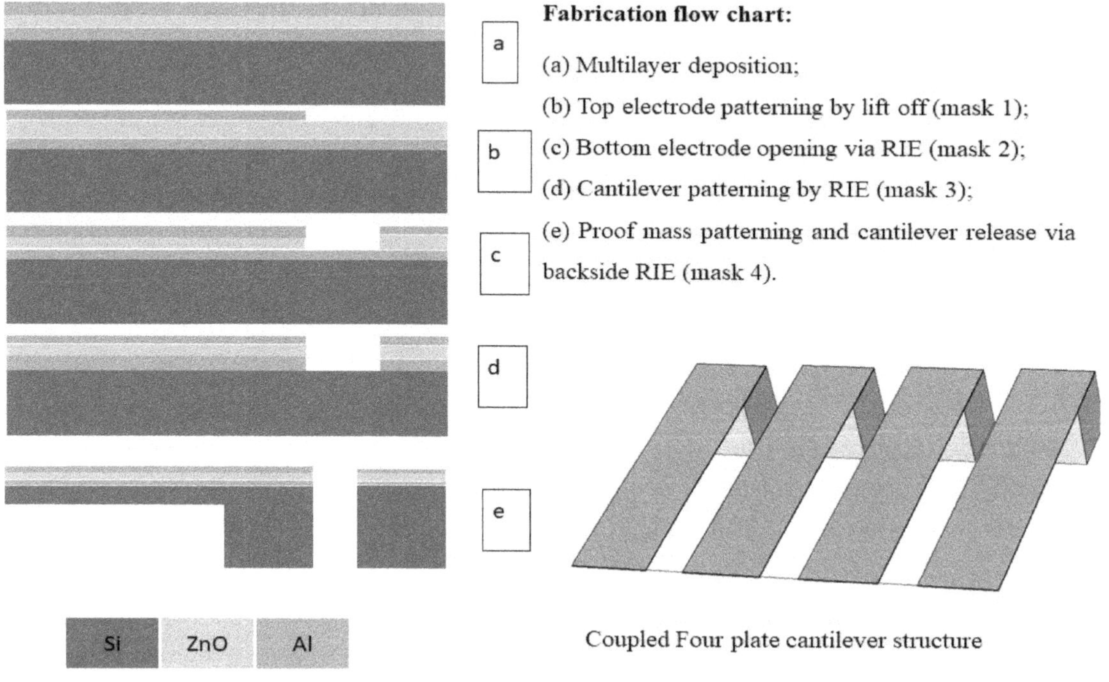

Figure 6.17: Fabrication process of four beam cantilever

Table 6.6: Comparative study of the proposed structure with the existing literature

Ref	Dimension	Bandwidth	Electrical output		Remarks
			Voltage	Power	
[127]	17.1×16.2 mm^2	10 Hz to 90 Hz	563 mV	0.423 mW	Large harvester area and low output voltage
[128]	160 mm^2	153 Hz to 219 Hz	655 mV	-	Large area, Low output voltage
[119]	11×12.4 mm^2	231 Hz- 237 Hz	7.04 V	66.75 μW	Large area and higher frequency range
[129]	13×18 mm^2	141.6 Hz to 191.1 Hz	-	1.06-3.24 μW	Large area, low output power, higher frequency range
This work	$5.15x7$ mm^2	133 Hz to 153 Hz	8.25 V	22.7 μW	Smallest fabricated area and highest output voltage

6.4 Applications

One significant phenomena in the case of the multi-plate construction is the coupling effect. There are numerous significant uses for this, which are addressed below:

1. Interactions within multi-plate structures: The majority of MEMS energy harvester devices are made up of several cantilever plates, as is widely known. Therefore, in order to construct the energy harvester structures correctly, it is vital to understand the interactions that take place between the neighbouring plates. It is possible to forecast the output of these multi-plate processes with accuracy once the coupling interactions between the neighbouring plates are taken into account.

2. Determining the resonant frequency of a multiple PZ structure: We can determine the resonant frequency of the entire multi-plate construction, or the frequency at which peak output is achievable, by utilising the coupling effect between the plates. The resonance frequency of each individual plate typically varies from this highest output frequency.

3. Extending the multiple PZ structure's bandwidth: Knowledge of the coupling effect aids in estimating the ideal difference between the resonant frequencies of adjacent plates, which raises the net displacement of the plates and generates a significant voltage across a broad frequency range. Therefore, the overall bandwidth of the numerous structures can be expanded by merging several plates with the optimal frequency difference.

6.5 Summary

The coupling effect, which illustrates how the vibrations of one plate in a multi-plate structure affect the vibration of the adjoining plate, has been covered in this chapter. The suggested mathematical approach is validated by simulating coupled two-plate, three-plate, and four-plate structures on the COMSOL Multiphysics platform. It is evident from Eqs. (6.7) and (6.8) that the voltage produced by the multi-plate structure as a whole is different from the voltage produced by the individual plates vibrating at that specific frequency. The difference between a plate's resonant frequency when vibrating alone and its resonant frequency in a multi-plate structure is described by equations (6.11) and (6.17). Ultimately, it is evident that as the number of constituent plates increases, so does the bandwidth of a coupled-multi-plate structure. It is important to consider the coupling effect between the plates while selecting the resonance frequencies of the individual plates.

Chapter 7

Bandwidth and output power enhancement in PZEH using magnetic proof mass

The potential for PZEH miniaturisation contributes to extending the lifespan of numerous low-power devices, hence facilitating the widespread deployment of IoTs. PZEH's limited bandwidth and frequency dependence limit its performance. At the resonance frequency, the piezoelectric energy harvester (PZEH) may produce its maximum output voltage and power. A PZEH's efficiency can be significantly decreased by even a little shift in the surrounding frequency. Many studies are being conducted to remove this restriction. Using non-linearity in the EH design is one such technique [67], [130].

Using magnetic tip mass as a proof mass in a magnetic environment is one way to induce non-linearity [67]. Non-linearity may be introduced into the system by the magnet's relative alignment, position, and arrangement. PZEH's efficiency and operating bandwidth can be increased in a number of ways. In the EH system, the permanent magnet has been utilised to produce monostable, [68], [69] bi-stable, tri-stable state, [70], [71], [72] [131], [75], [74], [73], and thus capable of expanding the operating frequency range.

Challa and colleagues [67] created an EH with a 34 mm diameter, and they adjusted the magnets' respective positions to adjust the resonant frequency in relation to the magnetic force. Zhou et al. [76] want to increase efficiency by modifying the permanent magnet's location and orientation in order to produce a penta-stable state. In their attempt to devise a method for calculating magnetic force in the vibration and energy harvesting efficiency of the piezoelectric energy harvester, Tan et al. [77]. For the electromagnetic micro-generator, Zhu et al. [78] designed a (13 x 5) mm^2 cantilever beam. The attractive force of an axially aligned permanent magnet has been used to tune the cantilever's resonant frequency. In order to improve the bandwidth of the EH using a permanent magnet on a dual cantilever, Wei-jiun et al. [79] created a 98 mm dual cantilever. Additionally, a 12-cm-long array of cantilevers was designed by D. Guo et al. [80] to improve the frequency bandwidth with the magnetic tip mass and boost EH performance.

This chapter discusses how to boost bandwidth in the EH system by utilising the multi-beam structure concept and the magnetic field intensity. In this chapter, a twin cantilever system with two magnets is introduced. Two magnets are affixed to the outer beam and the proof-mass of the inner beam, respectively. To establish the magnetic field intensity and to interact with one another, both magnets are attached close to one another. This inclination contributes to the enhancement of the EH's frequency bandwidth.

7.1　Mathematical modelling

Previous chapters have demonstrated that the distribution of stress on the cantilever beam determines the electric voltage that develops across the PZ layer. Therefore, the cantilever structure with the larger stress distribution yields a higher voltage than the others when all other design factors are equal. With the aid of the magnetic tip mass, the PZ cantilever system's introduction of a magnetic field will enhance the PZEH's performance by increasing the distribution of stress.

7.1.1 Mechanical modelling of PZEH with magnetic proof mass

A permanent magnet that is axially aligned with the fixed magnet is fastened to the proof mass of the PZEH. The system is modelled using Kirchhoff plate theory plus added magnetic force. The non-linear restoring force is generated by the magnetic force within the PZEH.

Eqs. (2.17) or (2.18) [20], [110] can be used to express the mechanical deviation of the cantilever plate in a perpendicular direction, as illustrated in Fig. 7.1.

The biharmonic operator in Eqs. (2.17) and (2.18) is Δ^4, which is provided in Eq. (2.19). The vertical displacement of the plate is denoted by $w(x,y,t)$, the density is ρ, and the flexural rigidity is D_r, as found in Eq. (2.20). The magnetic force $f(x,y,t)_m$, which is determined by Eq. (7.1), is applied externally to the system at any deflection $w(x,y,t)$.

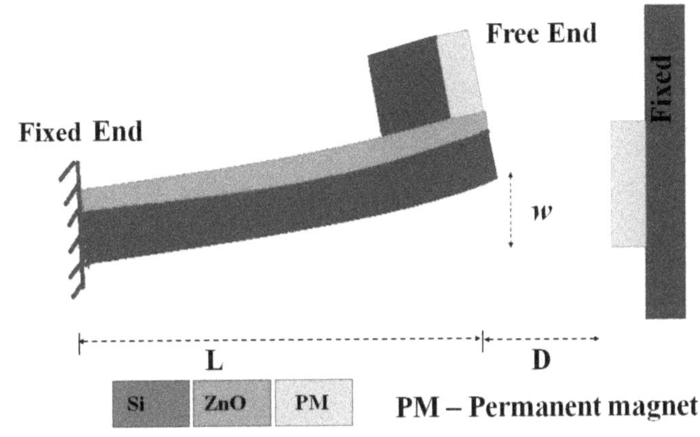

Figure 7.1: Typical vibrating piezoelectric cantilever with magnetic proof mass

$$f(x,y,t)_m = -\frac{3\mu_0 m_1 m_2}{2\pi(D+w(x,y,t))^4}, \tag{7.1}$$

In this case, two magnets are D distance apart, V_y is the volume of the magnets, and $m = \frac{2BV_y}{\mu_0}$ represents the magnetic dipoles m_1 and m_2. μ_0 is the air permeability. When two magnets have the same magnetic polarisation, there will be an attracting force; when they have the opposite polarisation, there will be a repulsive force.

In the event that the cantilever system is not subject to any magnetic force, $f(x,y,t)_m$ is interpreted as zero in Eq. (2.18). This is an example of the cantilever plate vibrating freely, as described by Equation (7.2) [20], [110].

$$D_r\nabla^4 w(x,y,t) + \rho t_p\frac{\partial^4 w(x,y,t)}{\partial t^2} = 0, \tag{7.2}$$

The free vibration of the PZ cantilever is already solved in Section 2.3.1. So, the free vibration of the PZ cantilever will not be discussed here. Here, the derivation of vibration of the PZ cantilever under the magnetic influence will be discussed.

Given that the rectangular plate has length L and width b, respectively, the boundary limit changes along length from x = 0 to L and along width from y = 0 to b. The displacement of the rectangular cantilever, or Eq. (2.18), will be taken into consideration when the external magnetic force $f(x,y,t)_m$ is taken into account, as shown in [20] and [116].

$$D_r\nabla^4 w(x,y,t) + \rho t_p\frac{\partial^4 w(x,y,t)}{\partial t^2} = -\frac{3\mu_0 m_1 m_2}{2\pi(D+w(x,y,t))^4}, \tag{7.3}$$

The vertical displacement of the plate will determine the value of Eq. (7.4).,

$$w(x,y,t) = \sum_{m=1}^{\infty}\sum_{n=1}^{\infty} W_{mn}(x,y)T_{mn}(t), \tag{7.4}$$

wherein For all $m,n = 1,2,3,$, $W_{mn}(x,y) = B_{1mn}\sin\frac{m\pi x}{L}\sin\frac{n\pi y}{b}$. The normalisation condition, provided as Eq. (7.5), is followed while normalising the normal modes.

$$\int_0^L \int_0^b \rho t_p w_{mn}^2 dx dy = 1,$$ (7.5)

$B_{1mn} = \frac{2}{\sqrt{\rho t_p L b}}$ is the result. The normalisation condition in Eq. (7.4) may be used to obtain the equation regulating the generalised coordinates $T_{mn}(t)$ by substituting it into Eq. (2.18).

$$\frac{\partial^2 T_{mn}(t)}{\partial t^2} + \omega_{mn}^2 T_{mn}(t) = N_{mn}(t); m, n = 1, 2, 3..,$$ (7.6)

Given the natural frequency ω_{mn} and the generalised force $N_{mn}(t)$,

$$N_{mn}(t) = \int_0^L \int_0^b w_{mn}(x,y) f(x,y,t)_m dx dy,$$ (7.7)

$$\omega_{mn} = \pi^2 \left(\sqrt{\frac{D_r}{\rho t_p}} \right) \left[\left(\frac{m}{L} \right)^2 + \left(\frac{n}{b} \right)^2 \right]; m, n = 1, 2..,$$ (7.8)

Eq. (7.9) can be used to express the solution of Eq. (7.6).

$$T_{mn}(t) = T_{mn}(0) \cos\omega_{mn}t + \frac{1}{\omega_{mn}} \frac{\partial T_{mn}(t)}{\partial t} \sin\omega_{mn}t$$
$$+ \frac{1}{\omega_{mn}} \int_0^t N_{mn}(t) \sin\omega_{mn}(t - \tau) d\tau,$$ (7.9)

The vibration of a rectangular plate under magnetic force can be solved in its entirety using Eq. (7.10).

$$W(x,y,t) = \sum_{m=1}^{\infty} \sum_{n=1}^{\infty} T_{mn}(0) \sin\frac{m\pi x}{L} \sin\frac{n\pi y}{b} \cos\omega_{mn}t$$
$$+ \sum_{m=1}^{\infty} \sum_{n=1}^{\infty} \frac{\partial T_{mn}(0)}{\partial t} \frac{1}{\omega_{mn}} \sin\frac{m\pi x}{L} \sin\frac{n\pi y}{b} \sin\omega_{mn}t$$
$$+ \sum_{m=1}^{\infty} \sum_{n=1}^{\infty} \frac{1}{\omega_{mn}} \sin\frac{m\pi x}{L} \sin\frac{n\pi y}{b} \int_0^t T_{mn}(\tau) \sin[\omega_{mn}(t - \tau)] d\tau,$$ (7.10)

It can be observed, therefore, that the magnetic force (from Eqs. (7.7), (7.9), and (7.10)) determines the deflection of the end mass of the vibrating dual beam cantilever structure. Thus, the cantilever structure's vibration is influenced by the magnetic effect.

7.2 Design of the cantilever structure

7.2.1 Design of the single beam structure

Zinc oxide serves as the PZ layer and silicon serves as the substrate in the creation of the rectangular cantilever structure. As seen in Fig. 7.2, the proof mass at the free end of the cantilever is made of Si and a permanent magnet (PM1), which serves to lower the resonant frequency [20], [116]. The first magnet is surrounded by another stationary magnet (PM2) that is positioned axially to produce an opposing magnetic force. The system may become non-linear as a result of the permanent magnet acting as a spring. Table 7.1 lists the dimensions of the single rectangular cantilever construction. Table 2.2 lists the various characteristics of the materials that were used to design the cantilever plate. The magnets utilised in the construction of the straightforward rectangular structure have a magnetic field intensity of 5 mT. There are 500 μm between the two magnets. The cantilever structure is designed with COMSOL Multiphysics. The structure has been meshing using standard meshing methods. The mechanical and electrical characteristics of the intended cantilever construction are obtained by applying the principles of electrostatics and solid mechanics. The single simple rectangular cantilever structure (SRC) has a resonance frequency of 95.5 Hz. In accordance with the previous discussion, the resonant frequency of a basic single rectangular cantilever with a magnetic tip mass of 5mT (RCWM@5mT) construction is 95 Hz. The names and abbreviations of all the cantilever structures covered in this chapter are displayed in Table 7.2.

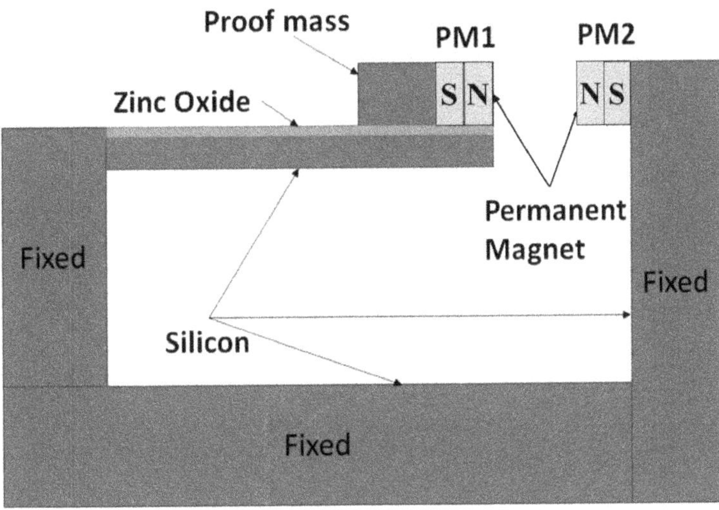

Figure 7.2: Block diagram of piezoelectric energy harvester with a magnetic proof mass of single beam system

Table 7.1: The geometry of different materials used in the single beam cantilever

	Si	ZnO	*Proof mass*		
			Si	PM1	PM2
Length (μm)	5000	5000	800	200	200
Width (μm)	1000	1000	1000	1000	1000
Thickness (μm)	12	2	850	850	850

Table 7.2: Name and abbreviations of different cantilever structures

Name of structure	Abbreviation	Resonant frequency (Hz)
Simple Rectangular cantilever	SRC	95.5
Rectangular cantilever with a magnetic proof mass of 5mT	RCWM@5mT	96
Dualbeam without magnetic proof mass	DBWOM	115.18
Dualbeam with magnetic proof mass of 5mT	DBWM@5mT	115
Dualbeam with magnetic proof mass of 10mT	DBWM@10mT	114.81
Dualbeam with magnetic proof mass of 20mT	DBWM@20mT	114.61
Dualbeam with magnetic proof mass of 30mT	DBWM@30mT	114.31

7.2.2 Design of the dual beam structure

The preceding chapter covered the topic of how the multi-beam cantilever structure might increase bandwidth. Therefore, the dual-beam EH with a rectangular shape and magnetic proof mass is intended to increase the EH's bandwidth. ZnO is the PZ material and Si is the substrate of the cantilever. To lower the resonance frequency, the proof mass is fastened to the dual-beam structure's free end. Each proof mass has a permanent magnet attached to it so that the proof masses repel one another through magnetic force. A permanent magnet is used to position the proof mass, as shown in Fig. 7.3. The magnet utilised in the single beam cantilever construction and the dual-beam structure have the same magnetic field intensity. The outer beam (L1) and inner beam (L2) have lengths of 5000 μm and 4200 μm, respectively. The outer beam (W3) attached to the fixed end has an arm width of 500 μm, while the arm at the free end (W4) has a width of 600 μm. The inner beam (W2) has a width of 1000 μm.

Table 7.3: Dimension of dual beam cantilever structure

SNo	Parameter	Dimension (μm)
1	Length of inner arm (Both Si and ZnO)	L2 = 4200
2	Width of inner arm (Both Si and ZnO)	W2 = 1000
3	Thickness of inner arm	Si=12, ZnO = 2
4	Length of outer arm (Both Si and ZnO)	L1 = 5000
5	Width of outer arm (Both Si and ZnO)	W3 = 500, W4 = 600
6	Thickness of outer arm	Si = 12, ZnO = 2
7	Proof mass on inner arm (Si+PM3)	Si = 800 × 1000 × 850, PM3 = 200 × 1000 × 850
8	Proof mass on outer arm (Si+PM4)	Si = 400 × 1000 × 850, PM3 = 200 × 1000 × 850
9	Perforation on inner arm	L3 = 1000, W5 = 400
10	Perforation on outer arm	L4 = 800, W6 = 100
11	Total width of dual-beam	W1 = 2500
12	Gap between inner and outer beam	D1 = 200
13	Gap between the two magnets	D2 = 250

The dual-beam (W1) has an overall width of 2500 μm. The twin cantilever beam has a total thickness of 14 μm. ZnO thickness is 2 μm and Si substrate thickness is 12 μm, respectively. The ZnO is evenly dispersed across the cantilever surface. The proof mass, which consists of Si and a permanent magnet (PM3), has dimensions of 1000 x 1000 x 850 μm^3 when it is coupled to the inner beam (IPM). The width and thickness stay the same, but the Si and permanent magnet lengths are 800 μm and 200 μm, respectively. Si and a permanent magnet (PM4) are also components of the outer beam (OPM) proof mass. The outer beam's proof mass has a net dimension of 600 x 1000 x 850 μm^3. The Si layer has a length of 400 μm, while the permanent magnet has a length of 200 μm. The thickness and width stay the same. There is a 250 μm gap between the inner and outer beam (D1) and a 200 μm distance between the two magnets (D2). To lower the resonant frequency and bring the inner and outer beams' resonant frequencies closer to one another, the perforation is inserted at the appropriate location [49], [116]. The perforations in the outer arm have lengths (L4) and widths (W6) of 800 μm and 100 μm, respectively, while the inner arm has lengths (L3) and widths (W5) of 1000 μm and 400 μm, respectively. Table 7.3 lists the dimensions of the materials utilised in the dual-beam design.

7.3   Mechanical output of the cantilever structure

Equations demonstrate how the average stress distribution in the cantilever structure affects the PZEH's electrical output. (2.9), (1.4a), and (2.11). Therefore, it is vital to confirm the impact of the magnetic field intensity on the stress distribution before delving into the specifics of the stress distribution of all the cantilever constructions. In order to do that, a straightforward rectangular cantilever with the dimensions displayed in Table 7.1 and Fig. 7.2 has been designed. To confirm how the strength of the magnetic field affects the distribution of stress, a stationary study is used to the cantilever structural design. First, a fixed load of 1g $(= 9.8 m/s2)$ is used in the stationary research. The effects of the magnetic field are then gradually introduced into the system to examine their effects. The stress distribution along the cantilever structure's arc length is depicted in Fig. 7.4. Fig. 7.4 shows that the stress distribution increases as the magnetic field intensity increases, which is consistent with the mathematical approach that was previously stated.

This section now discusses how the dual beam structure is affected by magnetic intensity. The comparison of the stress distributions of several cantilever structures at their respective resonance frequencies is shown in Fig. 7.5. Figure reffig:Stress in Cantilever illustrates the plotting of the dual-beam stress distribution to different intensities of the magnetic field. At its resonance frequency, the DBWM@30mT exhibits the maximum stress distribution. Based on Fig. 7.5, it can be inferred that as the magnetic intensity of the tip mass increases, so does the distribution of stress within the cantilever.

As the permanent magnet's magnetic intensity rises, so does the cantilever beam's stress distribution. When designing cantilever beams, the materials' Young's modulus should be smaller than the maximum stress that can be created in the beams. The cantilever's elastic and mechanical strength will be compromised when the tension exceeds Young's modulus. The stress distribution of each cantilever is shown in Fig. 7.5, indicating that each cantilever has adequate mechanical strength.

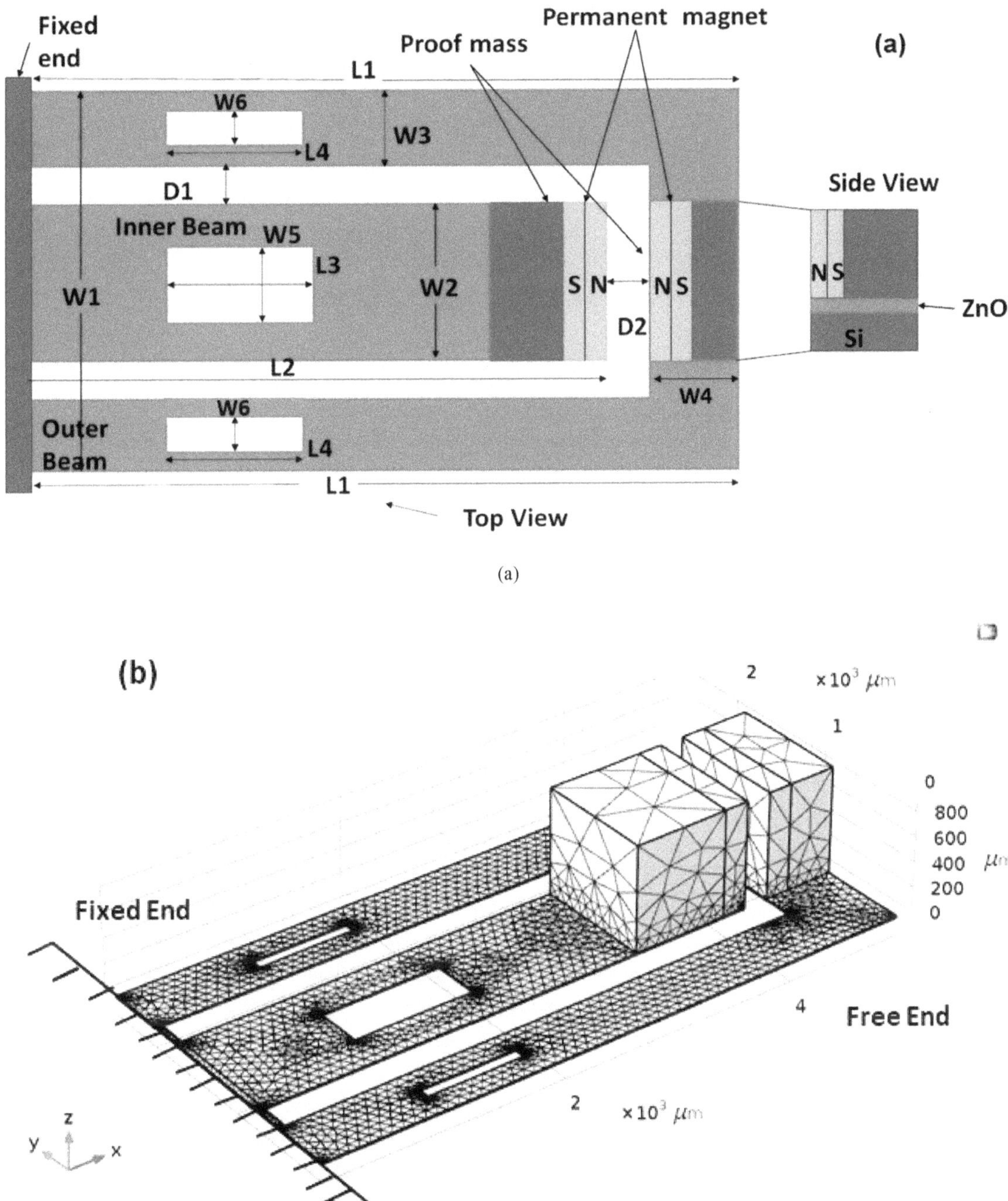

(b)

Figure 7.3: (a) Top view (b) 3D view of meshed PZEH with magnetic proof mass of dual beam structure with perforation

7.4 Electrical output analysis of the cantilever structures

7.4.1 Output voltage analysis of the cantilever structures

At the resonance frequency, the PZ-based energy harvester produces the maximum output voltage and output power. Therefore, for each of the discussed cantilever structures in COMSOL Multiphysics, a time-domain analysis is performed at the corresponding resonance frequency. The time-dependent voltage is provided via the transient analysis. For each structure, a sinusoidal acceleration of 1g ($g = 9.8 m/s^2$), where g is the acceleration caused by gravity, is applied at the resonance frequency of each structure. The time-varying output voltage of each cantilever structure at its resonance frequency is displayed in Fig.

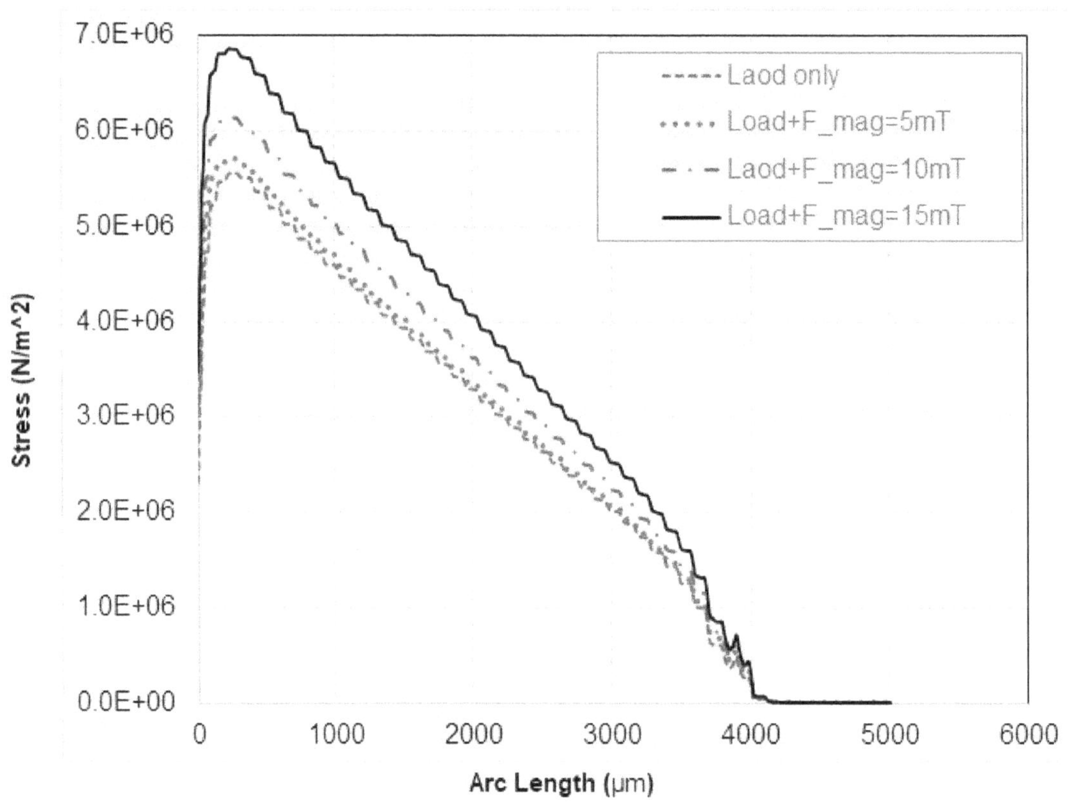

Figure 7.4: Variation of stress along arc length with magnetic field intensity

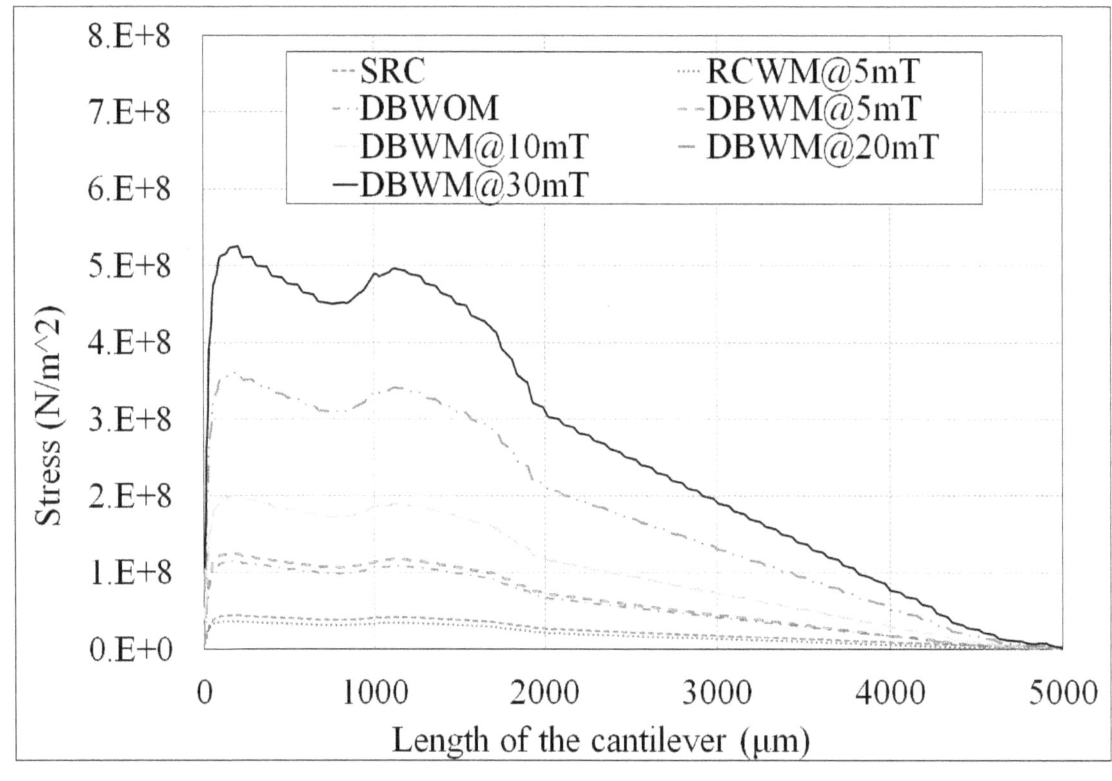

Figure 7.5: Stress distribution in different cantilevers

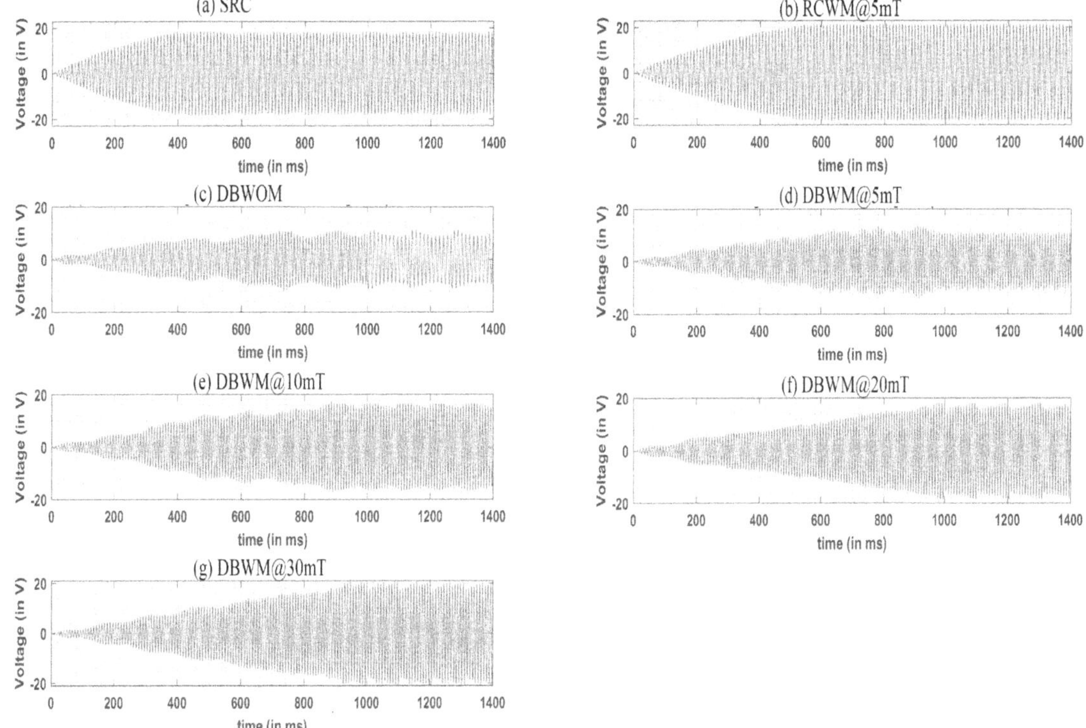

Figure 7.6: Transient Voltage of (a) SRC (b) RCWM@5mT (c) DBWOM (d) DMWM@5mT (e) DMWM@10mT (f) DMWM@20mT (g) DMWM@30mT

At its resonance frequency of 96 Hz, the SRC beam's peak output voltage is 18.4 V. At its resonance frequency of 95.5 Hz, RCWM@5mT exhibits a peak output voltage of 21.2 V. It is evident that the output voltage rises as the cantilever structure's magnetic influence is introduced. Only the dual-beam cantilever construction uses the higher magnetic field strength because the chapter's main goal is to increase bandwidth.

Similar to this, transient analysis is done on the dual-beam by altering the cantilever structure's frequency and applying a sinusoidal acceleration of 1 g. It can be shown that the peak output voltage of the DBWM@5mT at 115 Hz is 14 V, and the peak output voltage of the basic DBWOM structure is 12 V at 115.18 Hz. When DBWM@10mT, DBWM@20mT, and DBWM@30mT are used, their max output voltages are 16.4 V, 18.5 V, and 20 V, respectively, for 114.81 Hz, 114.61 Hz, and 114.31 Hz of resonant frequency.

7.4.2 Output power analysis of the cantilever structure

When the structure's resonant frequency coincides with the surrounding frequency, PZEH produces its maximum output power. The value of optimum load resistance, which is equal to internal resistance [18], [20], [116], is the other prerequisite. Given that both designs have the same dimensions, the internal resistance of the SRC and the RCWM@5mT will be the same. Similarly, regardless of the strength of the magnetic field, the internal resistance of every dual-beam cantilever construction will be the same. Fig. 6.5 illustrates the electrical equivalent of a single beam piezoelectric cantilever.

The dual-beam's inner and outer beams are joined in a parallel arrangement. Thus, as seen in Fig. 6.8, the electrical equivalent of the connected plate structure can alternatively be expressed as a parallel combination of two current sources, two capacitors, and two resistors.

The total of the individual capacitors is the equivalent capacitor in the equivalent circuit. The total of the reciprocals of each individual resistance is the reciprocal of equivalent resistance. The internal resistance will be determined indirectly because there isn't a direct way to determine it. When the load resistance equals the internal resistance of the PZEH, the PZEH will produce its maximum power. The term "optimal load resistance" refers to this load resistance. By altering the load resistance, the PZEH at the resonant frequency is simulated, and the optimal load resistance is computed. Plotted is the output power graph for several cantilever constructions at various load resistances. The ideal load is determined by finding the point at which the highest output power is obtained for the specified load resistance. The graph illustrating the relationship between the variation of output power and load resistance is presented in Fig. 7.7. The graph shows that the optimum load for the dual-beam's inner arm is 1.6 $M\Omega$, while the optimum load for the outer arm is 1.3 $M\Omega$. The optimum load for the simple rectangle and rectangular with magnetic tip mass is 2 $M\Omega$. Therefore, the dual-beam's corresponding internal resistance is 0.72 $M\Omega$.

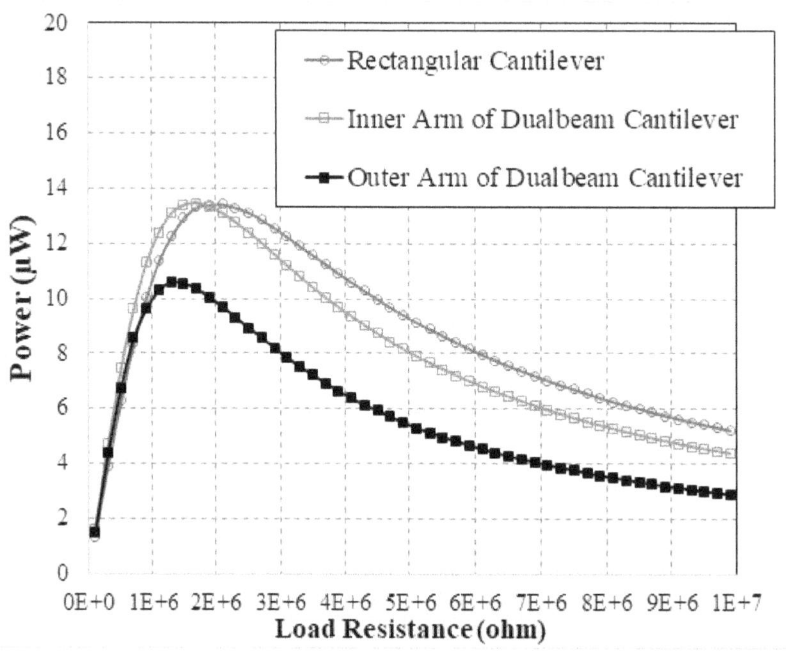

Figure 7.7: Variation of output power with load resistance

At this ideal load resistance, the maximum power is computed. The average output power is determined by adding the average square of the transient voltage measured at a specific frequency to the cantilever structure's ideal resistance. The average output power variation with frequency for each of the several cantilever structure types is displayed in Fig. **??**.

As can be seen in Fig. reffig:Stress in Cantilever, the stress distribution grows as the cantilever's magnetic field intensity increases. Thus, as the magnetic field intensity increases, the cantilever structures' output power also increases, as Fig. reffig:Variation of output power with Frequency for all cantilever structures illustrates. Furthermore, as the magnetic field intensity increases, the stress distribution throughout the cantilever's length increases, as seen in Fig. reffig:Stress in Cantilever. Thus, when the magnet's magnetic intensity increases suddenly, there's a chance that the cantilever's strength could be jeopardised. Thus, when developing the EH system, the ideal magnetic field strength can be used.

Every cantilever structure's combined output voltage plot is displayed on the same frequency scale. The frequency range or working bandwidth for each cantilever structure is displayed in this plot. Fig. 7.9 displays the output voltage for each cantilever construction.

There are two peaks in the dual-beam's output voltage and power at around 104.5 Hz and 107.5 Hz. At 110.5 Hz, there is a drop in both the output power and voltage. The dual beam's out-of-phase motion could be the cause of this drop in voltage and power. One possible explanation for the peak voltage and power at frequencies of 107.5 Hz and 114.5 Hz is that the dual beam is moving in phase.

Since most low power devices can operate efficiently with a 2 V power supply, the bandwidth of operation is believed to be the frequency range at which the output voltage is greater than 2 V. Table 7.4 tabulates the bandwidth of all the structures covered in this article. The single cantilever structures, SRC and RCWM@5mT, have bandwidths of 4 Hz (94 Hz–98 Hz) and 4.5 Hz (93 Hz–97.5 Hz), respectively, as can be shown. The DBWOM operates within a 14 Hz bandwidth range (104.18 Hz–118.18 Hz). The twin beam structure's addition of the magnetic tip mass expanded the cantilever's working frequency range. The DBWM@5mT, DBWM@10mT, DBWM@20mT, and DBWM@30mT have respective bandwidths of 15 Hz, 16 Hz, 17 Hz, and 18 Hz. It is important to remember that each beam in the dual beam configuration has an own resonance frequency.

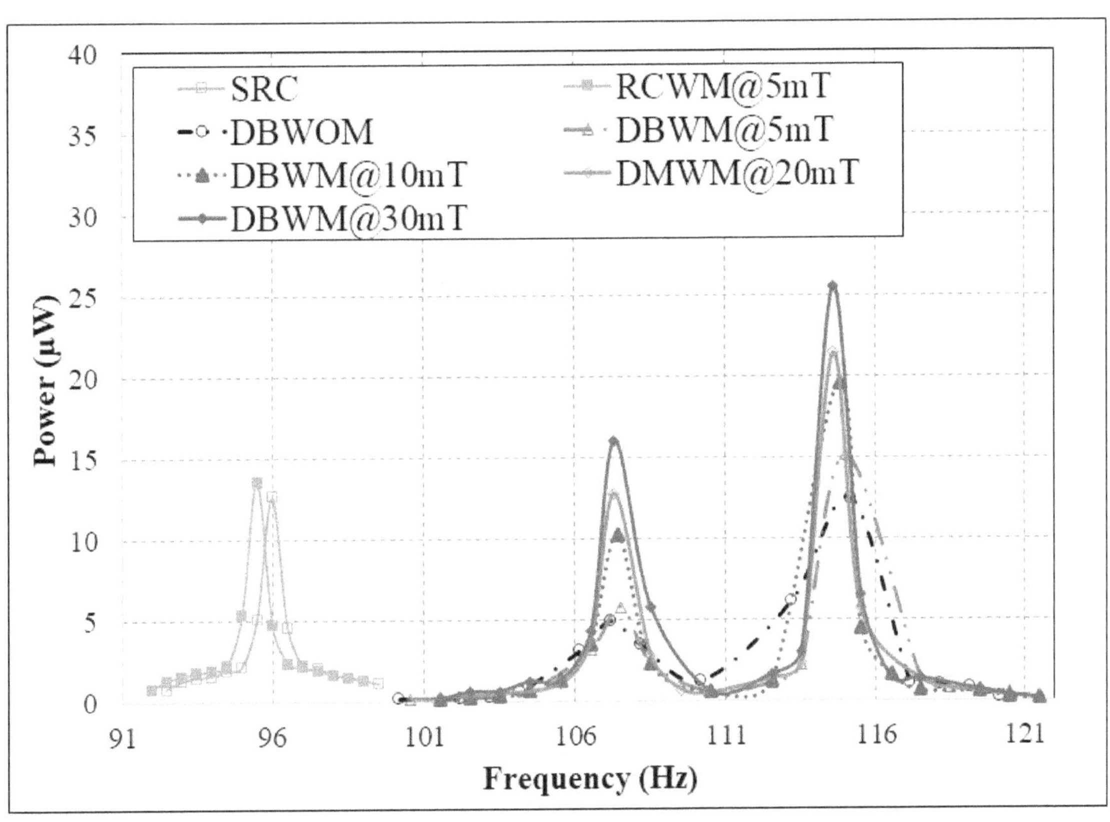

Figure 7.8: Variation of output power with frequency for all cantilever structures

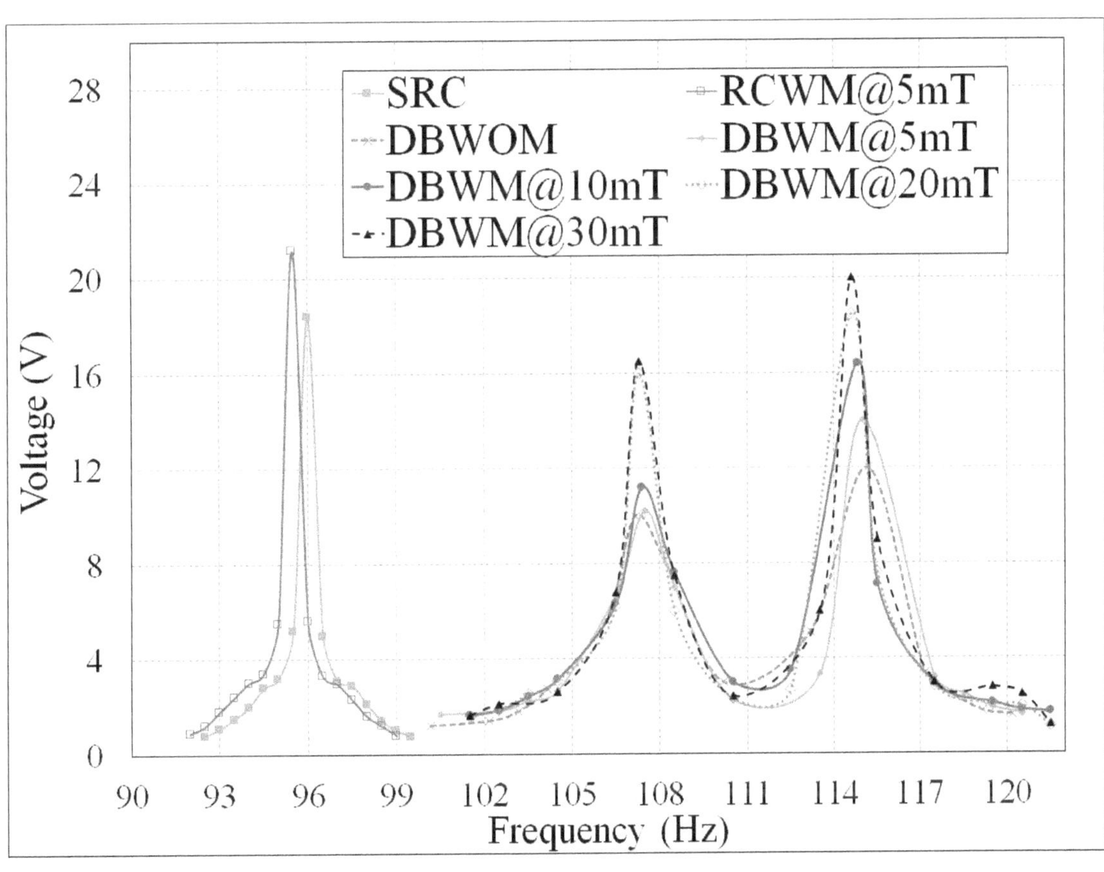

Figure 7.9: Variation of output voltage with frequency for all cantilever structures

In order for the structures to generate voltage across a broad frequency range, the resonant frequencies of each arm of the dual beam should be near to one another. Thus, a wideband energy harvester will not be obtained if the wrong cantilever beam is chosen during the dual beam design. Lastly, Table 7.5 presents a comparison between the suggested work and the body of existing literature. The table indicates that compared to the published literature, the current study has improved the performance using EH with a smaller dimension and has been able to obtain a higher or comparable bandwidth.

The tapered multiperforated cantilever structure's potential fabrication process is fairly comparable to that of that structure.

Table 7.4: Bandwidth of all structures

Structures	Bandwidth	Peak Voltage (V)	Average Power (μW)
SRC	4 Hz (94 Hz - 98 Hz)	18.4	12.614
RCWM@5mT	4.5 Hz (93 Hz - 97.5 Hz)	21.2	13.52
DBWOM	14 Hz (104.18 Hz- 118.18 Hz)	12	12.42
DBWM@5mT	15 Hz (103.51 Hz -118.51 Hz)	14	15.12
DBWM@10 mT	16 Hz (103.51 Hz -119.51 Hz)	16.4	19.58
DBWM@20 mT	17 Hz (103.51 Hz -120.51 Hz)	18.5	21.4
DBWM@30 mT	18 Hz (102.51 Hz -120.51 Hz)	20	25.5

Table 7.5: Comparison of the proposed work with the existing literatures

Ref (year)	Dimension	Bandwidth	Electrical output
[67] Challa et.al. (2008)	Beam- 34x20x0.6 mm3	10 Hz (22 -32 Hz)	Power - 240–280 μW
[78] Zhu et.al (2010)	Beam- 13x5x0.12 mm3	30.4 Hz (67.6 - 98 Hz)	Power - 61.6–156.6 μW
[79] W. Su et.al. (2014)	Length 98 mm, width 20 mm, thickness 0.531 mm	3.8 Hz (10 - 13.8 Hz)	Power – 1.8 mW
[80] Guo et.al. (2016)	Beam 1- 120 $\times$ 20 $\times$2 mm^3; Beam 2- 120$\times$ 20$\times$ 1 mm^3	28-42 Hz	Beam 1- Voltage – 24.84 V, power 81.97 mW/g^2; Beam 2 Voltage - 18.36 V, Power -44.78 mW/g^2
This work	5x2.5x0.014 mm3	18Hz (102.51-120.51 Hz)	Voltage – 20 V, Power 25.5 μW

7.5 Summary

This chapter has covered the topic of magnetism's effect in piezoelectric cantilever beams with magnetic proof masses. It demonstrates an enhancement in the electrical output, including the harvester's output voltage and output power, and contributes to expanding its working frequency range. The electrical output of the harvester is increased by simulating an SRC and RCWM@5mT cantilever structure. Additionally, the COMSOL Multiphysics simulates the dual-beam constructions with and without the magnetic tip mass, improving the output voltage and power. By applying a magnetic field, the dual-beam structure also exhibits an improvement in the frequency bandwidth. The dual-beam structures' output voltage and power are enhanced by the stronger magnetic field. When comparing the dual-beam constructions to the rectangular single-beam structures, there is a noticeable increase in frequency bandwidth. More than twice as large as the bandwidth of SRC or RCWM@5mT cantilever structures, which are 4.5 Hz and 4 Hz, respectively, is the operational frequency bandwidth of the DBWM@30mT, which is 18 Hz. The suggested DBWM@30mT has an operational frequency range of 102.51 Hz to 120.51 Hz. The output voltage and power of the suggested DBWM@30mT are 20 V and 25.5 μW, respectively.The bandwidth is increased by employing the idea of a multi-beam structure that makes use of the EH system's magnetic field strength. The efficiency of EH can be further increased by using an efficient electrode design. Another method to further increase the bandwidth is to flip and orient a permanent magnet.

Chapter 8

Conclusions and future scope

8.1   Conclusions

This book explores the benefits and drawbacks of the various energy collecting mechanisms while providing a brief description of each. It methodically describes the goals and breadth of the book that served as inspiration for the investigation and goal.

The goal of this book was to create a low-resonant-frequency MEMS-based energy harvester for low-power devices. The following lists the various conclusions that can be made after reading this book.

A simple rectangular cantilever construction was created at first. The purpose of adding the proof mass is to lower the resonance frequency. A separate dimensional parameter is used for the parametric analysis. It was discovered that, with the cantilever structure proof mass, the resonant frequency increases with an increase in cantilever length but drops with an increase in cantilever structure thickness and width. It has been noted that changing the structure can change the resonance frequency. The resonance frequency is decreased by the tapering and perforation, which can be single or multiple perforations. Additionally, by increasing the stress distribution inside the cantilever structures, the hole enhances the PZ device's performance. The PZ cantilever structure's many discontinuities are introduced with the aid of the multi-perforation. Compared to the perforated cantilever structure, it helps lower the resonance frequency and enhances stress distribution. Out of all the cantilever designs that have been studied, the multi-perforated cantilever structure provides the best stress distribution. It also produced the maximum output voltage and power and worked the best. As the thickness of the piezoelectric layer and excitation acceleration rise, so does the output power of the tapered multi-perforated cantilever structure. On the other hand, it falls when the damping coefficient rises.

In the second section of Chapter 2, a non-uniform cantilever structure is built and its impact on the output power, voltage, stress distribution, and resonant frequency is discussed. The resonance frequency is altered by the cantilever structure's variation in thickness and shape. The cantilever structure's stress distribution is enhanced and the resonance frequency is decreased by the tapered substrate thickness. The PZ cantilever structure's output voltage and power are additionally improved by the cantilever's tapered thickness. The suggested tapered down trapezoidal cantilever structure has the lowest resonance frequency and can produce the highest output voltage and power.

The L-shaped PZ cantilever beam is intended for PZEH applications that require low frequencies. Low power gadgets' batteries can be recharged using the mechanism that was developed for them. The wireless sensor node for the machine monitoring system is mostly included in this. The EH is within 5 mm of its size. A voltage of 11.6 V is generated at a frequency of 79.5 Hz when the suggested structure is simulated with a 1g acceleration. At its resonance frequency, the suggested L-shaped PZEH generates an output power of 10.8 μW.

Lengthening the piece will lower the resonance frequency. Significantly lowering the resonance frequency, the spiral-shaped cantilever structure helps extend the effective length without sacrificing compactness. The spiral-shaped cantilever harvester's dimensions are compatible with the majority of contemporary pacemakers. As the spiral cantilever structure's number of turns increases, the resonance frequency lowers.

A multi-beam construction has assisted in increasing the PZEH's bandwidth. The output and vibration of adjacent beams or plates are impacted by the vibration of a single beam or plate. The 'coupling effect' provides an explanation for this reliance between the nearby beams or plates. When a plate cantilever structure vibrates alone, its resonance frequency is different from that of the structure when it is designed with many plates. The voltage produced by the several plates vibrating independently at that specific frequency is different from the voltage produced by the multi-plate system as a whole. As the number of constituent plates in a connected multi-plate system increases, so does its bandwidth.

The book makes another attempt to use magnetic proof mass to boost bandwidth. In a magnetic environment, a cantilever with a magnetic proof mass produces more output power than a regular cantilever construction of the same size. The cantilever system's increased magnetic field intensity boosts output electrical power. But it also significantly raises the cantilever's tension. Compared to basic dual-beam structures without magnetic proof mass, the dual-beam structures with magnetic proof mass have a wider bandwidth.

Thus, it is evident from the findings and recommendations drawn from this work that low-power devices' reliance on batteries can be decreased by using a MEMS-based piezoelectric energy harvester. The integrated PZEH system can be successfully used in many different industrial applications, such as oil and gas pipelines, concrete constructions, biomedical devices, building health monitoring systems, and machine monitoring applications.

8.2   Future Scope

The study described yields some theoretical and simulated results, but raises issues that need to be further investigated. It is anticipated that some of the viewpoints will take several years to implement because they are more expansive and ambitious. On the other hand, the remaining ones can be considered as a logical progression of the ongoing project, which can be completed in the upcoming months.

The primary goal of this book is to include the PZ cantilever's 31 vibrational modes. Additional room exists for the 31 and 33 modes to be implemented concurrently in the same PZ cantilever structure. Consequently, the cantilever can move in both the Z and XY directions, which is advantageous.

The final viewpoint that can be attained in the next years is the non-linear energy harvester's adaptation to the lead-less pacemaker capsule's dimensions.

A hybrid EH system is conceivable, and it is possible to create the system utilising two or more separate EH systems.

Moving in the opposite direction and creating a larger-scale electrostatic or electromagnetic energy harvester for low-frequency applications is an intriguing area now awaiting investigation.

Bibliography

[1] J. Heidemann, M. Stojanovic, and M. Zorzi, "Underwater sensor networks: applications, advances and challenges," *Philosophical Transactions of the Royal Society A: Mathematical, Physical and Engineering Sciences*, vol. 370, no. 1958, pp. 158–175, 2012.

[2] M. H. Rehmani, A. C. Viana, H. Khalife, and S. Fdida, "Surf: A distributed channel selection strategy for data dissemination in multi-hop cognitive radio networks," *Computer Communications*, vol. 36, no. 10-11, pp. 1172–1185, 2013.

[3] M. H. Rehmani, A. C. Viana, H. Khalife, and S. Fdida, "A cognitive radio based internet access framework for disaster response network deployment," in *2010 3rd International Symposium on Applied Sciences in Biomedical and Communication Technologies (ISABEL 2010)*. IEEE, 2010, pp. 1–5.

[4] G. Werner-Allen, K. Lorincz, M. Ruiz, O. Marcillo, J. Johnson, J. Lees, and M. Welsh, "Deploying a wireless sensor network on an active volcano," *IEEE internet computing*, vol. 10, no. 2, pp. 18–25, 2006.

[5] F. Michahelles, P. Matter, A. Schmidt, and B. Schiele, "Applying wearable sensors to avalanche rescue," *Computers & Graphics*, vol. 27, no. 6, pp. 839–847, 2003.

[6] I. F. Akyildiz and E. P. Stuntebeck, "Wireless underground sensor networks: Research challenges," *Ad Hoc Networks*, vol. 4, no. 6, pp. 669–686, 2006.

[7] C. Wang, K. K. Fu, J. Dai, S. D. Lacey, Y. Yao, G. Pastel, L. Xu, J. Zhang, and L. Hu, "Inverted battery design as ion generator for interfacing with biosystems," *Nature communications*, vol. 8, no. 1, pp. 1–7, 2017.

[8] R. D. Prabha and G. A. Rincón-Mora, "0.18-μm light-harvesting battery-assisted charger–supply cmos system," *IEEE Transactions on Power Electronics*, vol. 31, no. 4, pp. 2950–2958, 2015.

[9] M. K. Van Veen and R. E. Schropp, "Amorphous silicon deposited by hot-wire cvd for application in dual junction solar cells," *Thin Solid Films*, vol. 403, pp. 135–138, 2002.

[10] V. Leonov, T. Torfs, P. Fiorini, and C. Van Hoof, "Thermoelectric converters of human warmth for self-powered wireless sensor nodes," *IEEE Sensors Journal*, vol. 7, no. 5, pp. 650–657, 2007.

[11] A. S. Holmes, G. Hong, K. R. Pullen, and K. R. Buffard, "Axial-flow microturbine with electromagnetic generator: design, cfd simulation, and prototype demonstration," in *17th IEEE International Conference on Micro Electro Mechanical Systems. Maastricht MEMS 2004 Technical Digest*. IEEE, 2004, pp. 568–571.

[12] J. B. Burch, M. Clark, M. G. Yost, C. T. Fitzpatrick, A. M. Bachand, J. Ramaprasad, and J. S. Reif, "Radio frequency nonionizing radiation in a community exposed to radio and television broadcasting," *Environmental health perspectives*, vol. 114, no. 2, pp. 248–253, 2006.

[13] S. Beepy, M. Tudor, and N. White, "Energy harvesting vibration sources for microsystem applications," *Measurement Science and technology*, vol. 17, pp. 175–195, 2006.

[14] R. Torah, P. Glynne-Jones, M. Tudor, T. O'donnell, S. Roy, and S. Beeby, "Self-powered autonomous wireless sensor node using vibration energy harvesting," *Measurement science and technology*, vol. 19, no. 12, p. 125202, 2008.

[15] M. El-Hami, P. Glynne-Jones, N. White, M. Hill, S. Beeby, E. James, A. Brown, and J. Ross, "Design and fabrication of a new vibration-based electromechanical power generator," *Sensors and Actuators A: Physical*, vol. 92, no. 1-3, pp. 335–342, 2001.

[16] S. Roundy, E. S. Leland, J. Baker, E. Carleton, E. Reilly, E. Lai, B. Otis, J. M. Rabaey, P. K. Wright, and V. Sundararajan, "Improving power output for vibration-based energy scavengers," *IEEE Pervasive computing*, vol. 4, no. 1, pp. 28–36, 2005.

[17] M. Miyazaki, H. Tanaka, G. Ono, T. Nagano, N. Ohkubo, T. Kawahara, and K. Yano, "Electric-energy generation using variable-capacitive resonator for power-free lsi: efficiency analysis and fundamental experiment," in *Proceedings of the 2003 international symposium on Low power electronics and design*, 2003, pp. 193–198.

[18] A. Anand and S. Kundu, "Design of a spiral-shaped piezoelectric energy harvester for powering pacemakers," *Nanomaterials and Energy*, vol. 8, no. 2, pp. 139–150, 2019.

[19] W. H. Ko, "Piezoelectric energy converter for electronic implants," Jul. 15 1969, US Patent 3,456,134.

[20] A. Anand, S. Naval, P. K. Sinha, N. K. Das, and S. Kundu, "Effects of coupling in piezoelectric multi-beam structure," *Microsystem Technologies*, vol. 26, no. 4, pp. 1235–1252, 2020.

[21] S. Roundy, "On the effectiveness of vibration-based energy harvesting," *Journal of Intelligent Material Systems and Structures*, vol. 16, no. 10, pp. 809–823, 2005.

[22] S. Roundy, P. K. Wright, and J. Rabaey, "A study of low level vibrations as a power source for wireless sensor nodes," *Computer communications*, vol. 26, no. 11, pp. 1131–1144, 2003.

[23] P. Glynne-Jones, S. P. Beeby, and N. M. White, "Towards a piezoelectric vibration-powered microgenerator," *IEEE Proceedings-Science, measurement and technology*, vol. 148, no. 2, pp. 68–72, 2001.

[24] P. Glynne-Jones, M. J. Tudor, S. P. Beeby, and N. M. White, "An electromagnetic, vibration-powered generator for intelligent sensor systems," *Sensors and Actuators A: Physical*, vol. 110, no. 1-3, pp. 344–349, 2004.

[25] M. Mizuno and D. G. Chetwynd, "Investigation of a resonance microgenerator," *Journal of Micromechanics and Microengineering*, vol. 13, no. 2, p. 209, 2003.

[26] H. Tiersten, "Electrostatic interactions and the piezoelectric equations," *The Journal of the Acoustical Society of America*, vol. 68, no. S1, pp. S40–S40, 1980.

[27] J. Cao, M. Ling, D. J. Inman, and J. Lin, "Generalized constitutive equations for piezo-actuated compliant mechanism," *Smart Materials and Structures*, vol. 25, no. 9, p. 095005, 2016.

[28] S. Roundy and P. K. Wright, "A piezoelectric vibration based generator for wireless electronics," *Smart Materials and Structures*, vol. 13, no. 5, pp. 1131–1142, 2004.

[29] D. Shen, J. H. Park, J. Ajitsaria, S. Y. Choe, H. C. Wikle, and D. J. Kim, "The design, fabrication and evaluation of a MEMS PZT cantilever with an integrated Si proof mass for vibration energy harvesting," *Journal of Micromechanics and Microengineering*, vol. 18, no. 5, 2008.

[30] M. Kim, S. Hong, D. J. Miller, J. Dugundji, and B. L. Wardle, "Size effect of flexible proof mass on the mechanical behavior of micron-scale cantilevers for energy harvesting applications," *Applied Physics Letters*, vol. 99, no. 24, p. 243506, 2011.

[31] W. G. Li, S. He, and S. Yu, "Improving power density of a cantilever piezoelectric power harvester through a curved L-shaped proof mass," *IEEE Transactions on Industrial Electronics*, vol. 57, no. 3, pp. 868–876, 2010.

[32] Q. C. Guan, B. Ju, J. W. Xu, Y. B. Liu, and Z. H. Feng, "Improved strain distribution of cantilever piezoelectric energy harvesting devices using h-shaped proof masses," *Journal of Intelligent Material Systems and Structures*, vol. 24, no. 9, pp. 1059–1066, 2013.

[33] L. M. Miller, P. Pillatsch, E. Halvorsen, P. K. Wright, E. M. Yeatman, and A. S. Holmes, "Experimental passive self-tuning behavior of a beam resonator with sliding proof mass," *Journal of Sound and Vibration*, vol. 332, no. 26, pp. 7142–7152, 2013. [Online]. Available: http://dx.doi.org/10.1016/j.jsv.2013.08.023

[34] M. F. Lumentut and I. M. Howard, "Parametric design-based modal damped vibrational piezoelectric energy harvesters with arbitrary proof mass offset: Numerical and analytical validations," pp. 562–586, 2016.

[35] Y. Jia and A. A. Seshia, "Power Optimization by Mass Tuning for MEMS Piezoelectric Cantilever Vibration Energy Harvesting," *Journal of Microelectromechanical Systems*, vol. 25, no. 1, pp. 108–117, 2016.

[36] R. Andosca, T. G. McDonald, V. Genova, S. Rosenberg, J. Keating, C. Benedixen, and J. Wu, "Experimental and theoretical studies on MEMS piezoelectric vibrational energy harvesters with mass loading," *Sensors and Actuators, A: Physical*, vol. 178, pp. 76–87, 2012. [Online]. Available: http://dx.doi.org/10.1016/j.sna.2012.02.028

[37] E. Köhler, P. Johannisson, D. Kolev, F. Ohlsson, P. Ågren, J. Liljeholm, P. Enoksson, and C. Rusu, "Mems meander harvester with tungsten proof-mass," in *Journal of Physics: Conference Series*, vol. 1407, no. 1.   IOP Publishing, 2019, p. 012121.

[38] M. A. Karami and D. J. Inman, "Parametric study of zigzag microstructure for vibrational energy harvesting," *Journal of Microelectromechanical Systems*, vol. 21, no. 1, pp. 145–160, 2012.

[39] O. Abdeljaber, O. Avci, S. Kiranyaz, and D. J. Inman, "Optimization of linear zigzag insert metastructures for low-frequency vibration attenuation using genetic algorithms," *Mechanical Systems and Signal Processing*, vol. 84, pp. 625–641, 2017. [Online]. Available: http://dx.doi.org/10.1016/j.ymssp.2016.07.011

[40] H. Liu, C. Lee, T. Kobayashi, C. J. Tay, and C. Quan, "A new S-shaped MEMS PZT cantilever for energy harvesting from low frequency vibrations below 30 Hz," *Microsystem Technologies*, vol. 18, no. 4, pp. 497–506, 2012.

[41] Y. Shindo and F. Narita, "Dynamic bending/torsion and output power of S-shaped piezoelectric energy harvesters," *International Journal of Mechanics and Materials in Design*, vol. 10, no. 3, pp. 305–311, 2014.

[42] H. W. Kim, A. Batra, S. Priya, K. Uchino, D. Markley, R. E. Newnham, and H. F. Hofmann, "Energy harvesting using a piezoelectric "cymbal" transducer in dynamic environment," *Japanese journal of applied physics*, vol. 43, no. 9R, p. 6178, 2004.

[43] N. White, P. Glynne-Jones, and S. Beeby, "A novel thick-film piezoelectric micro-generator," *Smart Materials and Structures*, vol. 10, no. 4, p. 850, 2001.

[44] L. Mateu and F. Moll, "Optimum piezoelectric bending beam structures for energy harvesting using shoe inserts," *Journal of Intelligent Material Systems and Structures*, vol. 16, no. 10, pp. 835–845, 2005.

[45] J. Baker, S. Roundy, and P. Wright, "Alternative geometries for increasing power density in vibration energy scavenging for wireless sensor networks," in *3rd international energy conversion engineering conference*, 2005, p. 5617.

[46] A. G. Muthalif and N. D. Nordin, "Optimal piezoelectric beam shape for single and broadband vibration energy harvesting: Modeling, simulation and experimental results," *Mechanical Systems and Signal Processing*, vol. 54, pp. 417–426, 2015.

[47] R. Hosseini and M. Nouri, "Shape design optimization of unimorph piezoelectric cantilever energy harvester," *Journal of Computational Applied Mechanics*, vol. 47, no. 2, pp. 247–259, 2016.

[48] S. Ben Ayed, A. Abdelkefi, F. Najar, and M. R. Hajj, "Design and performance of variable-shaped piezoelectric energy harvesters," *Journal of Intelligent Material Systems and Structures*, vol. 25, no. 2, pp. 174–186, 2014.

[49] D. Chaudhuri, S. Kundu, and N. Chattoraj, "Design and analysis of MEMS based piezoelectric energy harvester for machine monitoring application," *Microsystem Technologies*, vol. 25, no. 4, pp. 1437–1446, 2019. [Online]. Available: https://doi.org/10.1007/s00542-018-4156-z

[50] R. Sriramdas, S. Chiplunkar, R. M. Cuduvally, and R. Pratap, "Performance enhancement of piezoelectric energy harvesters using multilayer and multistep beam configurations," *IEEE Sensors Journal*, vol. 15, no. 6, pp. 3338–3348, 2015.

[51] S. Paquin and Y. St-Amant, "Improving the performance of a piezoelectric energy harvester using a variable thickness beam," *Smart Materials and Structures*, vol. 19, no. 10, p. 105020, 2010.

[52] D. S. Ibrahim, S. Beibei, O. A. Oluseyi, and U. Sharif, "Performance analysis of width and thickness tapered geometries on electrical power harvested from a unimorph piezoelectric cantilever beam," in *2020 IEEE 3rd International Conference on Electronics Technology (ICET)*.   IEEE, 2020, pp. 100–104.

[53] J. Zhang, X. Xie, G. Song, G. Du, and D. Liu, "A study on a near-shore cantilevered sea wave energy harvester with a variable cross section," *Energy Science & Engineering*, vol. 7, no. 6, pp. 3174–3185, 2019.

[54] S. Kundu and H. B. Nemade, "Piezoelectric vibration energy harvester with tapered substrate thickness for uniform stress," *Microsystem Technologies*, vol. 27, no. 1, pp. 105–113, 2021.

[55] J.-q. Liu, H.-b. Fang, Z.-y. Xu, X.-h. Mao, and X.-c. Shen, "A MEMS-based piezoelectric power generator array for vibration energy harvesting," *Microelectronics Journal 39*, vol. 39, pp. 802–806, 2008.

[56] H. Liu, C. Quan, C. J. Tay, T. Kobayashi, and C. Lee, "A MEMS-based piezoelectric cantilever patterned with PZT thin film array for harvesting energy from low frequency vibrations," *Physics Procedia*, vol. 19, pp. 129–133, 2011. [Online]. Available: http://dx.doi.org/10.1016/j.phpro.2011.06.136

[57] H.-C. Song, P. Kumar, D. Maurya, M.-G. Kang, W. T. Reynolds, D.-Y. Jeong, C.-Y. Kang, and S. Priya, "Ultra-low resonant piezoelectric mems energy harvester with high power density," *Journal of Microelectromechanical Systems*, vol. 26, no. 6, pp. 1226–1234, 2017.

[58] N. Jackson, F. Stam, O. Z. Olszewski, R. Houlihan, and A. Mathewson, "Broadening the bandwidth of piezoelectric energy harvesters using liquid filled mass," *Procedia engineering*, vol. 120, pp. 328–332, 2015.

[59] J. Twiefel, M. Neubauer, and J. Wallaschek, "C2. 1-bandwidth improvement for vibration energy harvesting devices," *Proceedings SENSOR 2013*, pp. 357–361, 2013.

[60] V. Meruane and K. Pichara, "A broadband vibration-based energy harvester using an array of piezoelectric beams connected by springs," *Shock and Vibration*, vol. 2016, 2016.

[61] A. Alomari and A. Batra, "Experimental and modelling study of a piezoelectric energy harvester unimorph cantilever arrays," *Sensors & Transducers*, vol. 192, no. 9, p. 37, 2015.

[62] H. Xue, Y. Hu, and Q.-m. Wang, "Broadband Piezoelectric Energy Harvesting Devices Using Multiple Bimorphs with Different Operating Frequencies," *IEEE transactions on ultrasonics, ferroelectrics, and frequency control*, vol. 55, no. 9, pp. 2104–2108, 2008.

[63] S. M. Shahruz, "Design of mechanical band-pass filters for energy scavenging," *Journal of Sound and Vibration*, vol. 292, no. 3-5, pp. 987–998, 2006.

[64] H. Liu, C. Lee, T. Kobayashi, C. J. Tay, and C. Quan, "Investigation of a MEMS piezoelectric energy harvester system with a frequency-widened-bandwidth mechanism introduced by mechanical stoppers," *Smart Materials and Structures*, vol. 21, no. 3, 2012.

[65] L. Dhakar, H. Liu, F. E. Tay, and C. Lee, "A new energy harvester design for high power output at low frequencies," *Sensors and Actuators, A: Physical*, vol. 199, pp. 344–352, 2013. [Online]. Available: http://dx.doi.org/10.1016/j.sna.2013.06.009

[66] K. Zhou, H. L. Dai, A. Abdelkefi, and Q. Ni, "Theoretical modeling and nonlinear analysis of piezoelectric energy harvesters with different stoppers," *International Journal of Mechanical Sciences*, vol. 166, no. June 2019, 2020.

[67] V. R. Challa, M. Prasad, Y. Shi, and F. T. Fisher, "A vibration energy harvesting device with bidirectional resonance frequency tunability," *Smart Materials and Structures*, vol. 17, no. 1, p. 015035, 2008.

[68] D. A. Barton, S. G. Burrow, and L. R. Clare, "Energy harvesting from vibrations with a nonlinear oscillator," *Journal of Vibration and Acoustics*, vol. 132, no. 2, 2010.

[69] S. C. Stanton, C. C. McGehee, and B. P. Mann, "Reversible hysteresis for broadband magnetopiezoelastic energy harvesting," *Applied Physics Letters*, vol. 95, no. 17, p. 174103, 2009.

[70] A. Erturk and D. J. Inman, "Broadband piezoelectric power generation on high-energy orbits of the bistable duffing oscillator with electromechanical coupling," *Journal of Sound and Vibration*, vol. 330, no. 10, pp. 2339–2353, 2011.

[71] S. Zhou, J. Cao, A. Erturk, and J. Lin, "Enhanced broadband piezoelectric energy harvesting using rotatable magnets," *Applied physics letters*, vol. 102, no. 17, p. 173901, 2013.

[72] S. Zhou, J. Cao, W. Wang, S. Liu, and J. Lin, "Modeling and experimental verification of doubly nonlinear magnet-coupled piezoelectric energy harvesting from ambient vibration," *Smart Materials and Structures*, vol. 24, no. 5, p. 055008, 2015.

[73] S. Zhou, J. Cao, D. J. Inman, J. Lin, S. Liu, and Z. Wang, "Broadband tristable energy harvester: modeling and experiment verification," *Applied Energy*, vol. 133, pp. 33–39, 2014.

[74] L. Haitao, Q. Weiyang, L. Chunbo, D. Wangzheng, and Z. Zhiyong, "Dynamics and coherence resonance of tri-stable energy harvesting system," *Smart Materials and Structures*, vol. 25, no. 1, p. 015001, 2015.

[75] J. Cao, S. Zhou, W. Wang, and J. Lin, "Influence of potential well depth on nonlinear tristable energy harvesting," *Applied Physics Letters*, vol. 106, no. 17, p. 173903, 2015.

[76] Z. Zhou, W. Qin, Y. Yang, and P. Zhu, "Improving efficiency of energy harvesting by a novel penta-stable configuration," *Sensors and Actuators A: Physical*, vol. 265, pp. 297–305, 2017.

[77] D. Tan, Y. Leng, and Y. Gao, "Magnetic force of piezoelectric cantilever energy harvesters with external magnetic field," *The European Physical Journal Special Topics*, vol. 224, no. 14-15, pp. 2839–2853, 2015.

[78] D. Zhu, S. Roberts, M. J. Tudor, and S. P. Beeby, "Design and experimental characterization of a tunable vibration-based electromagnetic micro-generator," *Sensors and Actuators A: Physical*, vol. 158, no. 2, pp. 284–293, 2010.

[79] W.-J. Su, J. Zu, and Y. Zhu, "Design and development of a broadband magnet-induced dual-cantilever piezoelectric energy harvester," *Journal of Intelligent Material Systems and Structures*, vol. 25, no. 4, pp. 430–442, 2014.

[80] D. Guo, X. Zhang, H. Li, and H. Li, "Piezoelectric energy harvester array with magnetic tip mass," in *ASME International Mechanical Engineering Congress and Exposition*, vol. 57403.   American Society of Mechanical Engineers, 2015, p. V04BT04A045.

[81] H. G. Çetin and B. Sümer, "A flexible piezoelectric energy harvesting system for broadband and low-frequency vibrations," *Procedia Engineering*, vol. 120, pp. 345–348, 2015. [Online]. Available: http://dx.doi.org/10.1016/j.proeng.2015.08.631

[82] S. Liu, Q. Cheng, D. Zhao, and L. Feng, "Theoretical modeling and analysis of two-degree-of-freedom piezoelectric energy harvester with stopper," *Sensors and Actuators, A: Physical*, vol. 245, pp. 97–105, 2016. [Online]. Available: http://dx.doi.org/10.1016/j.sna.2016.04.060

[83] J. L. González, A. Rubio, and F. Moll, "Human powered piezoelectric batteries to supply power to wearable electronic devices," *International journal of the Society of Materials Engineering for Resources*, vol. 10, no. 1, pp. 34–40, 2002.

[84] P. Niu, P. Chapman, R. Riemer, and X. Zhang, "Evaluation of motions and actuation methods for biomechanical energy harvesting," in *2004 IEEE 35th annual power electronics specialists conference (IEEE Cat. No. 04CH37551)*, vol. 3. IEEE, 2004, pp. 2100–2106.

[85] J. Kymissis, C. Kendall, J. Paradiso, and N. Gershenfeld, "Parasitic power harvesting in shoes," in *Digest of Papers. Second International Symposium on Wearable Computers (Cat. No. 98EX215)*.   IEEE, 1998, pp. 132–139.

[86] N. S. Shenck and J. A. Paradiso, "Energy scavenging with shoe-mounted piezoelectrics," *IEEE micro*, vol. 21, no. 3, pp. 30–42, 2001.

[87] K. Ishida, T.-C. Huang, K. Honda, Y. Shinozuka, H. Fuketa, T. Yokota, U. Zschieschang, H. Klauk, G. Tortissier, T. Sekitani *et al.*, "Insole pedometer with piezoelectric energy harvester and 2 v organic circuits," *IEEE Journal of Solid-State Circuits*, vol. 48, no. 1, pp. 255–264, 2012.

[88] Q. Niu, L. Wang, T. Dong, and H. Yang, "Application of a mems-based energy harvester for artificial heart wireless energy transmission," in *2009 ISECS International Colloquium on Computing, Communication, Control, and Management*, vol. 1.   IEEE, 2009, pp. 38–41.

[89] N. Li, Z. Yi, Y. Ma, F. Xie, Y. Huang, Y. Tian, X. Dong, Y. Liu, X. Shao, Y. Li, L. Jin, J. Liu, Z. Xu, B. Yang, and H. Zhang, "Direct Powering a Real Cardiac Pacemaker by Natural Energy of a Heartbeat," *ACS Nano*, vol. 13, no. 3, pp. 2822–2830, 2019.

[90] G. T. Hwang, Y. Kim, J. H. Lee, S. Oh, C. K. Jeong, D. Y. Park, J. Ryu, H. Kwon, S. G. Lee, B. Joung, D. Kim, and K. J. Lee, "Self-powered deep brain stimulation via a flexible PIMNT energy harvester," *Energy and Environmental Science*, vol. 8, no. 9, pp. 2677–2684, 2015. [Online]. Available: http://dx.doi.org/10.1039/C5EE01593F

[91] M. Deterre, "Toward an energy harvester for leadless pacemakers," Ph.D. dissertation, Paris 11, 2013.

[92] A. Zurbuchen, A. Haeberlin, L. Bereuter, J. Wagner, A. Pfenniger, S. Omari, J. Schaerer, F. Jutzi, C. Huber, J. Fuhrer, and R. Vogel, "The Swiss approach for a heartbeat-driven lead- and batteryless pacemaker," *Heart Rhythm*, vol. 14, no. 2, pp. 294–299, 2017. [Online]. Available: http://dx.doi.org/10.1016/j.hrthm.2016.10.016

[93] N. M. van Hemel and E. E. van der Wall, "8 October 1958, D Day for the implantable pacemaker," *Netherlands Heart Journal*, vol. 16, no. 1, pp. 1–2, 2008.

[94] T. Starner, "Human-powered wearable computing," *IBM systems Journal*, vol. 35, no. 3.4, pp. 618–629, 1996.

[95] H. Goto, T. Sugiura, Y. Harada, and T. Kazui, "Basic study of the automatic generating system (AGS) for quartz watches as a leadless pacemaker power source," *Japanese Journal of Artificial Organs*, vol. 28, no. 2, pp. 497–501, 1999.

[96] W. W. Clark and C. Mo, "Piezoelectric energy harvesting for bio mems applications," in *Energy Harvesting Technologies*. Springer, 2009, pp. 405–430.

[97] M. Deterre, B. Boutaud, R. Dalmolin, S. Boisseau, J.-J. Chaillout, E. Lefeuvre, and E. Dufour-Gergam, "Energy harvesting system for cardiac implant applications," in *2011 Symposium on Design, Test, Integration & Packaging of MEMS/MOEMS (DTIP)*.   IEEE, 2011, pp. 387–391.

[98] M. H. Ansari and M. A. Karami, "Modeling and experimental verification of a fan-folded vibration energy harvester for leadless pacemakers," *Journal of Applied Physics*, vol. 119, no. 9, 2016. [Online]. Available: http://dx.doi.org/10.1063/1.4942882

[99] M. H. Ansari and M. A. Karami, "Experimental investigation of fan-folded piezoelectric energy harvesters for powering pacemakers," *Smart Materials and Structures*, vol. 26, no. 6, 2017.

[100] G. T. Hwang, H. Park, J. H. Lee, S. Oh, K. I. Park, M. Byun, H. Park, G. Ahn, C. K. Jeong, K. No, H. Kwon, S. G. Lee, B. Joung, and K. J. Lee, "Self-powered cardiac pacemaker enabled by flexible single crystalline PMN-PT piezoelectric energy harvester," *Advanced Materials*, vol. 26, no. 28, pp. 4880–4887, 2014.

[101] L. Rufer, M. Colin, and S. Basrour, "Application driven design, fabrication and characterization of piezoelectric energy scavenger for cardiac pacemakers," *2013 Joint IEEE International Symposium on Applications of Ferroelectric and Workshop on Piezoresponse Force Microscopy, ISAF/PFM 2013*, pp. 340–343, 2013.

[102] S. Jay, M. Caballero, W. Quinn, J. Barrett, and M. Hill, "Characterization of piezoelectric device for implanted pacemaker energy harvesting," *Journal of Physics: Conference Series*, vol. 757, no. 1, 2016.

[103] N. Jackson, O. Olszewski, A. Mathewson, and C. O'Murchu, "Ultra-low frequency piezomems energy harvester for a leadless pacemaker," in *2018 IEEE Micro Electro Mechanical Systems (MEMS)*. IEEE, 2018, pp. 642–645.

[104] A. Kumar, R. Kiran, S. Kumar, V. S. Chauhan, R. Kumar, and R. Vaish, "A Comparative Numerical Study on Piezoelectric Energy Harvester for Self-Powered Pacemaker Application," *Global Challenges*, vol. 2, no. 1, p. 1700084, 2018.

[105] L. Beker, Ö. Zorlu, N. Göksu, and H. Külah, "Stimulating auditory nerve with mems harvesters for fully implantable and self-powered cochlear implants," in *2013 Transducers & Eurosensors XXVII: The 17th International Conference on Solid-State Sensors, Actuators and Microsystems (TRANSDUCERS & EUROSENSORS XXVII)*. IEEE, 2013, pp. 1663–1666.

[106] M. Yip, R. Jin, H. H. Nakajima, K. M. Stankovic, and A. P. Chandrakasan, "A fully-implantable cochlear implant soc with piezoelectric middle-ear sensor and arbitrary waveform neural stimulation," *IEEE journal of solid-state circuits*, vol. 50, no. 1, pp. 214–229, 2014.

[107] M. H. Ansari and M. Amin Karami, "Energy harvesting from heartbeat using piezoelectric beams with fan-folded configuration and added tip mass," *ASME 2015 Conference on Smart Materials, Adaptive Structures and Intelligent Systems, SMASIS 2015*, vol. 2, pp. 1–8, 2015.

[108] A. Anand and S. Kundu, "Design of Mems Based Piezoelectric Energy Harvester for Pacemaker," *Proceedings of 3rd International Conference on 2019 Devices for Integrated Circuit, DevIC 2019*, pp. 465–469, 2019.

[109] H. Kanai, M. Sato, Y. Koiwa, and N. Chubachi, "Transcutaneous measurement and spectrum analysis of heart wall vibrations," *IEEE Transactions on Ultrasonics, Ferroelectrics, and Frequency Control*, vol. 43, no. 5, pp. 791–810, 1996.

[110] S. S. Rao, *Vibration of continuous systems*. Wiley Online Library, 2007, vol. 464.

[111] A. Anand and S. Kundu, "Improvement of Output Power in Piezoelectric Energy Harvester under Magnetic Influence," *Proceedings of 3rd International Conference on 2019 Devices for Integrated Circuit, DevIC 2019*, pp. 382–385, 2019.

[112] S. Naval, P. K. Sinha, N. K. Das, A. Anand, and S. Kundu, "Wideband piezoelectric energy harvester design using parallel connection of multiple beams," *International Journal of Nanoparticles*, vol. 12, no. 3, pp. 206–223, 2020.

[113] Y. Jia, S. Du, and A. A. Seshia, "Cantilevers-on-membrane design for broadband MEMS piezoelectric vibration energy harvesting," *Journal of Physics: Conference Series*, vol. 660, no. 1, pp. 6–11, 2015.

[114] I. Kanno, T. Ichida, K. Adachi, H. Kotera, K. Shibata, and T. Mishima, "Power-generation performance of lead-free (K,Na)NbO 3 piezoelectric thin-film energy harvesters," *Sensors and Actuators, A: Physical*, vol. 179, pp. 132–136, 2012. [Online]. Available: http://dx.doi.org/10.1016/j.sna.2012.03.003

[115] P. Muralt, M. Marzencki, B. Belgacem, F. Calame, and S. Basrour, "Vibration Energy Harvesting with PZT Micro Device," *Procedia Chemistry*, vol. 1, no. 1, pp. 1191–1194, 2009. [Online]. Available: http://dx.doi.org/10.1016/j.proche.2009.07.297

[116] A. Anand, S. Pal, and S. Kundu, "Multi-perforated Energy-Efficient Piezoelectric Energy Harvester Using Improved Stress Distribution," *IETE Journal of Research*, 2021.

[117] P. D. Mitcheson, P. Miao, B. H. Stark, E. Yeatman, A. Holmes, and T. Green, "Mems electrostatic micropower generator for low frequency operation," *Sensors and Actuators A: Physical*, vol. 115, no. 2-3, pp. 523–529, 2004.

[118] S. Nabavi and L. Zhang, "Portable wind energy harvesters for low-power applications: A survey," *Sensors*, vol. 16, no. 7, p. 1101, 2016.

[119] H. Yu, J. Zhou, L. Deng, and Z. Wen, "A vibration-based mems piezoelectric energy harvester and power conditioning circuit," *Sensors*, vol. 14, no. 2, pp. 3323–3341, 2014.

[120] V. S. Mallela, V. Ilankumaran, and S. N. Rao, "Trends in cardiac pacemaker batteries," *Indian Pacing and Electrophysiology Journal*, vol. 4, no. 4, pp. 201–212, 2004.

[121] D. S. Chew and V. Kuriachan, "Leadless cardiac pacemakers: Present and the future," *Current Opinion in Cardiology*, vol. 33, no. 1, pp. 7–13, 2018.

[122] K. Tao, H. Yi, L. Tang, J. Wu, P. Wang, N. Wang, L. Hu, Y. Fu, J. Miao, and H. Chang, "Piezoelectric ZnO thin films for 2DOF MEMS vibrational energy harvesting," *Surface and Coatings Technology*, vol. 359, no. February, pp. 289–295, 2019. [Online]. Available: https://doi.org/10.1016/j.surfcoat.2018.11.102

[123] T. Galchev, E. E. Aktakka, and K. Najafi, "A piezoelectric parametric frequency increased generator for harvesting low-frequency vibrations," *Journal of Microelectromechanical Systems*, vol. 21, no. 6, pp. 1311–1320, 2012.

[124] F. Khoshnoud and C. W. de Silva, "Recent advances in mems sensor technology–biomedical applications," *IEEE Instrumentation & Measurement Magazine*, vol. 15, no. 1, pp. 8–14, 2012.

[125] M. Ansari, C. Cho *et al.*, "A study on increasing sensitivity of rectangular microcantilevers used in biosensors," *Sensors*, vol. 8, no. 11, pp. 7530–7544, 2008.

[126] M.-H. Hsu, "Dynamic analysis of electrostatic microactuators using the differential quadrature method," *Advances in Acoustics and Vibration*, vol. 2011, 2011.

[127] W. Zhang, Y. Dong, Y. Tan, M. Zhang, X. Qian, and X. Wang, "Electric power self-supply module for wsn sensor node based on mems vibration energy harvester," *Micromachines*, vol. 9, no. 4, p. 161, 2018.

[128] S. Nabavi and L. Zhang, "Design and optimization of wideband multimode piezoelectric mems vibration energy harvesters," in *Multidisciplinary Digital Publishing Institute Proceedings*, vol. 1, no. 4, 2017, p. 586.

[129] Y. Zhang, A. Luo, Y. Xu, T. Wang, and F. Wang, "Wideband mems electrostatic energy harvester with dual resonant structure," in *2016 IEEE SENSORS*.   IEEE, 2016, pp. 1–3.

[130] M. F. Daqaq, R. Masana, A. Erturk, and D. Dane Quinn, "On the role of nonlinearities in vibratory energy harvesting: a critical review and discussion," *Applied Mechanics Reviews*, vol. 66, no. 4, 2014.

[131] P. Kim and J. Seok, "A multi-stable energy harvester: dynamic modeling and bifurcation analysis," *Journal of Sound and Vibration*, vol. 333, no. 21, pp. 5525–5547, 2014.